DIFFERENT NATURES

Road Dog Publications was formed in 2010 as an imprint of Lost Classics Book Company and is dedicated to publishing the best in books on motorcycling, motorsports, and adventure travel. Visit us at www.roaddogpub.com.

Maps by John Hepburn

UK Edition of *Ureka* Copyright © Graham Field, 2015
Originally published in the UK by Little m Press, Colchester, UK 2015.

This North American Edition of *Eureka* published by arrangement with the author. Copyright © Graham Field, 2018
All rights reserved.

ISBN 978-1-890623-59-3
Library of Congress Control Number: 2018930233

An Imprint of Lost Classics Book Company
The UK Edition of this book is available in e-book format at online booksellers.

DIFFERENT NATURES

And the Spaces in Between

by

Graham Field

Publisher
Lake Wales, Florida

ABOUT THE AUTHOR

Author and travel writer Graham Field was "born at a very early age, and independent travel began shortly after he learned to crawl." During obligatory but inadequate schooling he spent the majority of his time looking out of the window and escaping into his favourite daydream—the freedom of the road. Making restless dreams become a reality has been his single-minded talent.

Graham's life of travel really started with his first motorbike, obtained way before he was old enough to have a licence. By the age of eighteen he was living in the US, working in construction, in strip clubs, and riding a 1960 Harley-Davidson. In 1990, he set off around the world with a backpack, and this was followed by challenging solo cycling trips in India and China.

For over a quarter of a century, Graham has had three constants in his life: motorcycles, travel, and diary keeping. He appeared on a national TV game show, where he announced he would use his modest winnings to ride to Mongolia. This was when all three of his obsessions came together. On a thousand-dollar KLR 650, he rode 15,000 miles east from his home in the UK—105 days on a $7,500 budget. This journey, the people met, the challenges, and the startling contrasts of both the cultures and landscapes became the subject of his hugely popular and inspirational diary-format book, *In Search of Greener Grass*.

A few years later, his KLR, with the same budget, distance, and time-frame, took him to Iraq and Azerbaijan. A "eureka moment" occurred during this journey, and that epiphany became the topic of his enthralling second book, *Ureka* [*Eureka* in the North American edition]. His third book, *Different Natures*, takes the reader on earlier motorcycle trips from the Alaskan Arctic Circle to southern Mexico. Delving into diaries packed with tales of naivety, and at times eyebrow-raising debauchery, the reader soon discovers that Graham's mantra is "You never lie to your diary."

Graham writes regularly for *Overland Magazine*. His articles and columns are published in British national papers and motorcycle publications in both Europe and North America. His presentations are widely regarded as some of the funniest in the genre, and in radio interviews he is well known for his passion for travel and his off-the-cuff comments, which both challenge and amuse. He makes regular contributions to *Adventure Bike TV*, where he was nominated as "most inspirational adventurer." Graham has a residency on *Adventure Rider Radio*, alongside travel writers Brian and Shirley Hardy-Rix, Grant Johnson of Horizons Unlimited, and myself. He currently lives in Bulgaria, with a variety of iconic motorcycles, a cluster of KLRs, and some gold-digging cats.

—Sam Manicom

Sam is the author of a four-book series (*Into Africa*, *Under Asian Skies*, *Distant Suns*, and *Tortillas to Totems*) about his eight-year journey around the world by motorcycle.

For Madalynn
Not an explanation, just an insight

Acknowledgements

From scribbling some notes about a day on the road to seeing your book on a shelf is a far harder journey than any I've done on a motorbike. The dedication and determination required is immense.

Like any journey though, you learn as you progress. Again, like a motorcycle trip I inevitably encountered situations beyond my abilities and that's when I called upon the literary and publication skills of certain individuals in my virtual support truck. So, in the order in which I needed them, I would like to thank Rebecca Legros for her impeccable, professional and punctual copyediting, Barbara Horde for her equally efficient proofreading and Nathan Millward for his general ability and skill at turning a word document into a book. And to John Hepburn for the finishing touches. Also thanks to Brigitte Crawley, Fil Schiannini, Sam Manicom, Tammy Howard and Michael Strah for their input with the cover design . . . which I mostly ignored. Also thanks to Trevor Angle who, despite being on the road, found time to add shine to this polished finished product.

Finally a massive thank you to you, the reader. If no one bought or liked reading my books, the stories contained within these pages would remain a scrawl in my diaries, but now, once again with utter vulnerability, I can display my innermost thoughts across the pages for the world to see. If you read on, I'll ride on and write on, deal?

CONTENTS

PREFACE

I wanted to call this book *The Motorcycle Dairies—Milking the Success of the First Two Books*; however, I was advised by authors of experience and wisdom to choose a more sensible title. You would know the people in question, but it would be wrong to start name dropping in the first paragraph. The reason for my original, tongue in cheek title was because instead of riding off in search of new subject matter, I delved into my diaries to recall past trips, however I ended up totally reliving the journeys (which is why, I suppose, I keep a diary). As I read and reflected, I saw patterns, insights, and events that instigated what was to come.

This is a book of three different journeys. Each pave the way to my other books, filling in gaps and answering questions. They all start in Colorado, where, for a while, I lived my other life; the place I'd run to when I needed to escape my Essex existence.

The first journey was in 2001, ten states in thirteen days. Reading through that diary, I was slightly disturbed to see how debauched my life was then. Looking back with wiser eyes, it's no wonder that I struggled to cope with reality, when I put so much effort in trying to avoid it. However, I found myself both smiling and cringing as I recalled those self-indulgent, mostly innocent days.

The second journey was in 2007, a 12,000 mile trip to Alaska, with two friends, at least on the way there. Up there I found a wilderness I didn't even know I was missing, and this sowed the seeds for the search for greener grass.

The third story is from 2012, solo to Mexico. My expectations weren't great, but the events far exceeded them. A motorcycle ride is always remarkable, this one was the precursor to my journey to Iraq that inspired *Eureka*.

These are, as always, my diaries; they are brutally honest, exposing myself, my thoughts, emotions, observations, and ultimately, my life on and off the road—

1

the different natures of growing older and reflecting on past experiences, as well as the environmental transitions through the awe of Arctic tundra, high altitude existences, geological phenomena, desolate desert, Pacific Ocean escapism, and everything that happened in between. So you see, it's still a pretty clever title, and it has the approval of Mr. Simon and Mr. Manicom.

ESCAPISM AND DISCOVERY

"My nature just changes.""
Jimi Hendrix

DENVER, COLORADO, USA, 2001
HOW LIFE WAS BACK THEN...

THE INVITATION

He'd been talking about it and preparing for it all summer. I watched his plans and piles of paraphernalia grow. I listened, like you do, but I didn't imagine, not until he said:"You want to come? I'd planned it as a solo trip, but it doesn't have to be, I just assumed you wouldn't."

"Well, you'd have to buy me a bike and lend me some money," I said. Surely he knew that would be the price of my company.

It had been a long friendship, started in the school playground. However, I'm not sure what that history entitled me to. Turns out the full package was on offer. My timing was perfect. What we have here is feeling beyond communication; it's the sentimentality of a lifelong acquaintance, combined with the brief, but truly genuine sense of love, brought on by what was, judging by how many lines it takes up in my diary, a bit of a regular habit. I mean, this was a Monday night—a school night—we're both thirty-five now, both living in the US, and one of us is enjoying the prosperity of the post-millennium boom: the one who has citizenship.

So there I was, sitting at the round table that was the centre of so many memorable and unremembered nights. The dealer had left, and we played cards, pushing the mirror and the envelope into the night. VH1 was on the TV, its rocking broadcast filling in the occasional silence that occurs when my thoughts turned from straights and full houses to the possibility of a bike trip.

In the warm, bright reality of an August morning, I drag my rock 'n' roll body out of bed. It is time to stop trying to sleep and start trying to work; work this morning is prepping a deck for staining. The can of deck preparation said that, once applied, I have to wait twenty-four hours before I'm able to stain it, or was that sustain it? Anyway, I do what it says on the can and I'm finished by 10 A.M.

I head over to my girlfriend's, where my Harley is stored, a tatty Shovelhead built from scratch with randomly sourced parts. It's complete now, running, and ready to be sold to someone who has the time, money, facilities, and interest to rebuild it properly. At the agreed time, a couple of bearded bikers ride out of a Dave Mann poster to have a look at it. They know their shit, but then so do I, and with a mutual respect of our combined knowledge, we have a good rapport, but I decline their offer. An Englishman in America has to try harder at everything to be considered equal at something he is actually better at. Like English.

When I get back home, I wonder if Jonathan might be having second thoughts about inviting me along for the ride. I fear the warmth, love, thrill, and camaraderie could well have faded along with the other traits associated with and experienced by the cocaine user. But soon we're sitting, squinting at lines on a map, and I realise with absolute certainty that I was born to ride the Pacific Coast Highway, and I'm meant to do it next week.

I have an extensive knowledge of a few select motorbikes, which consists of a thirty-year window in the ninety-year history of Harley-Davidson, which ends when they stopped making Shovelheads, and the only other bike I am very familiar with is the Yamaha XT500. That knowledge leaves me with no doubt at all that I would be needing a bike I knew nothing about, if it was to keep up and be compatible with Jonathan's two-year-old Triumph Sprint 955. He suggests an FJ1100.

"Ah, a shaft drive," I say quite confidently.

"No."

"Oh really. What am I thinking of then?" A question most people who know me shy away from.

The evening continues, and we talk of nothing else.

The next morning as I get on with the task of staining the deck, every thought I have is a good one. I am experiencing a momentary peak in what had basically been a disastrous eighteen-month relationship—my girlfriend and I are actually getting on quite well for once. My Shovelhead that is for sale is finally getting some serious interest. I have the bike trip to consider and look forward to. And in November we will be heading back to the UK for a big fireworks party en route to Thailand and Cambodia for a little backpacking trip. The sun is shining. Life is good. I almost have enough money, but none to spare, not until I sell the Harley. Everything is perfect.

This is at a time when the Internet is an alternative tool, rather than an essential one. I spend the afternoon looking through the paper at the touring bikes for sale. My overwhelming ignorance has me looking first at price and then at mileage and accessories before make, engine size, or any of the refinements, necessities, or luxuries. I don't know and I don't care about such things, and time isn't on my side. We are leaving in four days. This is also a time when most people don't have phones in their pockets. I would leave a lot of messages and then go out. So if they did call back, I'd miss it.

I go to my girlfriend's for dinner, it is like a date, she even bought some beer for me. I used to live there, but it hadn't worked. Instead we'd exchanged the complacency and presumption of cohabitating for the excitement, effort, and enthusiasm of dating.

I'd been considering how to bring up the trip to California and on up to Seattle. I know what she's going to say. I've been wondering who is most manipulative: her in making me stay or Jonathan in getting me to go. I know her well, well enough to know for all the reactions I'd contemplated and prepared for, she would always hit me with one I'd not seen coming. Surprisingly she's cool about it. Unbelievable! Such an uncharacteristic reaction, it is so refreshing it makes my mind wander back to the possibilities of living together and fucking everything up again. You can't improve on the perfect scenario, why try? If a situation is working, stick with it. She'd been married three times before, surely she could understand this was the way forward. That evening, I let myself think she could. As we eat, I keep her pacified, speaking of the sights and experiences the trip to Southeast Asia would bring.

Thursday, and no one seems to have to work.

Looking back, I'm not sure how we managed the lifestyle we had, but we did, and we did it well. No one had kids or commitments. We balanced the ratio of disposable income to free time with a nonchalant precarity. Reflecting on those days when I read my old diaries, they seem to smile back at me with a Charlie Brown innocence and permanent blue skies. Desires were met, and needing seemed to be a brief niggle, that only resulted in more desires being met.

Driving with the top down, we take off in Jonathan's Mustang to check out a ZR1100. The journey takes longer than we expected. The bike's forks are bent and it really isn't that practical. Besides, I don't fancy riding it back with just my shades and a T-shirt, as it is getting dark. Now the pressure is on to find a bike. Buying a bike is the trip preparation; there is nothing else to do. There are no other options, if I couldn't get a bike, the trip, for me, is off. And that is not an option.

I'm woken by the phone at 6:30AM.

"Yeah, you left a message about my bike. It goes really fast. It's got a special chain because it's so fast. Oh, and it's really fast."

"OK, thanks."

A Yamaha Venture has just become available. I go to have a look. It looks like a Gold Wing. It is massive and eighteen years old, but the guy says he is the original owner. It comes with a trailer. In my inexperienced and misguided way, I think it would be ideal for the job. I take it round the block. It is so big, and the brakes are shit. He wants $3,000 for it, but says he would do it for $2,500 without the trailer, and he would fix the brakes. I get him down to $2,450 and said I'll fix the brakes. I need to sort out the documents; it's Friday and I have to get it registered today. However, the ownership papers show he wasn't the original owner, so I let him squirm with embarrassment and then I knock the price down a bit more.

The pressure is mounting. I spend a day driving round to organise insurance and registration, as well as doing some paying jobs and picking up payment for the deck job. I even find time to buy and deliver some flowers to my girlfriend, just because she's being so cool about the whole thing.

When Jonathan and I pick up the Venture, he is torn between humouring me and blatantly taking the piss, but as it is his money paying for the bike he has to be a bit careful. Pulling up alongside him at a set of lights with my onboard radio playing, he just diplomatically says that he never thought he'd live to see the day. I don't care though. I'm going to ride the Pacific Coast Highway next week, and no shit anyone gives me is going to stick on this Teflon-coated dream.

Back at Jonathan's, we discover there are some musty rainsuits in the panniers along with tools and all sorts of other extras. It even came with a lid; a bit too big, but useful for some of the states we'd be travelling through.

This should be where my bike bonding begins—the stripping, maintenance, packing, and preparing. But I just leave it in the garage, pick up my girlfriend, and drive us up into the Rocky Mountains in my campervan for the weekend. She's tired and falls asleep early, so I sit under the stars and have a beer before climbing into the van and cuddling up to her naked body. I look out the back widows at the profile of the pine trees, black against the midnight blue of the light-pollution-free mountain sky, and for the second time this week, I think just how good life is.

Without opening my eyes, I visualise the near future: bike ride, parties, and foreign travel. When I open them, I see beauty both inside and outside the van. Our preferred camping space had been occupied last night, and the spot we settled for is a compromise. However, the consolation of less seclusion means a far better view. I cook the traditional Saturday morning bacon and eggs on the stove and place them inside some bagels. I have a big, old, heavy, black cast-iron frying pan which takes a while to heat up, but when it does, it holds the heat for ages, much like the rocky cliffs the morning sun is shining on and warming up. We went to the mountains almost every weekend; not for any physical pursuits. In fact, at this stage in life and relationship, the only physical pursuit is in the van while the back seat was still folded down into a bed. It is frequent, passionate, and particularly uninhibited out in the wilds, especially when a passing storm hammers on the fibreglass roof. During a mountain cloudburst no one can hear screams.

After breakfast, I go and spy on the people who are in "our" space and see that they are settled in for the weekend, so I build a fire for later. That's all we did: make fires, make love, and make food. When the late summer sun begins losing height and heat, a car drives up looking for somewhere to camp. I play my Ministry CD through large speakers that are on deliberately long wires so I can place them outside. It has the desired effect, and our obnoxious behaviour has them turning round in search of more congenial neighbours. When I turn off the music, we realise just how loud it was. A vacuum remains where the sound had reverberated round the forest. Silence floods into the void; it seems even louder.

We giggle with a shrug at our overreaction to the possibility of unwanted company. I light the fire, the warmth is instant in the fresh, cold, dark, low-humidity, high-altitude atmosphere, and we watch the flames light up our little patch of darkness, absolutely oblivious to everything beyond our illuminated territory. Throwing caution and money to the wind, I light the propane furnace in the van. Its output is only ever noticeable when standing up, as the heat hovers just below the uninsulated roof, and what doesn't escape cools and drops down in the form of moisture that mists up the windows. Under double duvets we huddle together for shared body heat, the chill adding to the romance of it all.

Man, that was a cold night; the morning is obscured by icy windows. I scrape it off to unveil a frost outside, which indicates this will probably be the last camp of the year. We decide to skip breakfast in exchange for the van heater and head off, picking our way between the rocks and trenches and back to the track where, once reached, I can pay more attention to the crisp, clear morning. We wind our way through the crunchy frozen shadows cast by the yellowing leaves of the aspen trees. The track leads to the road that takes us to the highway and back into Denver for breakfast at a Mexican restaurant that remains one of my favourite dining experiences on the planet. It does seem to be a life of self-indulgence and satisfaction. The scenery, the climate, the company, and pastimes all brought together in one idealistic lifestyle; no cynicism and not much awareness beyond our self-satisfying little circle. Living in a bubble designed for us by powers we never considered, either ill-informed or uninformed, we exist in blissful ignorance of modest extravagance and affordable luxuries. Then there is the Yamaha Venture. It is time to try and find some desire and pleasure in this ugly, heavy beast.

As I arrive at the house, a woman with a ring on her finger is just leaving. Jonathan was never one to kiss and tell, so there are no questions asked. I have servicing of my own to do. I give the bike new tyres, battery, and oil. I bleed the brakes with new fluid, and the stopping power improves tremendously. My work is carried out with a constant supply of refreshment. There is a keg of beer in the kitchen that has to be drained before we leave; I do the best I can. Packing the bike is easy. I've been transient for over a year: backpacking, living with my girlfriend, thrown out, staying with Jonathan, then living in the van. I just throw my possessions in the panniers and that's me ready.

The weekend ends with a roast dinner and the omnibus edition of *EastEnders* on BBC America; a touch of English Sunday tradition. The preparation has been pretty painless; it remains to be seen if it is adequate.

Day 1

Moab, Utah

440 miles

If the term *overlanding* was invented back then. I wasn't aware of it.

Twenty years of bike fanaticism, riding, and camping had, until now, just involved going to shows and rallies. Never more than a day away, and always with facilities at the arrival point.

We'd planned to leave at 8AM; I can't see it happening. There is a motto that you should always have a holiday in hand. So that morning, with a few long distance calls, I book the tickets to Bangkok with a travel agent in the UK, then call my parents and tell them a few half truths about my plans as I finish loading the bike. Just as well it's so big. Along with the panniers and hot tub-sized top box, I manage to fill up every available space. It's not so much a case of taking what I need as taking what I have.

Finally, I prepare sandwiches with the last of the food in the fridge; always the resourceful, industrious, and frugal Englishman. *Waste not, want not.* I know what the saying implied, but am not really confident enough to actually voice it, I just act upon it. At 9:30AM, I get the neighbour across the street to take a "before" photo of us both, and then we're off.

Lidless, sunblocked, and bandana'd—the contradiction of my appearance to the bike I'm riding doesn't bother me in the slightest. Neither does my forward-blowing hair flapping around my face from the vortex caused by my wind-blocking, aerodynamic-eliminating, and view-inhibiting screen. Within half an hour we're in the foothills of the Rockies, continuing into the mountains along the same road I'd driven yesterday. Different transport, different company, different mission. I'm a bit concerned by how quickly my fuel level is dropping; the bars of the LCD gauge seem to be fewer each time I glance down, and because of that, I'm glancing all the more. However, I feel a flood of relief when the tank overflows unexpectedly, and the pump has only clocked up $5.

After the first mountain pass comes a long stretch of straight road. I hold the bike at full throttle, and very slowly the needle on the speedo creeps up to the magical triple figure of 100mph. It's not the sort of high performance acceleration that makes for exciting line graphs; this is more a relentless determination of momentum. With a need to wring a greater thrill out of this momentous achievement, I poke my head over the screen and realise just how much wind it's deflecting. I grab for my bandana, instantly becoming aware that both hands are needed on the bars at such speeds to keep them from slapping the tank or whatever this plastic bulk between my legs is. Still, I have no intensions of taking it up to this speed very often; I just want to test its capabilities. They certainly seem to exceed my experience and level of skill, leaving me with room to grow and surely that is the point of travel, to grow.

After a sandwich stop, which, thanks to my forethought, lightened my load and not my wallet, we head to Gunnison, a place I've always romanticised about living in. It's a mountain town of adequate size, big enough to have facilities but small enough that I'd be known as the English handyman. Winters are cold at an elevation of over seven and half thousand feet, but the scenery spectacular, especially in late summer. Against the clear sky between the pines are clusters of aspen in varying stages of autumn shades from light green to yellow and orange. They look like a colour blindness test on a mountainous scale.

My ton-up speed test has come at a price: my fuel gauge is once more out of bars and I've only done a hundred miles. Fuck it; I'm not filling up again! If I run out, it means I'm only getting twenty mpg and that could have serious implications to the affordability of this trip. With fatalistic thoughts and a temper brewing, I consider what my reaction will be if I splutter to a halt. If this trip is denied me due to the thirst of my bike, I'm going to be inconsolably disappointed. That sorrow may well reveal itself in a kicking, stomping tantrum. Calculating furiously, I estimate the distance to Seattle and back and divide it by twenty. The estimated fuel cost is a daunting figure that is beyond feasible. The money for this trip is borrowed, not gifted. The river and canyons on route to Montrose are not as deep or dark as my thoughts. When we stop to fill up though, I find I've got thirty-six mpg, and all that concern is left behind on a road I barely noticed as I worried along it. There is a lesson there, I think.

Graciously, Jonathan offers to swap bikes. I've actually been pleasantly surprised with the Venture's handling, and it has even pulled quite well above 4,000 rpm. Perhaps it's not such a good idea to get on Jon's Sprint. So this is what power is like. Triple figure speeds occur as accidentally as daydreams, my senses scream, and my wide eyes stream. As I turn my head, tears mix with sun block and then flow back to sting behind my shades. With one eye shut, I take a fast hairpin, the forgiving Triumph lets me lean lower to correct my line of misperception. It's a lovely bike, but compatibility is not a word that springs to mind whilst I wait for him to catch up. We stop off at a one-horse and two-motorcycle town for a beer. Sitting at the bar, the locals enthuse about the road ahead, but I think it's something they say to every passing road warrior, "It's better over there; off you go now."

With dulled down reactions, I decide for the first time ever to wear earplugs. Back on the Venture, its wallowing seems in keeping with my reduced senses, and in a semi-silent trance-like motion, we wind along river-flanking roads towards the next state. Paradox lays at the Utah border, unless you are already in Utah, in which case it's on the Colorado border. Regardless, it's time to don the helmet. It's a cheap, nasty, old model; under-padded and oversized. It reminds me of being a kid and cycling round with the helmet some cool youth on a FS1-E let me wear, whilst he rolled a cigarette and chatted to a village girl who suddenly wasn't interested in me and my bicycle anymore. It took more than a helmet to turn a bicycle into a motorbike. Even through the misted up visor from the exertion of high-speed pedal pushing, I could see an engine was the only way forward if I wanted to catch the girls' attention now. I may be inside a helmet of nostalgia, but I'm also in a state of apprehension. I have an outstanding warrant in Utah. It's a long story and a small crime, but I never went to court or paid the fine, and the implications of a meeting with the law could amount to quite captivating consequences.

The temperature increases as the day ends, and we stop in Moab, one of Utah's few towns with alcohol available. In fact, it has its own microbrewery. This is where the end-of-day consumption of beer and a burrito occur. In the washroom, I wash my wind-burnt face, noticing in the mirror I have a scarlet strip where my centre parting is. It has headache-inducing qualities. I also have a red crescent shape on my leg where my boot stopped and my trousers had been flapping. I'm undoubtedly road weathered; unnecessarily so, in fact.

Keeping the red theme, we camp by a river in a canyon, the walls radiating their crimson colour as the setting sun reflects off them. It's a stunning spot, and when the stars come out, stoned and dream-like, I stand up to my knees in the temperate flow and stare at the unfathomable sheerness of the cliffs opposite me, the moon shining off the canyon walls. It's a wondrous sight. It convinces me I'm meant to live outside. My being, I believe, is supposed to be surrounded by natural beauty. Man-made house enhancements are nothing but conditioning, a poor substitute for nature, generated as an alternative to the natural beauty of the planet; a planet their production is destroying and depriving us of. My stoned inspiration flows through my mind like the water over my feet, and both are equally irretrievable.

To live an outside existence in England is to be a martyr to comfort; it is too damp, too grey, and too dull too often. But in this near-desert environment of Utah, the sky is big and the air dry, the land immense and unspoilt. At least on the face of it. The reds and oranges are not the brick and terracotta invasion of development on my overcrowded island of Britain, but the rock formations that reach up to dawn and evening skies. I could handle the cold and the snow, if it didn't come with incessant grey moisture. I could forgo my green and pleasant land for these barren surroundings, because it is natural in a liveable way. This would explain why the Native Americans worshipped the land.

I may be stoned, but I know tonight that there are places in life where I should be and situations that I should avoid. And right here, right now, under the stars, facing the cliffs, feeling the rushing river over my feet and the warmth of the air on my uncovered skin, I know that the simplicities of nature are all I need in life. A hunter-gatherer lifestyle would fulfil my needs; a daily existence of sustaining life, while simultaneously respecting, appreciating, and living it. Tonight I can honestly say that for the first time since my suicidal misjudgement, I'm glad I'm still alive.

Tonight I'm whole. I can see the path I should take; it's the one that led me to this place. I'm older than I'd ever been and I'm in love with being me.

I write my diary nearly entirely by moonlight, I'm speechless, due mainly to a Maglite held between my lips. I'm 420 miles into a two-week trip with my best and longest friend. How could what's to come be anything but excellent?

Day 2

Las Vegas, Nevada

250 miles

The tent flaps in the morning breeze. Sand has blown in through the open door and accumulated in the folds of my sleeping bag, and my ears. This could be seen as a negative way to be woken, but I prefer to see it as true grit.

I go and bathe in the river. Somehow it seems colder this morning. The air temperature is cooler, and freshness floods over me. For the next few hours my body and all that surrounds it have the productive and infinite possibilities of a new day. I pack up vigorously to produce a little warmth, circulate the blood, and stimulate my motor skills. This morning we will head up to the highway and make some miles. Interstate 25 is the only road that crosses Green River, which predictably, yet confusingly, goes through a town called Green River. If a settlement is built by a river and then named after said river, I would imagine there will always be an element of misunderstanding as to an inhabitant's actual location.

"I'm drinking in Green River."

"At the bar?"

"No, on the bank."

"The bank serves drinks?"

"No, I brought some beer with me, and it stays cool here."

"From the air conditioning?"

And so it goes. It's as short-sighted as calling your book *Ureka* and forever explaining it's not spelt with an "E." Anyway, Green River is a place where some years ago, driving a dodgy-looking van through a California night into a Utah dawn, I was stopped on suspicion of "hauling guns for the mob." An accusation I was absolutely innocent of, but nevertheless, a search of the van revealed I wasn't entirely innocent, hence the outstanding warrant. My defence has not changed; I honestly didn't know the contraband was there, it was more of a shock to me than the police officer who found it. Obviously, if I had known it was there, I would have burnt it and inhaled the smoke. Utah is not a forgiving state when it comes to such crimes; multiple prepubescent wives, however, is far more acceptable than smoking a natural herb. Although, if I ever went to court, I doubt I'd use that line of defence. So with mild apprehension, both the day and my state of mind are beginning to heat up.

Throughout the morning, with increased highway speed and no earplugs, I become aware of a whining noise from the shaft drive. The sound is creeping in through my ill-fitting helmet and is soon seeking all the attention I have. Green River being the only town of any significance for miles around means this is my only chance to do all I can to stop this incessant noise. The whining has destructive connotations, and I don't want to think about where it might lead. Looking at the shaft, I see there is a grease nipple. I find a commercial vehicle servicing garage and borrow a truck-size grease gun.

Pumping away, I figure it would stop taking it when it's had enough. But like some wanton little shaft teaser, it takes the lot. God only knows where it's all gone. Surely there should be some strong-smelling EP gear oil in there somewhere. Somewhat sheepishly, I return the grease gun with its depleted ammunition and hand over a few dollars as a thank you. It certainly seems to have done the trick. Perhaps not the recommended cure or capacity, but at least the shaft is now spinning silently, encased in a combination of lubrication.

This is the gamble of heading straight out on an unknown bike. I suppose it's a bit like an arranged marriage. I will get to know and learn to love this one that was bought for me, as opposed to dating several bikes and choosing the one I like the best. Our honeymoon takes us onto a "scenic byway." The frequent signs informing us it's a scenic byway are, in fact, the least scenic part of it. I've driven this road several times; I love Utah's diversity in terrain. It has been the one time in my life when I wished I knew a geologist, someone who could mutter facts of unfathomable time and forces that brought about such a truly spectacular landscape—a voice of discovery, much like a satnav would do these days, only perhaps with dulcet tones in the style of a David Attenborough narration, gently informing the spectator of ancient sea beds, moving tectonic plates, long-dormant volcanoes, and weather so extreme it shaped the sandstone edifices into photogenic monuments of time perception. However, no such commentary is available to me, and along with my now silenced shaft, there is little in the way of audible distractions. Anyway, silent appreciation seems the most appropriate honour to give this desert environment.

The road takes us into a shallow canyon alongside a river of irresistible invitation. I stop for a blood-cooling dip, fully clothed. I soak my hair so as not to let the red streak on my scalp blister. I ride on with a brief shiver that quickly turns to comfort and then regret. There is lightning up ahead. With a little elevation, the immensity of the land is revealed and crowned with a moody sky. Ahead is a black anger, from this distance it is mute, but none the less imposing, its visuals scream the brutal conditions to come. Regardless of how indirect the road ahead is, we are heading west and therefore into an imminent soaking. I haven't quite dried out from my river dip and now I have to put on my smelly waterproofs over damp clothing.

The change in conditions has the hot road steaming, and the tar patching is really slippery. The sensation is similar to riding with a worn-bearing, flat tyre, or loose wheel. I decide it wouldn't hurt to check that I'm not. It takes longer to slow to a halt in these conditions than it does to check the bike. I jump off, and a brief count confirms both of the wheels are still there, holding fast and elevated from the road by inflated tyres. With renewed confidence, I resign myself to riding on into the downpour, giving it all the concentration it requires. As well as being denied a mountain vista, as we climb into the very core of this climatic outburst, it's very hard to see anything at all. It's not just the annoyance of missing out on the kind of views that are usually only witnessed with air travel, it would actually be quite beneficial to see where the road goes before the motorcycle inadvertently becomes airborne as it plummets off a cliff edge.

With forward and upward momentum, the summit of the mountain and the peak of the storm are reached. As is often the case with peaks, we don't know we reached it until we start our descent out of the clouds and towards the baked plains. Soon, the unwanted undulation and violent battering becomes a memory, like a squashed hamster under a newly laid carpet. Gone but not forgotten, the drying process begins.

We pass the outer hoodoos, which are a surreal shade of orange and a free taster to the national park that is Bryce Canyon, a geological phenomenon, but it's not going to stop us today.

The afternoon tiredness is dulling my reactions, and we stop for medicinal caffeine. Sitting outside, we witness a wind blowing into town; it proceeds the storm we thought we'd left behind. This is clearly a regular occurrence, as trash cans, tethered to posts, start to thrash around like a caravan about to overtake the inexperienced driver towing it. It's hard to keep my hat on, but I have to, as today my head has a centre line of blisters.

There was once this girl. For several years I never liked her much, then for several more I did, and we became really good friends. Whilst living in Colorado, I got a call from her. She was going to use her holiday to come over from

England and visit. I looked forward to it, as you do when a friend is coming to stay. What I didn't expect was to get shit-faced drunk on the night of her arrival and the friendship changed status. Still, it didn't seem to make things awkward, and we set off in my van to do a little winter road trip. It mainly consisted of being permanently stoned, driving long, empty roads through thrilling winter bleakness and stopping regularly for her to take photos with a rather large camera she had borrowed. We played Pink Floyd, sang Van Morrison, and laughed and loved each other for ten fabulous days.

One cold morning a few days into the trip, I woke up, put the kettle on the stove, and looked around to see what views were around the place we had surreptitiously parked in the night before. I looked at the map and realised we could do a small diversion and go through a National Park called Zion. The sun shone, and the scenery wowed us as the first smoke of the day tightened my forehead and simultaneously numbed and heightened various senses.

Having lived in the van for a few days by that point, there were several pungent smells all mixing with each other for dominance. We certainly didn't consider it to be a smelly, hippy van, but looking back, that description would have a degree of accuracy. So, righteously stoned, without any warning, we came to the entry pay booth. I had no option but to open the window. Looking exactly like what we were, undoubtedly, Mr. Ranger summed us up as he handed over a guide pamphlet in exchange for our entry fee. I wondered if the ranger knew we were about to experience the most memorable miles of our lives. It's quite possible he did. Zion National Park became and remains my favourite place on the planet. Around every corner of the breathtaking, burgundy, winding road is the most dramatic and diverse natural beauty I've ever witnessed. We were in utter awe. So it was with disappointment that we saw a sign announcing a tunnel ahead, as we assumed we would be deprived of our visual overload.

"Maybe it will be the best tunnel in the world," I stated optimistically. And it was. Cut into the tunnel wall at certain points, there were arched windows that looked out onto an overexposed valley of impossible vastness and beauty. It couldn't be real, but it was, and we spent the next twenty-four hours in the most extravagant magnificence nature has ever created. No place on earth has ever made me feel the way I feel in Zion, and although there can only ever be one first time, every time has had its own unique and quirky highlight. But making love under the towering, sheer cliffs that create Zion Canyon was the most wide-eyed visual excess imaginable.

There aren't any lustful bonuses today; the highlight of this visit is the lidless freewheeling, fully immersed in the scenery as we glide down towards the canyon made by the Virgin River. It being a summer visit, this time there are far more people around. On the plus side the river is warm and accessible. Deep in a canyon the sun stops shining on you early in the afternoon. So technically sunset is at 3:15PM. It still reflects off the peaks of the canyon walls, but it won't shine in the valley again until late tomorrow morning. Regardless of the light, I am still surrounded by 360 degrees of wow.

I spin around, taking in the vertical majesty: cliffs that sore into a narrow strip of blue sky. Clouds blow across, but as they come into view they appear to be stationary, giving the impression that the cliffs are falling down. Illusions like this make me lose my balance, and I love things that make me fall over. As the light fades, we opt to take the shuttle bus back. Jonathan chats up the girl who is driving, whilst I watch a pink cloud with a skirt of rain beneath drift over some distance mountains, which are equally inaccessible.

We ride west towards the sunset as my mind processes all the scenery we have just witnessed, wistfully recalling past visits and planning activities for future ones. Zion is an irregular constant in my life; not every visit gives me that unique feeling, but it is more likely to than any other place I have ever been.

As we approach the highway, big drops of rain start to fall, and I extend my legs beyond the fairing to feel the cooling moisture on them. It's been a day of futile avoidance and deliberate indulgence when it comes to water. The same could be said of alcohol over the last fifteen years or so. As we drop down towards Interstate 15, the temperature increases, and we weave through the top left-hand corner of Arizona and into a black, desert Nevada night.

100° Fahrenheit, heat radiating off the asphalt, inescapable and only intensified with speed—I've never ridden such a hot night; I just don't associate darkness with such stifling heat. It really is like riding the highway to hell.

Ahead, Las Vegas shimmers its unnatural presence, and like moths with a gambling addiction, we are drawn towards the light. We ride down "The Strip." It's gone midnight, and I'm wearing just a T-shirt. Vegas provides more visual stimulation but of a very different variety; we ride past greed, excess, and repulsion. This man-made environment was specifically built to attract the hopeful and gullible visitors, while trapping the luckless and the losers, of which there are many, forced to live in the shadows of the extravagance, taunted by the unfairness of wealth distribution. We opt for a fleapit hotel, and after a couple of drinks, I jump in the pool. I try to float on my back like Bob Geldof when he played Pink in the movie, *The Wall*. I look up at a neon-lit sky, pretending my wrists are bleeding and try not to stare at the dodgy dealings occurring on the balconies. With a second wind and refuelled on tequila sunrises, we have a little wander. Being brought up in a land that has a fruit machine in every pub, chip shop, and motorway service station, it's easy to resist what seems to be a mesmerising urge for some: to deposit all their wealth into a slot machine. Jonathan takes us on a shortcut back to the hotel, which leads through a closed and guarded Chinese textile exhibition. Cool, I thought we were going to miss that! Back at base, our accommodation offers a choice of entertainment: sex, drugs, or swimming pools. Tonight, I only indulge in one. Las Vegas is everything Zion isn't, and it's been twelve hours since we saw the sun set there.

Day 3

Riverside, California

250 miles

I tell myself that four hours' intense sleep is more rejuvenating then eight hours' casual sleep. If I want to avoid the full intensity of the desert furnace, half my usual sleep quota will have to be adequate. At 7:30AM, its only 90° Fahrenheit, so I pack up my bike in the shade of the balcony of nocturnal commerce. Opposite is the onyx-black pyramid known as Luxor. Supposedly, a beam of light shot from its apex can be seen from space. However, it can't be seen from the light-pollution-free Mojave Desert just fifty miles away, which makes such a claim somewhat dubious. Looking like a negative prism, it radiates the morning's heat with distorted definition. Brushing my teeth from my open door, I contemplate its mystery.

We head straight out of Vegas; one night is more than enough. I despise the place. It revolves around excess, greed, and money. The developments are simply stolen landmarks from established countries; misunderstood, replicated, and cheapened. It epitomises everything I dislike about America.

Soon, we are back on the long, straight, baking-hot, high-desert road. There is nothing fake about this; it's hot enough to sear the tyres passing over it without necessarily keeping the air in. This is evident from the constant curls of black rubber at the side of the road. There are some hardy types who capitalise on the victims of shredded rubber—scorched businesses in wooden shacks making a killing from the people who gambled on a visit to Vegas with tired tyres. I'm waiting for the worst to happen.

With so many people falling foul to these extreme conditions, it seems only a matter of time before things come unstuck. The highway stretches into a heat-haze horizon, where it looks like nothing more than a dirt road, the central reservation being the grassy strip between the tyre tracks. The bikes don't miss a beat, although my temperature gauge is the closest to red it's got. Our transition into California is uneventful and unsignposted.

The desolate terrain and blinding heat brings an unexpected urge, stronger than my need for a California beach, swaying palms, and the glistening Pacific Ocean. My insatiable desire is to listen to some 1950s' rock 'n' roll in a diner designed as if propelled forward from that era through a time tunnel. It must be a common craving, because just ahead a sign for Peggy Sue's 50s' Diner appears like a mirage in the Mojave Desert. I'm able to feast and refresh on water, coffee, pie, and ice cream, in that order. Whilst listening to music, I know I was born a generation too late to really appreciate. I prefer the bands who were inspired by the bands that were influenced by this. Well, this is going to sit comfortably in my stomach as it mixes and curdles through the San Bernardino Valley (that being the name of our route to Riverside, and not a part of my digestive system).

From this point on, we are in the urban sprawl that centres round Los Angeles. The towns and cities may have different names, but over an eighty-mile stretch from here to the Santa Monica shoreline is nothing but highways, concrete, and a very dense population. The Interstates grow wider, and the traffic increases, as does the smog. Regardless of how built up the area is, one of the more pleasurable sights to sprout from the ground is palm trees. I'm not what you would call a tree hugger, but I love palm trees, or more accurately, I love the climate in which palms grow. Their scruffy unkempt heads aloft skinny bodies, to me, say shorts and sandals, warm sea and no work. The palm tree represents leisure, and therefore I will metaphorically embrace every one of them. However, if there was ever a place that failed to be enhanced by their bedraggled beauty, it would be Riverside; a city named for its location rather than the river by which it is located. It feels rough here; like a hard place to live. It feels gangland, suspicious, irritable, and the cops that cruise the streets seem frightened, jittery, and unforgiving. The first motel we find has all the welcoming qualities of a turf war. We ride around for a hot and frustrating hour and realise we won't find anything better. It is without question that we give the bikes as low a profile as possible, remove all we can, and lock them up for the night.

It's an early stop, and we could have passed on through, but we both have a mutual acquaintance here, although the acquaintanceship holds a somewhat stronger bond with Jonathan. I head to the market for beer and bread, and we sit in the air-conditioned room. As Jonathan channel surfs, I drift in and out of sleep. It occurs to me that the last time I was in California was fourteen years ago. I was living in a van with a friend of mine. On Valentine's Day, he sent some roses back home to his girlfriend, and when we got back to Colorado via that little hiccup in Utah, he discovered that in his absence she had got engaged to someone else. Fourteen years and three marriages later, she was now my girlfriend. Funny how things turn out. The girl we are going to meet tonight was Jonathan's girlfriend. You can cross state lines, sometimes even oceans, but there are some connections that just can't be broken.

Our motel, like so many across the US, is owned and managed by immigrants. It's a recognised way to guarantee residency in the country; buying, owning, and running a business is a fast track to a green card, and motels seem to be a popular choice. However, I'm not sure these new nationals get to see anything of their adopted country beyond the ever-changing faces and circumstances of their transitory guests. Tonight they have two long-haired bikers resident at their Indian-run establishment. So how do these people pass their time? There seems to be little integration into the community, either due to overwhelming work responsibilities, possible religious beliefs, or in the case of Riverside, a fear of what is beyond the security gates and CCTV cameras. As the channels are surfed through, we come across an erect nipple. You don't get that on American TV; even bums are pixelated to keep the minds of the nation clean and healthy, which seems a bit ridiculous as every single American owns at least one. What we have surprisingly tapped into seems to be the kind of porn that only a subscriber has the privilege of viewing. The channel surfing stops, and for an hour and a half we watch as the scenes became more and more hard core. I ask Jonathan if he thinks there will be any cum shots; he says he'll try not to, and I laugh beer out of my nose.

I'm sure his ex can feel the tension. The poor girl has just walked into a room where two virile and highly charged guys have just moments before turned off a TV set. Trying to get a grasp on reality is not so easy when a blond girl enters your motel room; it seems like another unimaginative plot. His ex looks kind of trashy. She still has her strong will and assertive personality, although she is six months pregnant from a guy who is now in jail. Her pretty hair has a crooked, self-cut fringe; her eyebrows are badly plucked and redrawn with sloppy apathy; she has holes in her shoes and is smoking. She has left her other kids in her trailer to come out and visit us. I'm not judging, but the Coloradan bank cashier and strong single mother I once knew seems to have lost her way a little. If she has, she's a long way from knowing or admitting it. To hear her speak, it sounds like she runs Riverside. She takes us downtown for dinner and tells us how bad this place is, though I'd figured that out on arrival. However, it's only been a few years since I'd been wandering the streets of Manila in the Philippines. Riverside isn't the only tough place on the planet. It's just that to the hip fashion victims, who loiter with intent, this *is* the planet and nothing else exists.

I've got sea-level syndrome. Living at an altitude of a mile high for any length of time, as I have in Colorado, your body acclimatises to thinner air. So down here in California I can drink six Coronas and a jug of Newcastle Brown, and annoyingly, it has no effect at all. This means that when we get back to the room the conversation isn't flowing nearly as freely as the beer had. Jonathan books another room, probably for some nostalgic reasons. And I'm left to entertain myself, which obviously means turning the TV back on.

Day 4

Big Sur, California

378 miles

This morning, I get to slowly come to without interruption. It would appear the subscription has expired. Probably for the best.

I walk to the market for avocados, tomatoes and cheese, and some yummy bread. They just can't seem to bake a good loaf in Colorado. Must be an altitude thing. Presumptuously, I buy enough for three, but Jonathan comes to my door alone. I wasn't expecting that; I wonder if he was. I guess the journey into nostalgic sex soon leads to a wasteland of incompatibility and regret. The next time I am to see his ex will be between glass, six years later, when I visit her at a maximum security women's prison, where she will be serving a life sentence for murder.

I call my girlfriend who is keeping Jon's business running whilst he is away. She needs to speak to him about some work-related thing or other. I start to resent his monopoly with women, particularly as he uses up the credit on my phone in the process. Still, the fact that his most recent company had left before dawn means an extra avocado for me. It's a soft and perfectly ripe substitute.

The westerly part of our journey is almost done. We are about to leave the Interstates behind and start heading up towards the Canadian border.

24

First though, we have to ride the multiple lanes of the Los Angeles freeway system. I turn my built-in radio on briefly and listen to The Who's *Reign on Me*. Inappropriate lyrics for this road, but a powerful song nonetheless. It seems every signpost generates a song in my head: Hollywood, Melrose, Pasadena, Rodeo Drive; and when I read the sign "Santa Monica Boulevard" I just have to pronounce it in my head one syllable at a time. Eventually, we leave the Interstate for Highway 101—Ventura Highway. I knew a song about that too. As I sing it to myself, I realise with disgust and disappointment that in the chorus "sunshine" is rhymed with "moonshine"; what feeble and unimaginative song writing. I'd never noticed it before. I suppose actually riding the Ventura Highway had me exploring the lyrics to find a descriptive insight and empathy as I experience the road that presumably inspired the song. The next signpost of association is Auger Hills, the address I wrote to in the early '80s to renew my subscription to *Easyriders* magazine.

Once the song-inciting signs come to a stop, the road loses its thrill somewhat, but there is excitement to be found elsewhere. I've just recorded a personal best of forty-one mpg. I treat myself to a coffee to celebrate. We have the Sierra Nevada Mountains off to our right and the Pacific coastline to our left, yet we seem to have found the blandest, dullest stretch of road between these two spectacular landscapes. It's a little frustrating. The temperature has dropped too, and there is a need for more clothing. Just as the boredom is setting in, the road finally finds the coast. My energy and enthusiasm levels rise with the scenic, undulating route as cliff-hugging corners come at us one after another. A grey mist hangs over us, but it's still pretty, and anyway, on a road like this my eyes are fixed on looking ahead.

We wind up in Big Sur and find a "right on," organic hippy restaurant. Unfortunately, the leek soup I purchase goes right through me. This seems as good a reason as any to call it a day; a decision made all the easier by finding a camp ground with almost spiritual virtues. To say the place has good energy would be a very Californian hippy kind of thing to say, but tonight that's what I am, and I can really sense the positivity. There is an excellent vibe here. It isn't something I can specifically point out or consciously verbalise, I can just feel it. And that, by definition, is how good energy manifests itself. Regardless of this vibe, we are still of the opinion that alcohol can enhance it, so we sit outside on a wooden deck by a fire and take in the night under the shelter of some unfeasibly large redwood trees. We meet an Irish couple and drink Bushmills together. This only adds to the energy; it's like proper travelling.

The thing about America is that it's full of Americans. I live the lifestyle of a resident, not a tourist. I don't stay in hostels or motels, so I rarely get to meet other nationalities. A constant array of freaks come and go around the fireside, all trying to sell us something. One guy makes doughnuts, describing them so vividly I get the munchies. He explains where his place is and how we should stop by for breakfast, what wonderful gifts doughnuts make, and how we should send them home to our loved ones. Or maybe it is the guy selling wrought-iron art who says that.

There are so many sales pitches, it's like, "We interrupt this drinking session to bring you these messages." Or, "This round of Bushmills brought to you by freaky doughnuts, what can you see through the hole?" Despite the intrusions, we stay put all night and then move to our own personal fire by the tents when the bar closes at 2AM. It turns out that the Irish girl has been studying in California, and her brother has flown out to meet her. Brother? You're not a couple? Within minutes, Jonathan has his tongue down her throat. Her brother leaves his sibling to it, and I go to bed with my old friend, resentment.

DAY 5

LAYTONVILLE, CALIFORNIA

316 MILES

I have a Bushmills lie-in, which is pretty much the same as a hangover, and finally get up at 10:30AM. Jonathan is not around. He'd taken his tent mate for a ride on his Sprint. Well, I suppose a slim, fast girl would be attracted to such a sleek design. I can only assume the kind of pillion my fat, wallowing beast would appeal to. As my bike slowly lumbers down the misty, moistened dirt track, it confirms just how difficult it is to control obesity. I lose my balance, I can't get it back, and therefore, can't get my foot on the rear brake pedal. I grab for the front brake lever, and predictably, the front wheel locks, the forks turn full lock, and with a rapid lack of options and little grace but with great determination and a degree of strength, the bike slowly falls to the ground. It gives the obligatory rev to announce this to all within earshot, adding to the embarrassment of my pitiful shortfall. Without eye contact or help, I manage to lift it up, bend back the cruising peg, straighten the mirror, press the start button, and get out on the road where Jonathan is obliviously waiting for me. I feel a strong sense of unfairness and abandonment, and the only way I can fully express this is to shut up and sulk.

It is midday when we finally set off, and with the afternoon miles, my mood rises. We enter the town of Carmel, a place I always associate with Clint Eastwood, as he was once the mayor here. Maybe he still is. I don't know anything about his policies, but the fuel from the quaint and rustic service station has a disproportionately high price tag, due mainly to the owner having no competition. With last night's excitement, I've lost count of how much range I have left in my tank, but I've never got forty-four miles to the gallon. It's not the most powerful bike in the world, and I don't feel lucky. We have to pay the price; this isn't helping my mood lift at all. Other customers being held to ransom at the station ask us if we are heading to the Pig-Nic. I have no idea what they are talking about. But, apparently, somewhere north of San Francisco there is a music festival on a hog farm owned by Wavy Gravy, who was one of the Merry Pranksters. It is clearly attracting a lot of interest, as we are nearly 300 miles away and the buzz has already reached us. With my long hair, purple combats, tie-dye top, and smoky smell, I've obviously been mistaken for a hippy type. All the same, the thought of a festival is something to mull over, and we continue through the mist-piercing, redwood-lined highway. I wonder if it's called *mist* because, due to its presence, we've missed everything of scenic and photographic value.

As soon as the road moves a little inland, the sun blazes from a clear blue sky, but these ocean-side dwellings are located in a dismal dullness. It creeps up from the sea almost translucent, and when it has climbed the cliffs to the road it doesn't flood down onto it, but gently arches over our heads and into the treetops. It takes all the heat out of the sun and forces us to ride in all our layers of warmth and water resistance. However, given a break in the clouds, the temperature soars and overdressed discomfort is instant.

At a coffee stop in Santa Cruz (I'm sure there is another song here, but none come to mind), we are told by a dishevelled- looking youth that this is the most expensive place in the world to live. In his world maybe, but I'm increasingly realising that a Californian's view of the world is even smaller than those in the other parts of the US I have visited, and that's saying something. Nevertheless, I concur that this is the most expensive coffee I have ever had the misfortune to have purchased.

We manage to enter the outer suburbs of San Francisco at 5PM on the Friday of a three-day weekend. At first it's very pleasant as we approach the Haight neighbourhood; brightly coloured, square-box townhouses that still have the hippy culture feeling to them. Read any beatnik movement book or band biography that had a foot in the '60s, and a story or character would have undoubtedly been based around this area. It was synonymous with the flower-power, incense-burning, acid-dropping, tie-dye-wearing, peace-and-love era. Although it may have moved on from VW campervans to the yuppie Saturns, it maintains an air of tranquillity and calm. That soon disappears as we approach the Golden Gate Bridge and its thirteen lanes of frantic, frustrated traffic. As with so much of today's journey, the landmark bridge towers thirty feet into low cloud. It's windy and cold, as a San Francisco summer generally is. A visitor doesn't have to spend long here before being told how Mark Twain famously said: "The coldest winter I ever spent was a summer in San Francisco."

To divert the mind from the chill, at least California is one of the few, if not the only, state where "filtering" is legal. Being British and a former London dispatch rider, I therefore go into impossible deadline and possible bonus mode, weaving my way through the traffic. At least here the drivers half expect it. Filtering being illegal in Colorado, I find it infuriating to be sitting in a jam in the blazing sun when there is a wide and empty space between the stationary cars, but that's what all the other bikes do. They obediently sit and swelter. If you don't follow suit, not only are you breaking the law, but you are also as obvious to the police as a neon doughnut sign on a cold, wet night. I assume the stance and carefully pass the crawling masses. It just goes on and on, all heading north. Whether their destination is home, away, or perhaps festival bound, the endless crawl is passed with cautious satisfaction. I'm really enjoying this; I'm focused, in the zone, and making progress. Out of the corner of my concentration, I keep catching glimpses of parched brown hills, grapevines, and occasional palm trees. Despite these symbols of heat, the temperature has become agreeable. The sun is slouching in a purple sky, and a full moon rises into what is left of the subdued northern California mood lighting. This hundred-mile stretch meets many bike trip desires: world-class landmarks in the form of traversing the Golden Gate Bridge and visual surprises in scenery enhanced by the colours of dusk; and all experienced with a steady progression, taking advantage of my two-wheeled choice of transport through the confinements of congested traffic.

After much longer than expected, we reach signs for the Pig-Nic just as it gets dark. It seems to be a bit chaotic, but quite well-attended. Without charge, we ride into the camping area. I'm no stranger to the festival scene, but I feel like a stranger at this one, though not the strangest by a long way. There are the weekend hippies—ties replaced with tie-dye shirts—then the too-cool-for-y'all types, the dealers, the losers, and somewhere, I suppose, are some music fans. We make camp, and for some unfathomable reason, we drink gin before going to assess the ticket situation. Entry seems to be by wristband and clearly not being *au fait* with the English sneakiness, they have innocently hung bunting around the ticket area, the colour of certain flags identical to the entry wristbands.

With my Swiss army knife and some insulation tape making an internal and invisible clasp, I make us some gate crashing bracelets. They barely check us: just a brief glance at our wrists, and we're in. Standing out from the crowd, with intricate tie-dye patterned shirts over large bellies are two men with long, grey hair and beards. They are looking out over the event and no doubt discussing something about the scene. My immediate thought is, "This is not your first festival, is it?" In eyes, look, stance, dress, and general demeanour, these two guys have undoubtedly seen a lot of this type of thing. I think about approaching them, but unfortunately, my confidence has slowly been worn down over the last few days. It seems that every time I open my mouth, my words are repeated back to me, as though I'm talking to some demented parrot. Is my accent really such a novelty to this insular bunch?

I realise imitation is supposedly the greatest form of flattery, but for fuck's sake, it would be refreshing if just once I'm listened to and given a fitting reply instead of having everything I say parroted back in an insultingly bad impression of what the perpetrator thinks I actually sound like. I'm not here to educate or even entertain, I just want to communicate, and I don't seem to be able to. I've had more success in India. Anyway, one of the two aging hippies was Wavy Gravy, the hog farm owner himself.

This is usually a scene I feel most comfortable in. I'm wearing my festival purple combats, so all the ingredients seem to be right. Even the music is good, but I'm not feeling the festival affection. I think there is more to this awkwardness than accent paranoia. Usually, I would be mingling, making spontaneous quips and observations. Not here; I feel my cynicism rising. It's far easier to internally taunt and judge than it is to open up and interact. The observations I make are of falseness. The ambience is contrived, forced, not unlike the weekend warriors who replace their suits with embossed leather jackets and get on their showroom-shiny Harleys, thinking they are bad motherfuckers. Being the loudest mouth in the bar doesn't make you anything other than a loudmouth in a bar. At the Pig-Nic, the attendees just seem like they are trying too hard to be hippies.

My cynicism has all the qualities of perpetual motion. It wasn't going to stop. Jonathan, however, is of a completely different frame of mind. I'm not sure if its positivity, but he's at least accepting and has a willingness to enjoy the situation. So when he turns up with some magic mushrooms he's scored, I know without a shadow of a doubt, that this atmosphere is not right for me to be taking mind-altering drugs. They will not change this mood for the better. He is angry that I won't indulge with him, and his disappointment is reflected in some hurtful comments. I feel his insatiable need to get wasted has finally crossed the line from hobby to habit. And his words crush what little self-esteem I have left tonight. "You're happy to abandon me when there's a shag on the horizon, but when you need a tripping partner my refusal offends," I think to myself as I recoil to the sanctuary of my tent. For me, the escapism is the journey; I wonder why he's doing this trip.

Day 6

Brookings, Oregon

237 miles

Drums were banging most of the night, but that was to be expected really. I don't know if Jon was too, but he seems upbeat this morning. Everyone is talking about the guy who'd been having a bad acid trip. Apparently, he had spent all night in his tent cussing at the top of his voice. I'd missed it all, but he had obviously pissed off a lot of people. Apparently, on the fifth attempt, security finally removed him. A very stoned burrito seller bumbles through the camp ground peddling his gourmet wares, which smell far more appealing than the garments he wears. With his dumbed-down dealing abilities, he's incapable of working out the change I'm due and completely scoobied by my accent. Selling Mexican food is evidently the closest to international interaction he can handle.

Time to move on; the festival can continue without us. My packing has developed a strategy and rhythm that last night's drummers could only dream of. However, by the time we roll out it's still a late start. This festival cost me nothing at all, and it was almost worth it. With the money I've saved, I decide to up my tempo a little and take the winding Redwood Highway at petrol-glugging speeds peaking at eighty-five mph. Today I'm riding in the warmth of the sun and in the shade of the trees, whilst running alongside a river. The road twists round the hills, through tunnels, and over bridges. It reminds me exactly why I ride. This is the road and the day that all the other roads and days have led to. Wake up, pack up, ride out, and find the kind of route that leaves me knowing that only being here today on a motorcycle, with all that has passed and all that's to come, will generate the feeling that I'm experiencing right now.

There is a T-shirt with a slogan something along the lines of, "If I had to explain you wouldn't understand." To me, that T-shirt might as well say, "I'm very inarticulate." But when not being pedantic or literal, I could apply that phrase to this road. It's a bike thing, and I simply can't describe this feeling. Call me ineloquent, but I'm trying to concentrate on the road ahead, and quite frankly, I'm speechless.

At Eureka, we stop, and I put yesterday's savings in my tank. Jonathan, though, has a bigger expense and is in need of a new front tyre. Whilst it's fitted, to kill time we wander round a flea market and I buy a new bungee cord that snaps as soon as I stretch it over my load. I have spent much of my motorcycling life looking for the perfect bungee; they frequently lack elasticity and seldom perform the basic task required of them: to stretch, hold, and retain that grip until it is no longer required. I have no doubt that somewhere out there is a bungee cord that does just that, and holding on to this hope is what keeps me purchasing them.

We try to find a bar—a task we generally excel in—but it takes several trips up and down the main road before we are successful. No wonder the place is called Eureka. Jonathan's new rubber seems far more satisfying and grippy than my bungee cord had been. With no further need to stick around, we ride off into what's left of the day, through more redwoods that seem to have an even stronger aroma with the fading light.

With the last of the daylight, we cross the border into Oregon. There has been a signposted countdown for a looming fish and chip restaurant, and obediently, we decide to eat there. It's a half hour wait just to get a table, so we look around the gift shop, which sells everything from lampshades to playing cards with fish on them. When we finally get a seat at the communal table, the cod I order comes in a battered square slice. Hype alone is obviously what has made this place so busy; they haven't got a clue. Much like an American-themed diner on the A1 in Lincolnshire with an acne-encrusted teen mumbling, "Enjoy ya meal," as he slams down an oversized plate of grease and indifference onto your Route 66-themed, plastic tablecloth.

It's dark now, and we think we're lucky to get the last available space in a campsite of rumbling motorhomes and yelling kids. I do a beer run and take advantage of my loan status to call my girlfriend, who is clearly taking advantage of her lone status and isn't home. After a few beers and several late nights, I'm more than happy to perform the other on-the-road ritual I love so much—the rolling out and pitching of the tent bit—then laying down in the comfort of self-containment; cosy and sheltered, if not isolated from the obnoxious world of motorhomes.

They are crammed into this holiday weekend site, closer than benefit scammers on a housing association estate. However, these multi-axle status symbols have infinitely more luxuries, requiring generators, and plug-in hook-ups designed to draw so much power the cables are thicker than a failed bungee cord. I imagine the world class holidays you could take for the price of a $100,000 motorhome. I can only assume the owners lack any degree of imagination, and that would explain why they're plugged into the restrictions of the national grid of camping grounds. I admit America doesn't have the condescending class system my country of lineage and descent thrives on. Yet, there is a paradox in the fine line between the Walmart white trash, who so often come from trailer parks, but give that trailer an engine, granite worktops, a smaller dog, and a tree-lined parking spot and suddenly the inhabitants are propelled from the status of lazy and unemployable to permanent vacationers. I find the time to consider all this since I have to fully wake up in the night to find my flysheet. The patter of rain turns from soothing to soaking in the time it takes me to realise I can no longer see stars through my mesh roof. Jonathan is asleep on top of a picnic table, not unlike Snoopy on his kennel roof, so therefore he isn't alerted to the sound of rain on the side of his tent. He may have fallen asleep with stars in his eyes, but he'll wake up to a damp reality.

Day 7

Seaside, Oregon

346 miles

Actually, a damp reality awaits the both of us. It isn't even rain, but a relentless drizzle: the most depressing form of precipitation there is. Possibly the inhabitants of the air-conditioned vibrating boxes around us are unaware of the weather beyond their soft furnishings. But we are well and truly exposed to the elements, and this morning there is a cold, grey, thick moisture hanging beneath and dripping from the canopy of trees surrounding us. Escape is futile.

I roll up my soppy, sagging tent, stashing last night's undrunk beer bottle in the centre, and we move onto a road of dense sea mist that slows our speed like an open drag shoot. To add to this morning's theme, the pancakes at the restaurant seem to have the soggy consistency that suggests they, too, had been outside all night. The waitress, undeterred, has a bright outlook and is adamant this will burn off as the morning progresses; I assume she is talking about the mist. And with the accuracy of an assassin, we ride into her predicted blue skies. Although the weather had been cold and miserable, it had a comforting moody feel to it. Not that I want to wallow in such things, but the greyness does possess its own atmospheric "no quarter" appeal. However, blue skies are always better. This is how I would imagine Alaska to be: sawmills standing between mountains of woodchips; logged trees gathered together in rivers waiting to be picked out, processed, and loaded onto waiting trucks—*The Waltons* with a bit more modernisation and automation. We pass little fishing villages, wooden houses with peeling paint; it all feels very comfortable and communal. When we stop for fuel, we are told it is illegal to pump your own gas in Oregon. We have to wait for a youth to do it for us. I assume this law is to generate employment; an alternative to being a lumberjack or a fisherman. They probably have career advice at school on the subject. If you get seasick and don't like chainsaws, but love meeting people, perhaps you should consider a career in pumping gas.

At Coos Bay, we stop to buy bread and cheese and then ride to an ocean view to eat. I make a very appealing-looking sandwich and put my hand in my rolled-up tent and pull out a nicely chilled beer; the cold, wet bottle slips straight out of my hand and smashes on the ground. Amongst the wild crashing waves and surf, huge sea lions are bobbing around. After their ocean battering, they wallow onto the beach like they too have eaten some undercooked pancakes this morning. It's not a bad lunch spot; too lovely to leave broken glass lying around, so I get on my hands and knees and diligently pick up the pieces, put them into a plastic bag, and place it in my top box.

We are besieged by flies, so the scenery is best appreciated at a pace faster than a fly can fly. It's a rugged coastline of rocky pinnacles protruding from angry and destructive waves. Having grown up in various coastal towns, I still find mountains more thrilling than the sea. However, this is a very dramatic scene of unhindered energy: waves pounding into the land mass with a momentum they have gathered over thousands of miles. It reveals the might of nature, and this is a relatively calm day. Still, the sun is deceiving, and the chill air saps the comfort. I just about have enough clothes on to keep me warm. I'm wearing my leather work gloves, but by 4PM I'm ready to put my proper riding gloves back on, which I can do without stopping, thanks to my cruise control.

We come upon a continuous succession of small towns, slowing our progress by both dithering local traffic and constant speed limits. This is still Highway 101, although depending on the area it crosses, it has several different names, none of which have shown a great deal of imagination. The Oregon Coastal Highway is the current signposted road. The town of Seaside is another name with bleeding obvious connotations. It's got a wild side to it, which invites wild camping, although not yet, as there are still some people loitering around the dunes. So we take the opportunity to ride along the beach, mainly because a sign authorises it. It's a wide and uninhabited beach of flat, firm sand; perfect for land speed record attempts, but I'm not sure what a slight tremor of the bars would result in. I could imagine the front tyre being grabbed by a sudden soft surface, which would feel unforgiving as I was high-sided off my bike. However, this unobstructed length of beach makes for some excellent motion shots as we ride side by side, focusing on taking blurred speed photos. Speed is definitely the way to pass over this surface, as when I head towards the dunes to make my turning arch I ride past the high-tide hardening point, and the bike reveals all its bulk and sinks into the sand like a sea lion full of pancakes. I do what I can with my throttle and clutch control to get the thing moving forward, as opposed to its desire to just dig down. I'm not whinging about having a shaft drive now.

We ride back into the town. It's pretty tacky, not unlike an Essex seaside town. We find a laundromat so Jonathan can put his sleeping bag in a dryer, then we find a hotel for a drink. It's Jonathan's idea; full of hope that he can pick up a woman with a room. It is, I suppose, possible, but we've been on the road for quite a few days now, and we aren't looking our best. I've got a tent, I've found a place to pitch it, and a dry sleeping bag to roll out; I don't need to find "a woman with a room."

Back at the sand dunes, we notice there are "No Camping" signs all over the place, but agree that if we can ride our bikes up the sandy path unseen, then no night-cruising cops will spot us. There is no way I'm going to get mine through this soft sand though, especially uphill. Jonathan gets his a little way up, until his back wheel starts to spin and digs in. I jump off my bike and run up to give him a push. Just as I reach the back of the bike, he gives it a fistful of throttle, shooting sand straight into my face, gets a grip, and takes off. I stand there blinded, trying to wipe sand out of my mouth and eyes with my T-shirt. Oblivious and proud, he walks back down the dune.

"Got up there all right, didn't I?"

"Yeah, because I was pushing you!"

He talks me into trying to get mine up too, and although I know it won't go, I try anyway. I take a run up, and as soon as the front wheel hits the sand, it sinks, and I drop the bike. The foot board catches my leg as it goes down and cuts into it. I decide to leave the bike in the parking lot; I also decide my leg needs a plaster. I open the top box to get my first-aid kit and in the dark put my hand straight on the plastic bag with the broken glass in it.

Well, this is turning out to be fun! I erect my tent and call it a day. Jonathan snores, so in my underwear and bike boots, I stumble across the reeds holding my tent aloft and stomp around to make a flat spot to re-pitch further away. It must look like some weird tribal ritual under the full moon. As I trample the reeds down I notice a lot of them hang heavy, like unharvested grapevines, but the weight that makes them bow is big, brown slugs the size of turds. It really is like Clacton.

DAY 8

SEATTLE, WASHINGTON

239 MILES

The moon projects flickering shadows onto the walls of the tent, and the reeds sway and brush against it in the ocean breeze. These unfamiliar sounds are enough to convince me I have unwanted visitors, especially when I'm wild camping and without my bike by my side. So for the second time tonight, I get out of my sleeping bag. I don't find slugs threatening, and I've never had a vegetable plot so I don't find them annoying either, but any living thing with such a close resemblance to a turd does nothing to endear me. However, they are the only life form beyond my tent, and that puts my mind at rest. The next thing I know it's getting light, and there is the now familiar sound of rain hitting the tent with varying force as the wind gusts. I get dressed and put on my waterproofs before I unzip the door; not the easiest of manoeuvres. Again, I roll up the sodden tent, the moisture flows off the lid of the opened top box and onto the seat as I pack my bedding away. We both have very cheap dome tents, and given our unofficial location, we didn't bother to stake them out properly. Jonathan has also managed to get all geared up before leaving his tent; he even has his helmet on.

Forgetting he hasn't got a woman in his tent to hold it down this morning, he soon discovers how quickly they catch the wind once they are emptied of bedding and bike gear. It blows off across the dunes, a bit like Rover the ball of control in *The Prisoner*; only this one is out of control, and Jonathan is the one doing the chasing. I watch him jumping over knee-high reeds; it has great comedic value, especially the full body dives. All geared up in his leather jacket and helmet, he disappears from sight in the tall grasses momentarily, emerges, and continues sprinting across the uneven dunes, the taunting tent rolling on just a few steps ahead of him. When he does finally retrieve it and returns, he explains that he hadn't been diving for the tent, but kept falling flat on his face when the matted undergrowth caught his boots. This made it all the funnier. An image of slapstick hilarity, it really brightened my morning. Despite the dress of the day being full waterproofs, my big fairing combined with the smelly one-piece outer layer I inherited with the bike, I'm actually quite toasty, and my mood is bearing up well, even with the grim weather. I'm happy to be on the road; it's better than a lot of alternatives.

We come to a long bridge spanning the Columbia River, which separates Oregon from Washington. The divide in the states also seems to be where the blue sky begins. My first experience of Washington, the most northwesterly of what Alaskans refer to as the "lower 48 states," is some perfectly cooked pancakes. I'm really quite dirty now, but I'm not particularly worried about it, as I know today we will reach our destination and the comforts of someone else's home, where I can wash away the weariness of the road.

Next thing we know, with his well-practised entrapment technique, we are pulled over by a cop. We'd been following him at the kind of speed and distance you follow a police car on a single-carriageway road, and when he indicates to turn left, we ride past on the inside of him. This is exactly what he wants us to do. Lights blaze and sirens scream as he cancels his fictitious turn to chase us. Of course, he had never intended to turn. He solemnly informs us that in Washington State it is illegal to perform the manoeuvre of passing on the inside of a vehicle turning left. What a scam! Predictably, he can't make head nor tail of my green and photo-less UK driving licence and moves on to Jonathan, a fully fledged American, who he patronisingly informs "should know better." Well, at least we know the mentality of the authority we are dealing with in this state, and we'll adjust our behaviour accordingly.

Jonathan's half-brother had a wife who now lives in Seattle. And her brother has a daughter living in Olympia, a place, like the suburbs of Los Angeles, I know a song about. We swing by his half brother-in-law's daughter's apartment; it's small and arty, but it's still a bit of a novelty to be somewhere that the unconnected road traveller wouldn't otherwise get to see. We're only there to pick her up before all heading on to her auntie's place in Seattle, but not before some essential sightseeing. It may not be on everyone's list, but I want to go to the Evergreen State College, where Courtney Love was introduced to Kurt Cobain, when she went to school in Olympia. I'm a bigger Courtney fan than I am a Nirvana fan, but still, for me this is like an historian standing on a Hastings battlefield, and I swear that I don't have a gun.

I'm given pillion-carrying duties, which I'm more than happy to do, and back on the road we proceed, with the most highway miles of the trip, up to a city with a skyline familiar to anyone who has ever seen the show *Frasier*. Even more familiar are the faces in the apartment we're staying in: old drinking friends who have relocated from Colorado. We fill the apartment with all our clutter and have a beer. It's time for that wonderful, long-awaited shower. My clothes are put in the washer, and I spend far longer than my allotted time and hot water quota washing off over 2,500 miles and a week's worth of road-acquired character. Much like cleaning a bike or a kitchen, the longer you leave the job the more you appreciate the change when it is once again spotless. That's how good it feels to take this shower, even if I only have a towel to wear whilst the washer performs its arduous task.

Right, we are now ready for some vacation pastimes, which are not that dissimilar to our end-of-a-day-on-the-road pastimes. However, Jonathan and I now have the company of three girls and are driven downtown to a large gothic pub that sells Caffrey's, my current beer of choice. And that is it. Despite a guidebook full of alternate activities, we don't leave the pub. But man, was it a fun evening! There are now eight of us staying in a two-bedroom apartment. I get a pretty good deal, though, and share a big bed with my cuddly drinking buddy. Her kid is in the bed too, so we just watch a movie, and I bask in the clean, white, soft bedding and safe environment. Sometimes the best bit of a road trip is when you have a break from it.

Day 9

Day off in
Seattle, Washington

24 miles

It had been at least nine days since I checked my email. But in 2001 that was an acceptable amount of time to go without Internet interaction. Now just nine minutes of no connection means missing something of seemingly significant importance.

After checking email, I drink coffee and watch TV. Not really how I would choose to spend a morning, but as a novelty, much like packing up a wet tent, it's OK every now and again. It strikes me how I've done no research at all for this trip. There are the things I knew of, like national parks and the Hollywood sign on the hill. Then there are the things I was happily surprised by, like the sea lions and twisting roads through the redwood forests. Today, we are going to see something I have absolutely no knowledge of, and I'm not even sure how enthusiastic I am about it. North of Seattle is where the Boeing factory is.

The climate here is so much like home that even when the sun is out, you know that rain is possible at any time. So it's a grey ride up to the Boeing plant.

We book our tickets for the tour. I don't really have any expectations, but even if I did, this visit most certainly exceeds them. It's a tour of spectacular statistics. For a start, the building where the planes are manufactured is the largest in the world by volume: the size of seventy-five football pitches. It can probably be seen from space. People love to say that. We walk through tunnels lit by fluorescent strip lights. Although only every other one is switched on, there are so many that they save a million dollars a year on their electricity bill just by only using half of them. When we reach the vista point that looks down onto the shop floor, its sheer vastness is evident, as three jumbo jets in various stages of completion are lined up. From our vantage point, it's hard to believe they are full size; they are dwarfed by the scale of this complex. They turn out a plane every eight days, and the tour guide makes it very clear that the legroom between the seats is dictated by the customer ordering the plane and not the manufacturer. That makes sense. I'd love to know what airline requests the least legroom, and the most, for that matter (probably a Scandinavian airline, as they are such a long-legged race). The utter size of the Boeing plant and the implications of building flying machines make for an impressive infrastructure. Just being in charge of the light bulbs would be quite stressful, let alone being the test pilot who has to take each new-build up into the sky on its virgin flight to see if it falls out. All this contemplation has made me hungry for a big fat burger, and soon my life returns to its insignificant existence of indulgence in the pursuit of eternal gratification.

Back in front of the TV, we realise we don't have enough time, money, or enthusiasm to go to the Space Needle, so we go to a local bar instead; one of those awful characterless places located in a terrace of shops. It has all the atmosphere of an opticians, but with more glasses and less light. That's all I see of Seattle. Most of what I did see was viewed from the bottom of a glass. Once again, I share a bed and the second half of last night's movie. The best thing about a break in a road trip is the craving to get back on the bike.

Day 10

Saint Regis, Montana

434 miles

Shower, coffee, packing, waiting, goodbyes. A feeling of sadness. Back out into the cold and grey, but we are warm, clean, and rested. I feel like I could climb a mountain. I hope the bike does too, because actually, I'm just going to sit here and twist the throttle. In the US, highways with odd numbers go north/south, which is why we rode Highways 1 and 101 to get to Seattle; even-numbered highways run east/west, and so now with coincidental chronological order, we are taking Highway 2 through the Cascade Mountains.

The road is wet, and I'm getting colder and colder as we climb. We are heading back now, and I'm feeling the misery of the colourless day. I'm hoping for a break in the clouds to reveal some of the scenery being denied us. Sure enough, when we reach the summit, the Pacific moisture—the mist that's been hanging over us for much of the trip since leaving LA—seems to be buffered by this mountain range. The descent brings with it blue skies, warmth, and a very different landscape. We coast down into a dry and almost desert-like setting. The land is flat, and there is no longer much need for concentration, which means there is a need for stimulation, as the songs in my head are becoming repetitive and annoying. I try making up poems, but that isn't working either, as when I get to the fourth line I've forgotten the first and have to do the poem backwards, it's like thinking inverse.

Necessity being the mother of invention, I discover that I can fit my foam-covered Walkman headphones under my helmet. They are squeezed against my ears with a pressure that is the comfortable side of a throb and stops the wind from taking the music away. I can bear this for just about the time it takes one side of my The Who compilation C90 tape to play. The terrain turns arable, and there are twisters on the horizon. I can see for miles, and at any time, there are at least seven or eight whirlwinds whipping up the soil 200 feet as it's sucked into the sky. As they cross the road up ahead of me, with an unlimited and unobscured horizon, it's easy to judge my speed so as not to collide. All the same, I'm quite intrigued as to what it would be like to ride through one. I can't imagine I'm going to be sucked into a vortex and wake up in the Land of Oz; it would probably just block my air filter and sandblast my paintwork.

With no alternatives, we join Interstate 90. But it's not a dull highway; it runs through canyons, up mountains, and past lakes and has some lovely, sweeping curves. It's a fast and pretty road and more suited to fast and pretty bikes. My wallowing beast doesn't really like high-speed handling; it really doesn't like handling much at all. It's somewhat manageable at slower speeds, but at a highway pace it doesn't want to multi-task, and I have to fight to change the angle of projection. I consider checking the air pressure in the tyres and the forks, or at least wear some more protection in case I do come off, but it seems a lot of effort, so I end up just gripping the bars tighter. Despite this, I don't even put a foot down in Idaho. We are racing a sun that is setting earlier the further east we go. We have already lost an hour and just about manage to get fuel, whiskey, and bread before the shop closes and loses its convenience status. They tell us of a free place to camp on a sand bar in the bend of a big river. The advice benefited us all, because when they mention it's a great place for a campfire, we purchase a bundle of logs too. The spot is straightforward to find, but it would be easier to get to in the van than on the Venture. I can't see the potholes because the fairing is in the way. When the track reaches the sand, the bike sinks into it; deep, really deep. It's as if the bike has been lowered and stabilised. I just step off it. That'll do; I'll deal with it in the morning. What a beautiful spot it is. The moon rises and shines over pine-covered hills, the river flows past silently, and there isn't a soul around. We make a circle of rocks and stones and light a fire, have a smoke, drink some whiskey, and soon, as the setting is so idyllic and because he still has a few left over, we eat the last of Jonathan's Pig-Nic-purchased mushrooms.

This is perfect; it's so good to be back on the road. A warm night and a campfire, surrounded by natural beauty, tranquillity and isolation. The Pacific coast was good, but this is better. It's too bloody hip in California; the forced coolness, the desperate need to be what they think they should be leaving them just fake and insincere. Nature can't be faked, and I can't fake how it makes me feel. I love it out here, this is road-trip heaven. Ironically, our illegal substances are natural too; it's the taxed and legitimate whiskey that is blended and manufactured. We sit by the fire talking bollocks, and I laugh till I cry. At an undetermined time, with salt traces of dried tears lining my laughter lines, I lie in my sleeping bag and let my subconscious mind take a crazy train of thoughts.

Lewis and Clark National Park, Montana

419 miles

A bigger deterrent than a lock and chain is a bike that is buried up to its axles in sand. In the light of a new day, I manage to find an implement with digging capabilities and warm myself up by removing sand from under my tyres and the sump of the bike. I also find a couple of strips of wood that I can use as crawler boards when it's time to leave. But it isn't time, not yet. It's such a beautiful spot; if only we had food and more time. Actually, although I'm enjoying every moment of this, there is an underlying knowledge that we are heading back, and in a few days I'll see my girlfriend again. I've missed her just the right amount; enough to make the return something I'm looking forward to, but not enough to actually turn me round prematurely. That was until this morning, when Jonathan suggests we go up to Glacier National Park on the Canadian border. Of course we should; why wouldn't we? I had just not considered we would be diverting from the circle that was taking us back to the start. It's an interesting dilemma. There is no reason why I wouldn't go up to the northern border, but I'm just kind of stuck in the mindset of heading back now.

Although, I won't be heading anywhere if I don't get my bike out of this sand it's stuck in. So with an idea I got from watching a programme on how the pyramids were built, Jonathan takes the plank I've just ridden over and puts it in front of me, until, one bike length at a time, I get back to a surface that requires a side stand. The next surface that requires a side stand is outside a restaurant, and lacking the same sense of proportion I have for the sizeable state of Montana, I order way too much food. It's been said that owners often look like their dogs. Well, I'm rapidly resembling my bike, which also has proportions I'd initially underestimated.

When we head back out on the road north to Glacier National Park, we start to notice a large number of fire trucks. There are camps of fire fighters, blackened and exhausted. It turns out we have well and truly left the rains behind us; here in northern Montana they have suffered a summer of drought, resulting in a lot of forest fires. The fire fighters have got permanent campsites where they grab some sleep before starting another long and strenuous shift. They look shattered. I get the feeling they have been doing this for a while. As we approach the park, smoke fills the sky. Montana is known as the "Big Sky" state, yet there is still enough smoke to fill it. A lot of the park is closed, and although we don't intend to go off the main road and hike trails, it's not even an option.

With increased elevation, we can see the level of devastation. Northern Montana has been burning for most of the summer, and smoke hangs in the blackened valleys. Height, in both altitude and latitude, combined with the time of year, has brought the temperatures right down. We are very close to the Canadian border now. It isn't the most spectacular of experiences, and there is an underlying air of despair. Defiance has kept the park open, but we don't see the stunning scenes the park is named after. There are some beautiful, winding, cliff-hugging roads, but they just feel in the way of my homing instinct. In fact, there is nothing to divert my attention from this reluctant travel in the opposite direction to where my heart wants to go.

We prepare ourselves for some long-distance riding, but unfortunately, I don't prepare my bike; it probably would have been wise to have filled the tank. We have many miles ahead of us, and as we ride along, I discover there is a lot of nothingness both around me and inside my tank. A sign confirms this, saying the next town is eighty-nine miles away. There is no way I can make it there, and I'm not about to turn back either. I am saved from the humiliation of depleted reserves when we enter the tiny one-pump town of Dupuyer. We just can't seem to get going today; every shitty little town seems to require us to stop to address some need or other.

By 7PM, the sky no longer has the glow of the sun or the forest fires. We pick up our staples of whiskey and beer at Great Falls and head off to the national forest for some free camping. I find something that I have to assume is a campsite; it's by a river, but it's too dark to figure out what else is around, so it will have to do. I find some damp logs and, with a little persistence, manage to get a fire going, which soon gives out some much-needed warmth. With the consumption of whiskey, it doesn't take long for the warming of the insides to start, and soon they meet each other, and a comfortable glow is achieved. We've been dragging a set of speakers around with us the entire trip and not used them once. As this is probably the last night, we plug them in for a bit of live Floyd around the fire. When the wood is all gone and the bottle is empty, I go to my sleeping bag to insulate myself from the damp night. Since my excessive breakfast, I haven't eaten today, so my tent sort of spins a bit when I get in it. The last thing I remember is being on all fours with my head sticking out the door and wondering which breakfast I will see first: tomorrow's or this morning's.

Day 12

Casper, Wyoming

515 miles

The delicate sound of falling snow is not the sound I expected to wake up to; however, it is a cold and genuine reality. How can this possibly be? My mouth is dry, my stomach is churning, and I just want to go back to sleep. If the way I feel along with the thought of all the miles ahead of us isn't wretched enough, we now have to contend with the fact that it's bloody snowing. We need to get out of here; we need to drop our elevation. Packing up a snow-covered tent has my fingers numb before I've even turned the key in the ignition. When I eventually do force my frozen fingers into my bike gloves and am ready to leave, I find myself constantly whiping a layer of frozen slush off my visor. The thought of 500 plus miles in these conditions is daunting.

We head south out of the forest and drop in altitude, where the snow ceases . . . and turns to rain. The first town we come to is called White Sulphur Springs. We walk into a diner. Everyone is commenting on how wet it is out there and how cold we look. The main topic of conversation is the weather. A bunch of loud, fat ranchers is ecstatically pleased and expressing their joy with bellowing enthusiasm. They have been waiting for this for a very long time. When we have peeled off our layers and shuffled into a booth, I look through the condensation-covered and rain-streaked window. The whole town seems to be rejoicing in what I consider to be the misery of the weather. I suppose it's reduced the risk of fire and the fear they were living in. There is a sign above the hardware store that would usually say something like, "Save $$$ on new mowers," but someone has actually bothered to go up a ladder to change the slogan to, "So this is what rain looks like." We clearly are very lucky to have arrived at such a special time.

Jonathan needs some better gloves; the ones he has been riding in are just not up to these conditions. White Sulphur Springs not being a town that caters for bikers and their possible needs, he has to settle for some white, sparkly, spandex, disco under gloves, which he covers with brown, rubber gardening gloves. I have to tuck his jacket sleeves under the elastic cuff for him, as he has lost all dexterity.

We head on down to Livingstone. Progress is slow and the conditions miserable. There is no way we are going to get back today. We'd intended to go back via Yellowstone National Park but have unanimously decided, without any form of discussion with regard to the detour, that the appropriate response as to the possibility of prolonging the misery of these conditions is simply, "Fuck that!" The unappealing, but direct, alternative is to take the highway the 600 miles back to Denver. We get onto Interstate 90 and head east. The mesas to the north of us are snow covered; it's only a matter of a few hundred feet and a couple of degrees that has turned the precipitation to rain.

There is a clatter of plastic on concrete. My top box, which was always a little wobbly, has just dropped off the back of my bike like a used-up rocket booster. In my mirrors, I see it skidding down the highway, still with my tent and sleeping bag bungeed on top. It's going really fast, but not fast enough to catch me up. There's a campervan behind it wondering which way my top box is going to veer and if he should attempt to overtake it. Luckily, the top box decided to pull over on the hard shoulder. I stop, turn around, and ride the wrong way up the highway to retrieve it. The tent is grazed, but nothing is missing or broken. I stand there in the strong wind and pissing rain trying to refasten it. Jonathan has stopped too and is having trouble putting the Sprint on its side stand in this driving crosswind. As he makes his way over to me to see what the problem is, his bike blows over. I gesture to him what has happened, and he runs back through the spray of passing traffic to lift it back up. It's not a good day.

We continue on; the miles are going by so slowly. The rain seems to be set in for at least a week. There are no signs of hope. We stop for lunch at Billings. Like breakfast, our entry sparks comments of the bleeding obvious. We look wet and cold apparently, it's not good weather to be riding, and it's a long way to where we are going. I put myself in their place. What would I say to me? Nothing, just a sympathetic smile and perhaps an offer of a coffee. It would be a token gesture, a sign of some empathy. Because telling me I look a bit on the wet side is as useful as telling the patrons they are on the wrong side of slim. My feet are soaked, so I change my socks and put my trainers on. The waitress gives me two thick, black, industrial bin bags. They are like waders without form, and I tape them round my legs to stop them flapping.

With a warming chilli inside me and dry feet, the ride has gone up a notch in bear-ability. Nothing has changed outside, but my body has a little more resistance to the elements now. We cross into Wyoming—our tenth state in twelve days. My feet are feeling wet again, but it must just be the cold. Though when I glance down, I realise the bin bags have threaded in the wind. My feet really are wet again, despite the denial. The energy I have used to generate warmth in my body combined with the concentration the road conditions demand has left me feeling drained. I want to stop and get a motel, but am worried this rain could turn to snow overnight. We opt for a hot chocolate in Sheridan and force ourselves on. Another two and half hours; another 150 miles. I am really pushing my levels of endurance; not exactly helped by a two-week diet of alcohol, low-nutrition diner food and various other substances of questionable benefit.

As we approach Casper and embark on the last 50 miles of the day, it actually stops raining. Not that it makes any difference. It's a bit like the tide going out after you've already drowned. The clouds lift a little to reveal snow on the nearby hilltops. That was, I can say without any shadow of doubt, the longest, coldest, wettest ride I have ever done. It's been utter shit. Just as we get into the motel, the rain starts again, only now I am dry and warm, it goes without saying that it doesn't look like good riding weather out there.

Day 13

Denver, Colorado

288 miles

At 7:30AM, I look out the window. Yes, it's dry. It's grey. It's cold. But it's dry, and that is as much as I was hoping for. My boots are still damp, everything is, but nothing is going to get wetter, and that's the main thing. It's only 47° Fahrenheit. If we hadn't diverted up to Glacier National Park we may have avoided the soaking we got, but we can't change any of that now. The highway is as empty and grey as the sky. It's OK though. There's only one thing I'm looking forward to now, and that is the journey's end.

We clock up 110 miles on the flat, monotonous asphalt before we stop for breakfast. That says everything. Had it stayed dry, had we gone through Yellowstone National Park, had we followed the mountain roads back, then the journey would have wound down into Denver from a Rocky Mountain high. However, now all we are left with is a concrete highway that propels us into the outer sprawl of dense population. Catering to house the ever-growing populace has made all the outlying towns part of the extensive metropolis that Denver has become. There are more lanes and less room. The traffic increases, and the tolerance and attention of other road users proves that city minds have nowhere to grow.

Six hours after I woke up, 4,400 miles, ten states, and thirteen days since we left, we pull back into the driveway. I place my camera on the lid of the bin, and we pose for the "after" photo. The bikes go in the garage, and it's not long before I'm in control of four wheels, picking up my girlfriend and heading to my favourite restaurant. Jonathan and his part-time lover are already there. My girlfriend pays me for her flight to Bangkok that I'd booked before I left, and I give the money to Jonathan to pay for the trip we'd just taken. Paying for the past with money meant for the future, it is a precarious way to live, but I love it.

And that was it; the end of what had been my first proper tour on a motorbike. Would I do it again? Not if my girlfriend had anything to do with it. To me it was my maiden flight; to her it was my swan song. Nothing was ever going to be the same, and as if to confirm this, two days later two planes flew into two buildings in New York City, and then the buildings collapsed. The implications of the impact had repercussions that rippled out and shook the entire world.

Wilderness and Confinement

"On earth there is no heaven, but there are pieces of it."
Jules Renard

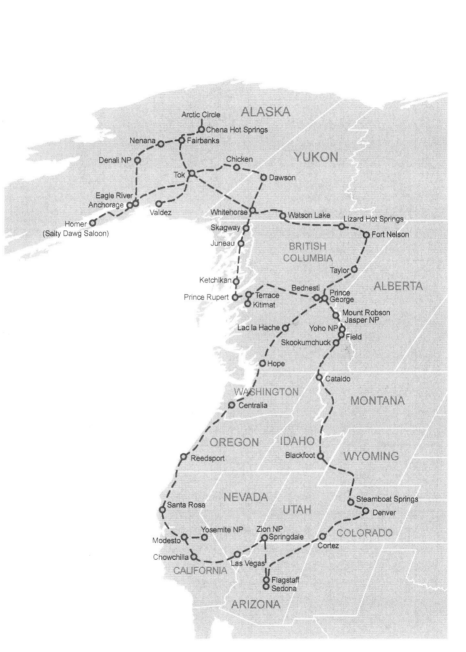

June 2007

By now, not only had I done a few significant bike trips, but also had some significant others. *The Long Way Round* had recently exploded into the consciousness of almost every motorcyclist. In fact, it had even got mainstream attention. It wasn't just a journey; it was a brand. For some, it was a dream. And for all, it had firmly become a phrase; a label with which to stereotype someone, much like anyone who rode a scooter heard the word *Quadrophenia*, or someone on a chopper was *Born to Be Wild*. Now, if you happen to have a set of panniers or a tent bungeed on your rack, the comment you got was always *"Long Way Round."* There were strong and varied opinions about the much publicised journey, but ultimately, you couldn't load up a bike for a weekend away and not hear those three little words.

Due to the fact that I don't recall how the plan to ride to Alaska was conceived, I have to assume it was alcohol-related. I'd spent the last month in Colorado in the planning stages. Always time rich and money poor, I was possibly the instigator, probably the motivator, and definitely the researcher and organiser. Some of the suggested research reading gave more insight into the idiosyncrasies of the American traveller than the actual destination, often written by the condescending tourist to inform the insular idiot. In one publication, it actually stated that to get to Alaska you had to ride through Canada. Well fuck me! Lucky I saw that. And there's me thinking we'd have to get there via Russia and across the Bering Strait like those two significant other guys had. Well, that makes things a whole lot easier! I had a Harley out in Denver; I'd bought it the summer before from a pawn shop. The pawnbroker, who specialised in jewellery, had been conned into repeatedly taking the bike in exchange for a gradually increasing but always repaid loan. The day came when the owner of the Harley, with his hard-earned and impeccable credit history, asked for and received a loan of disproportionate value to his collateral. He was never seen again. The bike had no place on the floor of a jeweller's shop, which was trying its hardest— despite a dodgy downtown location—to be as upmarket as its position would allow. The graffiti on the windows was at least spelt correctly, and the urine-soaked side passage had aromas of chardonnay; even the discarded syringes still had sharp needles in them. The bike brought down the tone of the place, potentially attracting the wrong type of punter, and was also a permanent reminder that the owner had been conned. It had a questionable history too. The ownership papers didn't really prove who the owner was, and the after-market engine cases suggested the possibility that someone somewhere may or may not still be looking for some of the bike.

The day I went to register it as mine, I sat in the government office clutching a ticket with a number printed on it. The pawn shop owner had agreed to take all responsibility if alarm bells rang. So there I was, waiting for my number to be called out, whilst rehearsing my innocent excuses as to the discrepancies in the paperwork. It was only a small office in a tiny town, where everyone knew everyone, except me. I overheard a conversation.

"Hi Candy, didn't expect to see you here. How long have you been working here?"

"Oh, only a few days. Just kind of getting the hang of it," came the response. So, I thought to myself, everyone knows Candy. I want Candy. When Candy called my number, I knew I was in with a chance. Inexperienced and eager to please, she processed my paperwork and gave me a crisp new ownership document. Any previous history the bike had was sent into the shredder of deletion.

It was a lovely bike, especially with its new Colorado licence plate; *OCD* were the first three letters. They contradicted its rat-black colour, mismatched parts, and other loud, obnoxious qualities. However, now that the paperwork proclaimed the bike's pedigree status, it was far more valuable than it was when I bought it. It was an outrageously enjoyable bike to ride. The model was basically a Fat Boy, which is what Arnold Schwarzenegger rode in *Terminator 2*. I left it in Colorado for the winter, as I knew I'd be back this summer. It was going to be the bike that would finance my next ride, the one to the Arctic Circle. All I needed to do was sell it. I have time; I'm just aware it's passing.

I'd never done this much research for anything. Research, like revision for a school exam, usually had me gazing unfocused at the words I was supposed to be reading and remembering, looking for patterns in vertical lines between the gaps. Maybe it was because my two travelling companions were counting on me;

maybe it's because if I didn't plan properly the trip would be a chaotic cluster fuck. Whatever the reason, the fact remained that the distance was long, and for the other two, timing was imperative. Flights had to be caught, careers had to be continued, and twenty-three days and 6,000 miles after our departure, we had a very important ferry to catch from southwest Alaska.

It had to be pre-booked, and it was vital we were all on it, because the Alaska Marine Highway is, despite my initial optimism, only traversable by boat. As if that wasn't enough pressure, Jonathan's girlfriend, Tammara, was also going to fly out and meet us in Anchorage. The schedule required that daily mileage quotas were reached, and there was little room for deviation. However, once we actually set off, I seemed to be the only one who cared about this, which is ironic, as it wasn't my girlfriend, my career, or my flight that was going to be missed. I had other plans, my only incentive to make the ferry, apart from proving my itinerary was faultless, was the fact that I had paid nearly $2,000 on my credit card for the three of us and our bikes.

Jonathan had just bought a BMW R1100 RT. He'd sold his Triumph Sprint to DRob, who was flying over from England for the trip. DRob is a doctor, and his name was (and still is) Rob. But there were several Robs in our circle of friends, so to avoid confusion, we always referred to him as Doctor Rob. He was not keen on this prefix, because as soon as someone knows they are in the company of a doctor, they usually want to talk about what ails them. The benefit of the abbreviation to DRob is that a name with such Neanderthal connotations doesn't inspire confidence in his ability to do anything, least of all practise medicine. Although, when it comes to mechanical aptitude, the Neanderthal insinuation is entirely accurate. Neither does he have the ability to give up smoking. But we all have our shortcomings; mine is forgiveness; however, I can at least forgive him this.

The 955 Triumph Sprint is a stunning bike; however, you don't have to delve far into any Triumph forum to hear how important the 24,000-mile service is. DRob decided he'd like it done before he set off. Personally, I have a strong dislike for dealerships, but it's not my bike, nor my money, so I took it down to the local Triumph people to do with it what they will. It came back with breather hoses hanging outside the fairing, and the expansion bottle looked like a hamster had been living in it. Still, the service book was stamped and in the eyes of the dealer, it wouldn't need official inept intervention for another 6,000 miles.

So there we have it: Flid (as I'm affectionately known) the organiser, Jonathan the womaniser, and DRob the compromiser. It was a match made inebriated, I may have been the common bond between the other two, but there was no pressure on my part to be the vine that held the grapes together. They would get on with or without me, and sometimes the latter may even have seemed preferable, I'm sure.

The bike I was taking was not dissimilar to the god-awful Yamaha Venture I rode on my first ever multi-state trip. The difference being I had brought this one myself, through choice, and like a Volkswagen Beetle or a 2CV, it came with camaraderie. It was a Kawasaki Concours. I'd ridden it to California a few times. It had a big fairing but was nimble, and when I used lower gears and higher revs, it unleashed a hidden power with screaming proclamation and would take off with sportsbike characteristics. Not that I'd had a lot of experience of a sportsbike's ability, but it was good enough for me. Occasionally, I even ground the foot pegs, the handling was so good. The Concours—or Connie—like KLRs, is very popular in North America, though practically unheard of on the British side of the Atlantic. I don't consider myself a Kawasaki man, nor do I see myself ever getting a green K tattooed on my body, I just seem to end up with them (Kawasakis that is, not green K tattoos).

As the planning and preparation progressed, I fell into the honey-trap that is out to catch and profit from so many riders in research mode. I was under the misguided belief that I needed to squander my travel savings on clothing, as well as bike and camping accessories. Luckily, there were two things that saved me. Firstly, at the time, the exchange rate was two dollars to the pound, and secondly a shop had sprung up locally selling bankrupt motorcycle gear at very-reduced prices. My best purchase was a pair of Gore-Tex trousers with a zip-in liner for fifty dollars. When I got them home and unzipped the liner, I found a price tag for $225. There isn't much in life that makes me happier than a bargain. If I ever won the lottery and money became plentiful, the thing I'd miss the most would be the satisfaction of saving a few quid.

Every day seemed to involve going to the army surplus store or the bankrupt stock shop. A valuable philosophy I once heard was, "A bargain is only a bargain if you need it." A classic example was when a friend's mum once came round with a beautiful fireplace tool set she had found at a car boot sale. None of us had an open fire or even a log burner. It was of no use to anyone we knew. But it was cheap, therefore she'd bought it. I tried to refrain from unnecessary accessories for the Alaska trip, but as is often the case with obsessive research, I inevitably came across some extreme stories, and warnings of prevention started to niggle—snow in July, bear attacks, landslides, killer mosquitoes, washed-out bridges, and even blood-thirsty truckers on unmade roads fuelled on crystal meth and speeding towards bonus-promised deadlines throwing up rocks the size of footballs.

The list was endless; but admittedly, "cold and wet" seemed to be a recurring theme. So I bought a heated waistcoat, leggings, and hand grips. In the garage, I had a dress rehearsal. I put on my thermals, heated clothing, jeans, sweatshirt, inner jacket, trouser liners, and then the Gore-Tex outer-armoured jacket, and finally, my bright-yellow, oilskin-type waterproofs. Yes, I could still move. Yes, I could swing my leg over the bike. And yes, I could sit comfortably on it in the riding position. However, this was June in Denver, so a frantic undress rehearsal followed soon after. Next, I had to wire the clothing in. I wasn't convinced my heated clothes were actually heating up.

It being so hot outside, it was hard to tell, so wearing just my underwear, I donned the waistcoat and attached the trousers around my legs with the Velcro, plugged them in, and sat on my bike in the garage revving the engine and trying to feel for warmth. Since embarrassment also manifests itself with a similar sticky heat, when Tammara came into the garage to see what all the noise was about, I discovered there was a flaw in my experiment. It seemed we've both got our wires crossed. But with a little adjustment to the power input, within less than a minute my clothing had all the qualities of an electric blanket. God knows how much energy that was drawing from the battery, but I reassured myself with the fact that the definition of *Arctic Circle* is that on the summer solstice the sun never sets. We might be a week late, but even so, I didn't think I'd need to use my lights, so more power to me.

Alaska has a three-month tourist window, so if there was something that we wanted to do, it had to be booked in advance. The whale watching was already sold out, and two months before we were to arrive, I booked the last of the camping spots in Denali National Park. Thanks to my industrious ways, a week before we were due to leave, I had little else to do. I had even printed out pack lists, as well as a calendar stating our daily destinations. I was so on top of this thing.

The trip had been the only topic of conversation for the last month, and in passing, I had mentioned the condescending guide book to some people, and the general response in all seriousness was, "Yes, Canada is a foreign country and you will need a passport to enter." "Well, how the hell do you think I got into America?" Of course, it would be wrong to judge the geographical ignorance of an entire nation based on such comments. And not everyone was of the same opinion. One guy I spoke to was convinced you had to cross an ocean to get to Alaska, and there was no alternative; perhaps he was thinking of Hawaii. It's a worry.

The other book, the bible if you will, for anyone going to the northernmost state is called *The Milepost*. It is of telephone-directory proportions and is ideal for the drivers of thirty-foot motorhomes. The passenger can sit with it on their lap, and mile by mile, every point from the Canadian border up the ALCAN Highway and into Alaska is explained in great detail. It's not exactly a bike-friendly publication in its size, but by all accounts we would be fools to attempt the journey without it. As well as its comprehensive mile-by-mile information, it's also full of hints and tips on survival.

Apparently, there are different defence tactics depending on whether you are apprehended by a grizzly or a black bear. If it's a black bear you should be prepared to fight back or at least use movement to show you are not a tree, thereby preventing the bear from attempting to climb up you. A little dance can work too. Then there's the Diana Ross hand gesture of *Stop in the Name of Love*, but instead of singing you say, "Whoa, Bear!" However, if it's a grizzly that's doing the attacking, the appropriate form of defence is to lie on the ground and play dead. This method sounds suspiciously like it's written by a grizzly bear. I had decided I would use the Billy Goat's Gruff approach and point out how much more meat there is on my two friends. I'm no bear expert, and somehow I don't think "Now, which species are you?" would be my initial reaction if I came face to face with one. Moose are easier to deal with by all accounts: you just run. Apparently, they have appalling people skills and are generally emotionally unavailable.

I re-advertised the Harley, dropping the price again. It was the cheapest bike of its sort in the for sale ads, which means it attracted the interest of the biggest wankers. There was a time when I was proud to be a Harley owner, a time before they became fashion accessories, before every posing tosser went out and bought one as a status symbol. There are probably still some genuine riders out there, but they are so diluted by a plethora of wannabes that the whole scene has left me very bitter. I can tell as soon as I speak to one prospective buyer on the phone what he is like, and when he fails to honour the viewing time, it only confirms my suspicions. Another potential buyer agrees to a price and the next morning is suddenly $1,000 short and full of excuses . . . "Well, it needs new tyres and . . ."

"It needed new tyres last night too, and they don't cost $1,000," I retort. He continues to whine like a dry prop shaft until I cut him short and hang up.

There was also a time when buying and selling a Harley was an enjoyable exercise; a way to meet genuine, passionate, enthusiastic people, regardless of whether a sale was achieved. You swapped stories and knowledge. I miss those days. It's all been completely ruined, just like when the BBC got behind the Glastonbury Festival and the whole thing got too popular. The way to avoid disappointment in change is to never go back; try something new. That's why we were going to Alaska.

THE DAY BEFORE WE LEAVE

Late one night, DRob arrives; we drink. In the morning, we all go to the big, posh outdoor and camping shop. It's pure porn for people like me. But I have to refrain, I've got everything I need. Everything that is except "six-week underwear," which sounds spectacular. OK, just one more purchase; we leave tomorrow.

One more phone call: a guy wants to see the Harley this evening. I'm really busy, but we arrange to meet. He's a fireman and is in uniform with a gun on his belt. "Wouldn't a water pistol be more useful?" I think to myself. I show him round the bike, and when I press the starter, what do you know, it won't bloody start! Totally dead. I fiddle with the starter relay, and eventually a connection is made, and it fires up. He makes an offer, which I accept, and off he goes. I don't have the money, and he doesn't have the bike. He'll bring the cash tomorrow, but then he would say that wouldn't he? Stupidly, I don't even think to take a deposit.

I leave the bike downtown in a locked workshop. Tonight we are packing. We all have our lists; we all have our equipment. All that's left is to put it in our panniers. I really expect this to be fun, but there's only silence; focused as we are on the task. No chat, no banter, no piss taking. There's anticipation and excitement, but it's not expressed in an audible way. It's a strange atmosphere, but as the panniers fill up and the boxes get checked off, the mood becomes more jovial, possibly helped by the William Shatner CD playing in the garage. Everything on my list fits on the Connie. I'm alright. All I have to do is load my sleeping bag, but I need to sleep in it first.

When I do get into it and lay my head down, my head's as full of thoughts as my panniers are with provisions. I can't say if I'm excited or more overwhelmed at the thought of what lies ahead. I'm glad I'm not doing the trip alone.

DAY 1

STEAMBOAT SPRINGS, COLORADO

201 MILES

I'm woken by the phone. It's the fireman. He's just finished his night shift and is going to the bank to withdraw the money to buy the Harley. I'm in shock that after its appalling performance last night he still wants it. It's to my advantage that he hasn't had a chance to sleep on the decision. I roll up my sleeping bag, load it on the Connie, and I'm off. So this is the start of my trip to Alaska. No time for breakfast, no tentatively seeing how the bike feels fully loaded, no send off. I'm just heading downtown with a preoccupied mind and trying not to rejoice prematurely at the sale that seems imminent. I go to the workshop, swap the Connie for the Harley, and meet the guy at the bank. There he is, with $7,200 in cash, which I count in the passenger seat of his pickup. However, he expects me to walk back from here. There are no taxies, no buses, and I'm a bit vulnerable. As a compromise, if I follow him to his mother's house; he'll give me a lift back in his pickup truck. I can get behind that. I'm chatting away constantly in the passenger seat of his truck. I can tell he doesn't like me, but I keep talking anyway. I can feel his disdain that I'm even in his truck. I don't care! I've got a massive lump in my pocket and a great way to blow it. When I get back to the Connie, Jonathan and DRob are already waiting, and I'm not even close to ready.

I have to go and get a spare ignition key cut; something I could have done weeks ago. I'm unable to exchange routine pleasantries this morning, I just can't help but blurting out, "I'm going to Alaska," to everyone crossing my path who asks, "How ya doin'?"

I buy a lock for the bike too. I've just got so much money; it's so unexpected and such perfect timing. Jonathan calls me. They're getting impatient. So I head back. I still haven't even eaten yet, let alone composed myself and considered what I'm about to embark on.

We get Tammara to take a photo of us. Then we all hug; she probably feels my big wedge press against her. Perhaps I should get a money belt. Finally, with a "See you in Alaska," we're off. No, wait! I need to get fuel. Well, what are they gonna do, they're not going to ride off without me. Are they?

Apparently, yes. But as I'm coming out of the pay kiosk, they head back for me. Now we're off. Officially. I follow them; full tank, empty tummy, laden bike, lots of money, and nothing left to fuel my manic disposition. What a rush! But this is how my life always turns out. What a way to start a trip! I remind myself that when I have a bad day—and I inevitably will—I have to remember this morning. It has every ingredient to thrill: the promise of a long-awaited sale, the last-minute preparation, the hyper-elation of leaving. And now I'm following my two best mates out of the city and into the foothills of the Rocky Mountains on the first miles of a trip for which we've been preparing since last year. And, of course, the sun is shining. They may have got irritated by my last-minute errands, but I would have left two weeks ago if I hadn't been waiting for them.

We stop in a foothills town for food. We've luckily missed the lunch hour rush. I'm so hungry. But with this burrito I have no more needs in the world. Well, not for the next few hours at least. A bit of highway and within an hour we're at 11,000 feet. Within two, we're in a high-altitude and highly priced camping supplies shop. I buy a money belt and soap, and then find a second-hand consignment camping shop nearby to buy a stove. Now I'm definitely ready. A busker is sitting in the sunshine playing Pearl Jam and Alice in Chains songs on his acoustic guitar. I want to listen—he's really good—but the others are keen to carry on.

None of us has grasped how to react with the actual start of this long-awaited journey. We have no method yet of dealing with the proportions we are to face. I suppose we're holding onto the last of the comfort and familiarity the trip has consisted of up to this point, which has basically involved buying shit in preparation for the journey. Now we are undeniably on our way, the transition feels too sudden. If I ever meet an astronaut, I will try and remember this moment in order to empathise with how it must feel to do all that training and then at last comes that giant step where you're suddenly thrust into space.

"Yes, mate," I'd say. "We had to stop in Silverthorne to get a stove, just to try and cope with the acclimatisation."

It's getting late, and we're getting nowhere. We're supposed to be in Salt Lake City by tonight. If we could just stay out of camping shops and actually get to our destination and down to some camping. We leave the highway onto some road I've never done before. I suppose this is something I'd better get used to. The road winds round perfectly placed mountains with clear, sweeping bends. It doesn't take long to realise that mine is the slowest bike. I keep thinking the Sprint is mine. I've got one at home, but I'm happy with the Connie, and I'd rather walk than take Jonathan's new bike. However, when I'm banked over at ninety mph on a perfectly consistent curve, the engine strong and the handling reassuring, the love for my Connie goes up a notch. This is just fine. We stop at some roadworks, and the adrenalin the road has generated no longer has any use, so I chat to the girls in the car next to us.

"We're going to Alaska," I say, because we are and I can't talk about anything else.

We eventually stop at Steamboat Springs, about 300 miles short of our destination. Oh, well. We cook bratwursts on a barbecue, then take a bottle of Jägermeister down to some hot springs and talk to anyone who will listen to us; same subject, only slightly more slurred. I look up at the stars, smell the pines, and listen to the running river. I can't stop smiling. I take my smile to my tent and lie on my sleeping bag with my head outside so I can still look at the stars, smell the pines, and listen to the river. I'm going to Alaska, I think to myself. Days don't get any better.

DAY 2

BLACKFOOT, IDAHO

513 MILES

God, I'm thirsty; what time is it? Where's my money belt? Where's my torch? Where's the toilet? It's inevitable, being the first night on the road; the bike sale, our scenic location, and the camaraderie; that there was always going to be an irresponsible amount of drinking involved. Pathetically, but productively, I find all I require, relax, and listen to the first bird song of the dawn, I am no longer unconscious. I am conscious, and the reality is good, I close my eyes and drift in and out of sleep.

Last night, in some drunken play fighting, I'd fallen against a rock. It wasn't a big deal, but the graze on my back is right where my waistband rubs. That's annoying. But DRob has some cream for such things. I put some on and then go for a morning bathe in the hot springs. The irresponsibility continues. I have the steaming rock pool to myself, and I don't recognise any of it. I'm not sure this was the one from last night. The Jägermeister oblivion; how can I remember to stop drinking the stuff when I have no memory of drinking it? The sun beams through the steam rising from the water. What a beautiful hangover I'm having! Unfortunately though, today we have to make up yesterday's lost miles, so it's time to stop basking and start biking. I get out my stove and realise I have nothing to boil water in, so we leave in search of a diner.

In the town of Craig, we sit in an empty restaurant. I read right through the *Craig Daily News*, where there is nothing of any great significance happening. In other news, the waitress eventually appears and informs us that they stopped serving breakfast at 10AM, and lunch doesn't start until eleven o'clock. It's a quarter past ten. So we leave the fucktard café, feeling a little irritated having wasted precious road miles. However, the dysfunction ends at the threshold. We are greeted with great enthusiasm by a bright and cheery passing local who recommends a restaurant that caters for people who are hungry for more than just the local news. That's all it takes to restore our faith in a town we thought was closed. It is unanimously decided we should start a kitty, and I am the nominated keeper; just what I need— more money on my person. I may be able to dissuade bears from eating me by pointing out the girth of my friends, but I'd certainly be the jackpot in a mugging scenario.

Breakfast is followed by a fuel stop, and somehow we all manage to lose each other. We have the progress of a herd of turtles. Whilst I wait in the shade at the side of the road for one of them to ride past, I discover I've lost the moulded earpiece on the end of my iPod earphones. It must be somewhere in last night's campsite. That'll teach me to get all drunk. Actually, no it won't. So now I'll have an eardrum-piercing tube of discomfort to contend with if I want to listen to anything other than mono on my journey.

Eventually the others find me. "C'mon, we're going to Wyoming." We have a ninety-two-mile stretch of straight northbound road ahead of us. I get out the map at breakfast, so we all know today's route. However, once we get going I seem to be the leader, and no one is taking it away from me. I don't mind being in front, but I prefer variety. Leader of the pack can get repetitive. This had better not be the case all the way to the Arctic Circle. Just because I've done all the research doesn't mean the others can't take the initiative, and we won't exactly be challenged with a huge choice of alternative routes.

In Wyoming, we pick up the highway. It's flatter, straighter, and faster than the stretch from Craig. The temperature has increased too, and we're buffeted by giant trucks. It's not the most pleasurable of rides. DRob indicates that he needs a drink, so we pull off when we see a sign for "gas, food, and lodging," which turns out to be nothing but a solitary warehouse. On the side in big letters, it says "Adult Store." I'm not sure we're going to find what we need here, but we stop anyway. Inside there is nothing but dolls, DVDs, and dildos. Not even a Coke machine. The girl behind the counter gives us a glass of water. It's not really enough. An old man walks in, whom she clearly knows.

"What's going on?" she says to him.

"Oh, nothing impotent," he replies. It's priceless; do they say that every morning, or was that a moment in time? You can't make that stuff up. Spectacular. A lone building off a parched and deserted fast highway, and in the five minutes of my life that I happen to be in there, I get to hear that golden comment. Let's move on.

At ninety mph in 90° Fahrenheit, my bike is drinking fuel like I should be water. When we get to Cokeville, I opt for a lemonade, just to be cantankerous. There is a brief respite from the heat as we ride a lesser-used, tree-lined road. The day is not cooling, yet it's passing fast. We always knew the first few days would be long, hot, and hard, even without the porn shop stop. We pull into Blackfoot at 8PM and cruise the blocks of the town until we find the house of an ex of Jonathan. I haven't seen her for years, and I've never met her husband. He's a freight train driver, and I go with him to the liquor store. This is ideal, as I happen to have a lot of questions about trains, which mostly arise when I wait at a level crossing for three engines pulling more than a hundred wagons and pushed by a further two engines to slowly clank past. The power of these engines is immense, and I'm told that they're actually powered by electric traction motors. I'm confused, as I was convinced they had diesel engines.

Apparently they do, which is what powers the electric motor. Still not getting it; why don't they just . . . ? Because an electric motor needs no clutch. The driver has control over all five of the engines. One of the duties of the guardsman at the back is to announce a derailment that can be more than half a mile away from the driver up front. The power output is nearly 4,500 horsepower per engine. Adjusting back to driving a car must be tricky. Maybe that's why he has the air conditioning on and the windows open. Or maybe it's just American excess.

The three of us seem to have come in and taken over the house. I have a simple request; my sheepskin seat cover keeps falling off, but, this not being a household of sheds containing tools of implementation, we have to get inventive and improvise. A pair of tights does the job, even if the gusset makes for an unfortunate and rather obvious focal point. It's funny. It's awkward. It's inappropriate. But ultimately it's functional, and therefore, it's staying. The table is laden with food, tons of it, and the rest of the evening is spent consuming steak and copious amounts of carbohydrates.

Day 3

Cataldo, Idaho

502 miles

I suppose if you're in a state so proud of its famous potatoes that it's proclaimed on every vehicle's licence plate, it should be no surprise to the visitor that your hosts will put their produce where your mouth is. In Idaho, we're fed to the point of rupture. I'm not sure how much of a benefit this is going to be with today's challenge: we are 600 miles away from our target destination. This itinerary is starting to cause me concern. If we don't pass through the bland segment of the trip on schedule, we'll be out of time to enjoy the outstanding parts. Then again, you can't rush hospitality, and this conflict of time versus company has a clear winner. It's 10:3AM by the time we're packed up. In a token gesture of sightseeing, we ride past the Idaho Potato Museum. Predictably, there is a large effigy of a potato outside, of the baked variety, and it has what I suppose is sour cream as a garnish and a pyramid of butter to crown it off. This incarnation must be the king of potato recipes, as the fry, being French, lacks patriotism one would assume. Enticing though the museum is, the call of the road has amplified to a scream of impatience.

We obey, and once again, I'm leading, but today it comes with a bonus I've never experienced before or since. The road is, as roads across plains often are, straight and flat, and there is no weather today, just clear skies and warm sun. There is no traffic either, not a single vehicle. Therefore, the air is as still as the mountains on the horizon. I'm thrusting myself at eighty mph into this invisible motionless tranquillity, and there's absolutely no buffeting at all. It's like being the first person to dive into a still swimming pool. The air parts around me with a hypnotic consistency, much like bikini-clad synchronised rollerbladers might skirt a drunk in a rain mac on an esplanade. I'm riding a wakeful dream, passing through time and space with flying-carpet propulsion. Careful what you wish for as, oblivious as a dog in a domino-toppling contest, Jonathan comes past me with his obtrusive horizontal cylinders, and my turbulent-free, carbohydrate-induced dreamlike state is gone forever. Bloody BMWs.

Arco is a very small town. Small towns always evoke the same question in me, particularly when there is nothing else around. What the hell do people do? The answer in this place is that once a year the graduating high school class climbs up the local hill and defaces it with a big white number depicting their year of graduation. It's quite striking, it's memorable, and in the few minutes it takes to pass through this place with a population of under a thousand, it's vaguely stimulating. But it wouldn't be something I'd want to look at every day. However, I suppose the whole town can be proud that there is a day in their lives when they make their mark.

Slowly, the scenery improves. The mountains are getting closer, and the road starts to curve in preparation. Some quad bikes come towards us, and I'm in a dilemma as to whether to wave or not. They have handlebars and are exposed to the elements, but they also have four wheels, and as I lean round another bend I realise it's a sensation they're incapable of experiencing. Therefore, there is no alliance, and I keep my waving hand on my bars and my nodding head still. We ride up over a mountain pass, and I scrape my foot as I curl round a hairpin and straighten up into the state of Montana. A Frank Zappa song comes into my head and I scroll through my iPod to find it.

With determined respect, we push the day as hard as we can, not wishing to break anything this soon on, but if we can't keep the pace then Alaskan days won't be long enough. The town of Wallace stops us; an old silver mining town with a Wild West feel to it. It sits underneath the elevated highway, and despite the shadow and noise coming from the viaduct, it maintains a charm and dignity. Unfortunately, it's been needlessly cheapened.

Perhaps it's me, but to declare a place "the centre of the universe" and have a manhole cover cast specifically to state this seems like the sort of gimmick more suited to Las Vegas. We're able to get supplies in town and are advised of a camping place twenty miles outside the centre of the universe. The recommended route takes us through a Deliverance-style community, where the eyes of men bore into us. The campsites we see are all on the other side of the river. The road turns to dirt and winds into a logged forest. Jonathan drops his bike, but nothing breaks. We're all tired. The only flat and hidden spot we find is under an electricity pylon. Its ugly, but it's already 10PM. It'll have to do.

Our arrival is met with two big streaks of lightning, and it occurs to me that it's not ideal to be camped out under the only metal on the mountainside. We're not going to move, as between us we have aching limbs, bad backs, and locked knees. We're only in our mid-thirties, but for the first time in my life I'm becoming aware of how age interferes with the youthful ability that was once taken for granted. Now I can relate to a woman's biological clock; you have to achieve your desires while the body will still cooperate. To do this trip later in life, in a campervan, would be tantamount to adopting a Chinese baby.

Day 4

Skookumchuck, BC, Canada

284 miles

It rained all night. It's still raining now. The power cables above our heads are buzzing, and the cloud hangs in the valley beneath us. I get fully dressed in the tent and exit arse first like a sack of coal falling through a rotten hammock. The others aren't up. I'm now homeless, and a gentle awakening is not an option for them. Like a drill instructor in a dorm of new recruits, I wake them and demand they get up immediately. It's absolutely miserable; rolling up a wet tent and damp sleeping bag and strapping it all on the bike. I then face the challenge of trying to get cold wet hands into dry gloves. We ride into a dull, horrid morning. Now, should we continue in the right direction on the wrong side of the river or double all the way back? We gamble on the former and come to a small, official camping ground. I approach the owner of a motorhome who is cooking breakfast under his awning. The interior looks warm and inviting, the lights are blazing, and the smell of bacon combined with my damp hunger motivates me to be far more affable than either of us expects. I ask if there is a bridge ahead, and he confirms there is. That's all; no invite for breakfast, a shower, or even a little doze on his couch. Well, we'll be off then.

We find the highway and head for the town of Coeur d'Alene, where bacon for breakfast is easier to come by. My waterproofs are doing exactly what they should; even the highway spray hasn't penetrated. I am, however, losing the impressive bug collection on my windshield in the downpour. At a diner, we disrobe and hang our dripping clothing over highchairs and other objects we don't understand. The mood is a subdued one, and we didn't even drink last night. Well, not much. All we can do is press on. With no warning, and more annoyingly, without replenishing our supplies of fuel and alcohol, we arrive at the Canadian border. We're not even processed out of the US, and our entry into Canada is straightforward.

"Do you have any alcohol?"

"Just a few Budweisers."

"Why would you import that shit into here?" was the implication of the offhand response.

My very first impressions of Canada are that it lacks an identity. There is no real difference between where we are and northern Idaho, other than that the signs are now in kilometres. We have no currency, and annoyingly, today turns out to be Sunday and no banks are open, assuming there even is a town nearby that might have a bank. Jonathan's prediction has unfortunately come true, and we find ourselves in a procession of motorhomes. But most annoying is that the cloud cover has taken away the scenery. It's at least stopped raining, but I'm feeling disappointed. Since we left Denver I've been driven by an inexhaustible excitement of what is to come. But now we've reached Canada, the urge to carry on to tonight's destination has completely gone. We're missing what we should be seeing, and that is the whole point of being here. On the plus side, we've caught up on ourselves and are only a hundred miles behind our intended stop. Even so, it's quite a significant one. We're supposed to be camping in the vast beauty of Banff National Park this evening; a place of unmissable magnificence. Not only would we be surrounded by lakes, mountains, and hot springs, but the following day would be a slow, short ride onto Jasper, a park with an equally stunning landscape.

It's decided that as our camping gear is so wet, perhaps we should get a room for the night and dry everything out. I can see the logic and try to quash my destination-driven truck driver instincts. I'm not sure what I'm hoping for, and once we find a place to stay, the sun comes out. This is ideal drying weather undeniably, but it's also good riding and sightseeing weather. Well, no point agonising over it; we're booked in, unpacked, and we may as well make the most of it. We have some jobs to do, DRob gets to sit in the laundromat putting coins into the drier. My errand involves a twenty-four-mile round trip to a familiar establishment—and now that we're in Canada, it has a familiar-sounding name too—the requisite off-licence. It's a mood-changing ride with no luggage and no waterproofs to weigh me down. I ride the now empty road through pines and alongside a river, and to the east there are dramatic snow-capped mountains.

This is what we came for. It's what I came for, and I'm glad I'm seeing it. I needed this. I reach a lake on the other side of which is the town of Wasa, where the beer is sold, only at much higher prices than in America, although US dollars are still accepted at an appalling exchange rate.

Everything is drying, and we sit at a picnic table in shorts, drinking beer and eating pizza. The day has turned out well. DRob has a new digital SLR that he bought specifically for this trip. He did a lot of research before deciding on a Nikon and then saved a lot of money by having it sent over from some East Asian dealer on eBay. Now he has his new toy, he can't stop playing with it. I'm pretty keen to capture most sights, but he's becoming obsessive. It's getting to the point where I think I'll leave it to him to take all the photos, and I'll just get copies later. As the alcohol flows, we scroll through his images, and I realise that not only does his camera not lie, but it has a far better memory than I do.

DAY 5

YOHO NATIONAL PARK,
BRITISH COLUMBIA

182 MILES

What was that thing we said that was so funny last night? It was golden; I can't remember. Other things that were also forgotten were to wash my clothes, myself, my hair; and catch up on my diary. I'd better get up then. When I've done all that, I'm still behind as the others have been doing bike maintenance. I'm feeling stressed, rushed. I roll up my dry tent and sleeping bag. I have to compromise on the day's preparation, mainly because I'm the one who's always pushing us on. We haven't been on time since we left. In fact, we didn't even leave on time; whose fault was that? Oh yeah, mine, well anyway. Due to warmth and sunshine, I decide to put my bike trousers on over my underwear, not just because the other way round would look silly, but I don't think I'm going to need the layer of my combats today. As I pack my bike, a Dutch couple chat to me, just when I really want to be concentrating. This is how things get left behind.

I'm too hot. Every day, I love these bargain bike trousers more and more, but I just can't seem to get the balance of layers and liners right. We ride into the first town of any importance and find a bank. Without thinking how stupid it makes me look, I voice my surprise to the bank cashier on seeing the queen on the banknotes.

"Wouldn't you rather have a Canadian face? Alanis Morissette, for example?"

The cashier responds that the queen is Canadian. I don't have an answer to that. Then at breakfast, I discover the best and most unexpected thing about being in a commonwealth country is the wonderful addition to the choice of condiments. The sauce that enhances any meal—brown sauce—is a recognised topping on every table in the restaurant. I think I'm going to like it here.

Our waiter looks how I would if I tried to look like Magnum PI, but he's very knowledgeable as to the local attractions. I hope his investigation into the disappearance of several sachets of peanut butter won't lead him to me, although there is indisputable evidence that I am guilty. Jonathan discovers he has left his earphones at last night's motel; I feel his frustration. The infuriation rises when they decide we will just continue the trip a day behind schedule. They don't fucking get it! If there was room for a day off or less mileage to cover don't they think I would have scheduled it in? I've worked so hard on this trip to end our days in beautiful and interesting places, and there will be a significant sacrifice at the end of the journey if we don't bother to go with the itinerary. This new and lenient majority ruling means that we can all stop at some hot springs to relax. Oh, really? They wouldn't want to relax if they knew what they were missing. Later, we meet an Australian couple with an Ural outfit who've been on the road for some time. The man has a calm wisdom about him, a road-learnt acceptance of how motorcycle travel really is. Next to him, we seem manic and underprepared, impatient and demanding. In our defence, he does have retirement and time on his side. I have a ticking clock, a rigid calendar, and a bulging money belt. We plainly have different perspectives on how the horizon will come to us. Maybe when I'm older I'll adopt his philosophy, but right now I don't have the time.

Eventually, we get to Kootenay, the first of many national parks, as we head through the Canadian Rocky Mountains. I still can't get my temperature right, and I'm either too hot or I've got a cold draught coming in through a vent. It keeps on raining, and the cloud is low. Some sunny peaks reveal themselves, but it's not really happening for me. I'm not getting the feeling. We make a stop, and Jonathan makes coffee. We're all feeling tired. A tour bus pulls up, and the tourists disembark; a seniors' holiday.

The women wander past chatting to each other, but the men are more interested in checking out our bikes and hearing about our journey than looking at the scenery. They're clearly envious of what they are seeing, but whilst the rain falls and they doze, reclined in their seats, their dreams of our journey possibly have more romance than our reality.

That stop has livened us up. We have to be alert, as deer have jumped out in front of us on several occasions. The trick is not to speed up after one has crossed your path, as they are invariably in groups and occasionally being chased by something that would really put a dent in your fairing. We don't stop at my points of interest, and I'm wondering if all my efforts of research have just made it worse for me. We go to Lake Louise, which is fucking awful! A tourist hell; and this in pre-season. There is nothing tranquil about it, just a motorcade to the car park and a procession to the vista point. People are actually pushing for space to stand at the prime spot for a photo opportunity. Capturing this contrived natural beauty in a crowded open space is a contradiction I don't want to be part of. Apart from that, a chill wind is blowing off the lake, rippling the water and depriving us of the famed reflection of the surrounding mountains; although they can barely be seen through the cloud, let alone mirrored in the water. It's absolute shite.

Off the well-trodden route, we opt for a mountain pass that takes us by the engineering phenomena that are spiral train tunnels, bored through the mountains so that the railway can traverse the range. We can sort of make out the tracks as we look down from the pass, but being tunnels, it does prove a bit tricky to actually see them, even from the viewing points. Looking at tunnels from the outside is like admiring carrots as they grow. It's just not very fulfilling. On the plus side, this visual disappointment has cut the tourist count. We have to go to the tiny community of Field. It's too close not to, and I get a photo of me by the sign. It may not be a very glamorous name, but you can't help what you're called, so you might as well accept it and enjoy the quirks when they occur. Being away from the vacation procession, we find an empty camp ground, which even has a shelter for our bikes. We light a fire and grill steaks, and when the clouds finally clear, we grab our cameras and photograph the looming snow-covered mountains that have been teasing us with their constant disappearing act. This is kind of working for me. I'm not quite there; not disappointed, just a little tormented by my tunnel vision to get the timetable back on track.

Day 6

Mount Robson Provincial Park, British Columbia

234 miles

The clouds may not have leaked overnight, but there is so much moisture in the atmosphere that the tent sags with dew, and condensation flows down the inside. I only have myself to blame; if I could just stop breathing! I boil some water for chai and make a sandwich with one of my stolen peanut butter sachets. This is a shudder-inducing morning, not just the chill air, but the peace, beauty, and solitude of our spot. My eyes explore the surroundings as my body recoils into my clothing. There's an old-fashioned water pump in the centre of the camping area, and with a few thrusts of the cold metal handle, clear icy water gushes from the spout, and I wash my face and shock my senses.

Field seems more popular this morning—not me, I wasn't woken in the night with anonymous texts of adoration—the fuel station in town is heaving. A dithering coach party has just been vomited from a tour bus; they congregate round the coffee machine like school kids round a fitting class mate, unsure of what to do, but preventing access to those of us who do. They seem incapable of coming to terms with any sense of the world beyond their reclining seats and temperature control. This morning's cold-water wash gives me the right to be condescending and intolerant. Whether they envy or despise me, the only real difference between us is the comfort level of the vehicle giving us our tourist status. Unless you're a trader with a commodity to sell, coaches and cruise ships are best avoided.

By lunchtime we're in Banff, the place we should have woken up in yesterday morning. It's dry but cloudy. It wasn't cloudy in the bloody photos of enticement and promotion. I know how this place can look under clear skies. DRob and Jonathan don't; therefore they're in awe of this spectacular, vast, endless range of snowy, rocky mountains. Once again, I just feel frustrated. From inside my lid, I try to work out why this is. Have I seen too much? Do I need blue sky and sunshine? Is my smile really solar-powered? Am I suppressing something? I recently split from my girlfriend, but it was my choice. I just feel sorry for her, but not for me. Is it the missed destinations or the late schedule? Perhaps that even here, in the second biggest country in the world, the planet still seems overpopulated and under appreciated. I'm not sure. Outside my helmet, I can fake it and make the appropriate noises. I'm just a little envious by how impressed the other two are with it all. There is a point, when I see some glaciers close up, that I almost feel the thrill. It's like a stirring in the loins, the promise of a second erection right after ejaculation; then you think about it too hard and it's gone again. I put some live Floyd on my iPod, as that never fails to induce goose pimples. It helps a little, but my mind wanders, and I don't really notice the scenery.

We stop at Peyto Lake. I pull into a space and park, but DRob is doing a second lap of the car park because he wants to park the Sprint in front of a snow bank for a photo. It didn't even occur to me. I keep my iPod on to drown out the chatter of the crowds as we take the path up to the vista point. We wait our turn to stare out over the glacier-fed turquoise lake. Although it's not written, the considerate among us acknowledge the queue and give ourselves an allotted twenty seconds to take in the timeless scene before stepping to the side to allow the next in line to do the same. As though providing fuel to my loathing, cynicism, and sarcasm someone asks, "Are you on bikes?" Our clothing and tank bags are a bit of a giveaway. They continue, "Only one has been knocked over" . . . Lakes, glaciers, photo opportunities all mean nothing. We rush back down the path, unsure of what we want the most, to catch the culprit or to see whose bike it is. A Dutch couple is standing nervously behind their rented motorhome.

They have stood up DRob's Sprint. Their manner is so apologetic and humble that it defuses the situation before it even erupts. The bike has a bent brake lever and a snapped foot peg, plus a lot of scratches to the fairing. It can be fixed. In fact, having a real situation to deal with focuses my mind. I need to convince DRob this will not affect the trip, and the best way to do this is by fixing his bike. So while he goes through the paperwork, Jonathan and I replace the peg with a redundant pillion one and bend the bike back into shape. Crisis averted, we can all carry on with our holidays. I say goodbye in Dutch; the relief on their faces is endearing. I may have been a bit dissatisfied, but at least I'm not an arsehole.

The incident puts everything into perspective; I'm hungry. There's a coach-load queue at the cafeteria, so it's crisps and milk for us; enough to keep us going on to Jasper. More lakes, glaciers, mountains, clouds, rivers, waterfalls. It's certainly dramatic; I'd love to see it in the winter. We head to a campsite at the foot of Mount Robson; a pretty place but absolutely infested with mozzies. They're swarming and relentless. We light a fire, but even that doesn't deter them. I soon tire of slapping myself around the head, and take my tent into the woods for a solitary and peaceful night's sleep, induced for once by exertion and not alcohol.

Day 7

Taylor, British Columbia

491 miles

I'm unsure as to what time zone we're in. All I know is it's undeniably early. I'd go back to sleep, but I hear Jonathan chopping wood. This is unlikely, but it needed to happen. I forgo my planned shower, pack up, and wander out of the woods. I get the feeling they might have had a little meeting last night in my absence. The time may be 6:20, and we are out on the road. There is a misty low atmospheric cloud; it brings about a feeling of discovery and isolation. It's how this land is meant to be experienced. There's a chill, but it's not uncomfortable; it just adds to the ambience; it puts an element of challenge into the trip. I realise that this is what was lacking.

My enthusiasm for this journey was not generated by thoughts of comfort and the company of the progressing throng. It was the thrill and the danger of the untamed, the barely traversable, being confronted with extremes and discovering my limitations, as though I were a nomadic road warrior on the edge of time. OK, I know I ran to my tent last night and sulked because there were a few mozzies about, but last night the wuss inside me died as I slept. I woke a new man. And right now, that man is riding his steed through the dawn mist, wide-eyed into the future on a road parting a dense forest, where only

84

the strong survive, leading his companions fearlessly . . . Fuck me! There's a moose. It's bloody huge. We slow down and watch as it crosses the road in front of us and disappears into the wooded world on the other side of the road. That was fantastic. This is what I want. Fuck that tourist scene; I don't care how prestigious the sights are, I much prefer to have a moose to myself in the deserted.

Heated grips, iPod, and wrapped up in multiple layers, we pass through an infinite amount of pine and spruce trees. Occasionally, a snowy mountain appears. It's not necessary, but it's an appreciated bonus. Then a second moose, this time with antlers. This is spectacular. My fuel gauge is the wrong side of red, but there's nothing I can do about it out here. A third moose; this one is dead on the side of the road. So by my calculations, one in three moose in Canada is dead. I reserve the right to change these statistics based on further research. We do 180 miles before breakfast and arrive at Prince George just as the town is waking up to a day it has already missed the best part of. This is the place where our itinerary says we should be waking up this morning. Oh joy! We're back on schedule, actually, make that on schedule—for the first time. This morning marks a week on the road, and at last, we are where we should be when we should be there. I can get behind that.

Prince George is a big town with small portions. We have justified ravenous appetites and consume multiple side orders. We all have phone reception too. There's a massive supermarket, the biggest we've come across since leaving. We stock up, and then a very available lady in the car park lets us follow her car to the off-licence. There was an invitation to stick around awhile, but we've only just caught up with ourselves. Do we want to blow it already? We settle for whiskey and Jägermeister, a comforting substitute. Jonathan and DRob go to a camping shop, and I sit outside on the wall and call home. It's still a novelty that I can pull a device from my pocket in a Canadian town and speak clearly to my mum in Essex. Every passerby has something to say, mainly apologising for the weather. It's not normally like this by all accounts; if we just waited a few days it would clear. If only we could. They joke, with an element of truth, that no one ever stays in Prince George. It's not that bad; it's really worth a stay. I show the itinerary as proof. Look, we had planned to, it's just . . . I'm sorry, but we really should be off.

So we've basked in the delight of being on time, and now we are behind again. To make it worse, we can't seem to find our way out of town. It's very humid, and I want some air around me. We've left the motorhomes behind. I'd feared the procession would lead all the way to Alaska. Some bravely continue past Jasper, but the majority are on a two-week vacation, and that means we have passed their point of return. We start today's objective: 230 miles. At this speed we could do it in three hours.

Once again, I lead, too late I realise the car coming towards us is a cop. I brake hard, and in my mirror I see he does too. Shit! I expect him to catch up with us. It always seems silly to slow after you've been seen; logic says speed up, get away, don't give yourself up. But we don't see him again. DRob and Jonathan don't see him at all. However, when we stop, they tell stories of moose in lakes and Jonathan even saw a bear. I seem to be looking out for the wrong things. But none of us fails to notice the black storm clouds ahead. We pull over and put on waterproofs. The last hundred miles had been flat and uneventful, but now, just as we head back towards an undulating landscape, the rain threatens again. As we head towards the city of Dawson Creek, the road takes us due east, and we run parallel to the weather front.

This is it: the start of the Alaska Highway, also known as the ALCAN Highway. This is where we stop and take the obligatory photo of the sign. Its only significance being that it is there; for us it means the exact point where the journey continues. None of us had wanted to carry *The Milepost* handbook, with its biblical proportions, and none of us wants to be the one who throws it away either. It's not easily accessible, and so we really aren't using it much. However, after having taken the time to refer to it, it tells us of an alternative route; the old, original route on dirt road that twists through picturesque mountains and over wooden bridges spanning rocky ravines of deep wild rivers. We decide we want some of that and soon find ourselves on a road untravelled. Today really has marked a turning point in the trip. The spectacular and the accessible may attract the hoards, but the boundless beauty beyond is where the real admiration is.

The wooden bridge is a talented piece of carpentry, being as it curves over the river; all the elongated planks have varying radiuses. From the railings, we watch a family of beavers going about their business. We watch them undisturbed until we've exhausted every single beaver joke we can think of. It's getting late, but it's not getting dark. Tonight is solstice night, and I have all the energy that this magical night generates. I could ride on into it, but we find a deserted camp ground on the side of a river. It seems as good a place as any to indulge in our own interpretations of ancient pagan rituals.

It starts with some Jägermeister and a game of Frisbee, followed by sending DRob across the river—via the bridge—to fetch beer. The landlady joins us; she sells us some wood for our ceremonial fire. She has her mobile phone clipped to the front of her skimpy top. The phone is pulling it down past the cleavage point. Surely she is aware of this. The only way to deal with the situation is to give her whiskey and take her photo. We play some groovy tunes on the iPod speakers and jump around enthusiastically. Later, she returns with her daughter, and we use the same strategy of sharing our alcohol and taking photos.

Although he only spent eleven years living in the UK, they were formative school years. And so, whenever he drinks, the thug in Jonathan comes to the surface, and I am usually the victim. His play fighting gets rough, and I come off worst. Our hosts come back a third time. They've printed off A4 colour prints of the photos they just took and brought more beer and firewood. I tell loud, drunken stories, the mother laughs raucously, and her daughter squirms between discomfort and flirtation. DRob is repeatedly telling me to shut up and go to bed. But that will never happen, not while I still have some Jägermeister and an audience. At 2:30AM, it's still light, or perhaps it got light, or maybe I've seen the light, or something. Before I go off to my tent, I make the unquestionable good decision to text an ex. What could possible go wrong?

Fort Nelson, British columbia

257 miles

I hear loud rain—loud enough to wake me from my coma. I consider what has been left outside but do nothing and go back to my preferred oblivion. The next thing I'm aware of is Jonathan's voice. He sounds distressed; it pulls me out of my dream and into my boots. It's been raining really hard. I had left my jacket, trousers. and helmet outside, along with the guidebooks and mosquito coils. Well, that was rather silly. On the plus side, the dirty dishes are practically clean. I'm fully alert now and go into some kind of manic survival mode.

We take the sodden things and put them in a convenient shelter. I must still be drunk, as I'm finding this really funny and have absolutely no hangover. As I'm hanging up the sad array of saturated belongings, I manage to kick myself really hard with my unlaced steel toe-capped boot. Even that doesn't bother me. Rather than pack up, I find other things to do. I write my diary and talk on the phone. Jonathan's dad is very ill, and I discuss the situation with someone in Denver. In the cloudy damp morning, I feel moisture in my eyes for his predicament, but I won't mention it. I'm not sure what Jonathan's coping strategy is, but I'll go along with whatever he decides. For now, it could be drinking and denial. Then again, this is familiar behaviour, and I could be reading too much into it. When the next downpour comes, I watch it from between hanging clothing in the shelter. *The Milepost* has tripled in weight from the water it's sucked up.

The weather this morning may be sobering, but I'm not sure what I am. I could have been looking at the longest hangover of the year, but for some inexplicable reason, I'm alright. Even putting on wet clothes isn't too much of a hardship. We don't see our hosts as we ride past their house and back to the road. Technically, Fort Saint John is where the itinerary said we should have stayed overnight. It's only ten miles up the road, so we stop there for breakfast. The car park is nothing but mud and puddles. It seems a popular place, and every single vehicle outside is a pickup truck. We're evidently in rancher country now—big trucks, big bellies, and big appetites. Why am I not hung over? I totally deserve to be, and this would be the ideal road. We have 240 long, dull, flat miles to do today. It would almost be nice to feel rough; at least it would keep my mind occupied. At a fuel stop, we meet some American Harley riders all branded up with their flamed sweatshirts and skull-embroidered denim jackets. They have piss-pot, open-face helmets and are desperately under-equipped for this journey. It's a thin line between cool and being an ignorant twat, and their inability to protect themselves against the elements leaves me doubting they will even cross into the Yukon Territory, let alone reach Alaska. It makes me feel quite smug about my informed and researched ways. Yeah, I had a Harley, but I sold it because it's really not the best tool for this job!

The scenery consists of nothing but pine trees. The cloud is low and the road is wet. We pass a bunch of stationary motorhomes at some roadworks, then follow a pilot car along the rough and unmade surface. When the sky ahead comes down to meet us, we stop to don the waterproofs. I can almost taste the conceit when the white boxes on wheels trundle past us, watching us perform our roadside yoga of standing on one leg and pulling yellow outer layers over our already overdressed bodies. I'm not feeling the love and camaraderie from my fellow travellers as we continue on our individual quests towards the permanent light of the North. At this point in the once-in-a-lifetime journey, the divide in the choice of vehicles seems stronger than the unification of the destination.

Once again and without discussion, I'm the nominated leader.

We couldn't take an alternative route if we wanted to, so what is this addictive fascination with viewing the back of my bike? I wish someone else would take the lead for a change. I could get behind that.

We aren't going to manage the 240 miles in one hit, and we don't have to. We're on time. It's OK to stop. It's a concept I'm finding hard to adjust to. After a hundred miles, we pull off for a coffee. The waitress is gorgeous, and her presence fills the room, leaving it in a stunned silence when she goes out to pump fuel. She has no idea how captivating she is, and that alone is the most beautiful of qualities. Is it coincidental that the girls seem to get prettier the longer I'm on the road? It's quite clear that the exact opposite applies to me.

As we approach Fort Nelson, I go onto reserve and ride in on fumes. It's been a day of monotonous scenery and wet roads; an altogether miserable ride. I put more fuel in my tank than I even knew it held, then we pay the high—but expected—price for a room for the night. These people only have three months in which to earn a year's living. It would be wrong to haggle or even begrudge them the price. It's understandable, and as my dad said, "You don't go on holiday to save money." Anyway, it's a much appreciated novelty not to camp. I have an en suite and can see my bike out of the window. It all feels very luxurious and decadent. This is Flid time. I do my laundry in the sink and have a long hot bath with a whiskey. I've given up waiting for the hangover. God knows what happened to it! I use the computer in the reception and speed-read through my inbox, but there's nothing worth opening—no correspondence delaying or distracting me from going back into the real world. Remember that this is still a liberating, honest, and undisclosed time before the necessity to post an exaggerated and enviable status update on a social media site. You just get on with your journey and tell people about it later.

I have to do a little bike maintenance. The landlady warns me not to use her towels to clean my bike.

"Why would I do that? What do you think I'm like?"

She apologises and says some of the Harley riders have been known to. Anyway, I still have a supply I took from a motel chain back in the US. Speaking of the devils; the skull-displaying, flame-decorated, piss-pot posers come waddling into the complex, too cold to talk and too cool to interact. I overhear (it's hard not to) that they have mechanical issues. If only they could open their tiny minds, they would see the benefit of friendship beyond their elite and cliquey circle. But they don't want my limey, Japanese-stained fingers delving beyond their dirty chrome to fix a fault they have no concept of. Loud of mouth and deaf to advice, they are beyond both their capabilities and accepting my help. I'm not going to persuade them to take good advice. I've owned and ridden Harleys for over twenty years, but if the only way to get their acceptance is to announce this then *Fuck 'em!* is the phrase that comes to mind. And a turned back says it in an accent they can understand perfectly.

DRob, Jonathan, and I have all been happily doing our own thing, catching up on what we individually feel is important to us. The clouds have broken up and it would be good to do something with this, the longest of days, like ride the light night and sleep through the wet hours. I probably would if I was on my own, and with today's attitude, I'm surprised I'm not. Instead, I organise myself and prepare my things for tomorrow. I put *The Milepost* over the hot-air vent in my room. Then I sit outside—warm, snug, and clean—with a whiskey in my hand, watching the sky change colour but never going dark. I'd like to squeeze more out of this permanent day, but my big bed has extremely persuasive qualities, so I reluctantly leave the temptation on the other side of my blackout curtains.

Day 9

Liard Hot Springs
British Columbia

196 miles

I feel a little guilty banging on DRob and Jonathan's doors at 7AM, but not so guilty that there is any feeling of remorse. I've been given leadership responsibility, and there's more to that than following my arse as the miles pass. Again, there is a misty chill in the air, and it would be a beautiful October day, except it's June. *The Milepost* is dry, but with wavy and crisp pages, it's also now three times its original thickness. I put it under the TV, hoping the weight of this unstealable box will compress it, then turn it on and watch the weather channel. It's not very positive. However, it does help me grasp just how big this country is. I love how they understate the size of the place. Hudson Bay is big enough to fit Spain in—at 650 miles wide, it's only 70 miles less than the Great Australian Bight—yet in Canada, it's just a bay, although not exactly your sunset, palm-lined evening stroll. Anyway, we aren't going there; we're heading up to the next state, the Yukon Territory, a far more modest area, just twice the size of the UK but with a population of only 33,000. It's so sparsely populated, I'm going to be hard pressed to find anyone to piss me off. However, that's no hardship today. The Harley riders have decided they're going to turn back. We try to help one of the fat bastards bump start his bike, but weight and a general lack of enthusiasm are against us.

The fuel station doesn't offer much in the way of breakfast snacks, and I find a glance turns into a stare as I pass a *Hustler* magazine on the shelf. Humm, I have a primitive yearning—"Flid needs woman" . . . or something. I've just checked out of my room too. Relief is not looking good. Still, at least her precious towels remain unspoilt. Jonathan can't log onto his email account, and DRob can't get money out of the cash machine, so it looks like we've all failed. I'm being alert to Jonathan's situation and looking for signs as to how he must be feeling about his dad, but he's giving little away. Just remaining aware is all I can do for now. As usual, hours have slipped past before we're ready to leave. However, something remarkable has happened. The skies have cleared. We get to ride in the sunshine at last, to see scenery, to wear fewer clothes. And with the sunshine, the cameras come out too. We stop for a "world famous cinnamon roll." Really? Do the Canadians, like the Americans, do this too? No one's ever bloody heard of you; no one who hasn't ridden past your roadside signposts. No one asked me or indeed told me over my months of research, "Well, if you don't make it to the Arctic Circle or even Anchorage and if the majesty of Banff and Jasper National Parks evade you along with the bear and moose, whatever you do, don't go to Canada and not have a 'world famous cinnamon roll' from that shitty little nondescript shop at the back end of nowhere, the one that puts more effort into hype than baking." In their defence, they have a distinct lack of competition. There is absolutely nothing with any stimulating qualities for miles around. That's why we stop for the half-baked and overrated cinnamon rolls. We get chatting to an old couple travelling in a large motorhome.

"We're going to Alaska," we say as we always do. However, we are speaking to seasoned and experienced travellers who ask us which route we're taking.

Jonathan and DRob look at me. "Umm, this one."

Apparently there are several, and we were cautioned by the lady as to the condition of the more northerly roads.

"You'll get some dirt up the Dempster," she warns. Sounds nasty.

But we take the advice on board, and when we get outside, we giggle like little boys. "Watch out, you don't want dirt up ya Dempster!" While we are having our meeting inside, outside some clouds have met up, and that's the end of the sunshine ride.

We should have stayed on our roll, not stopped for one. We get up to speed again on the now mainly empty road. Up ahead, a car is stopped in its lane. For once, I'm not leading, and it's Jonathan some way in front who passes it first. But as I approach, without indication, the car pulls a U-turn. For fuck's sake! With only the benefit of time on my side, I miss him, but the manoeuvre is only seconds away from ending in some severe impact.

This being the only road, any services—be them for rolls, fuel, or accommodation—are frequented by all who travel it. Later in the day, I see the car again. Luckily for him, my anger and adrenalin have subsided, and I let it go. We're both lucky. The cars do provide one useful service though, and we soon learn that if one is stopped in a seemingly illogical spot, it's because the vigilant passenger has seen some wildlife. We spot some caribou and horned sheepy things. But the best is when everyone is looking at a buffalo on the other side of the road, and being forever contrary, I look the other way and see a black bear wander off into the undergrowth. With fingerless gloves and a zoom lens, I'm able to get a photo of it before it disappears. At last, I get to see something no one else does. I needed that; it was a bear necessity.

Today's mileage has flown past, and with plenty of stops, some sunshine, and photos the mood's been upbeat. Perhaps it was a bit short-sighted to put the high mileage days right at the beginning of the trip; it reflected my impatience to get to the good bits though. But it's all working out now, and the itinerary means tonight, as planned, we get to stay at some hot springs. It's early afternoon as we approach. A herd of buffalo is loitering on the side of the road as if it's the most natural thing in the world, and in this world, it is. If your vehicle, load, and licence plate don't give you away, then taking a photo of buffalo says, "You ain't from 'round these parts, are you?" I decide to pay for a camping spot to myself, so I don't hear my snoring friends. This decision is made on account of a newly adopted road philosophy: no more self-inflicted hardships. The trip requires plenty of endurance; I see no point in making it harder than it need be.

One such hardship we could never have foreseen is the fact that the only permanent building here, which serves as a general store, and more importantly, a restaurant, has just discovered their water is contaminated. They are very concerned about it. As we're surrounded by rivers and thermal springs, I don't really see the seriousness; until it's pointed out that because of the contamination they have to close the restaurant. WHAT? This is serious! And what do you mean you only have a licence to serve alcohol with food? What if we buy a can of beans? Now what are we going to do? It's with a sinking feeling that I also realise I left three beers in the fridge of my room this morning. What an unfortunate string of tragedies! The insufficient consolation is that they have a few cans of food for sale.

We finish the last of my whiskey, which is also insufficient, and walk the elevated, wooden, decked path over a stagnant, steaming swamp to the hot springs pool. We get there just as a thunderstorm rumbles over. Surrounded by pines, vision distorted by the vapours and torrential rain, we sit up to our shoulders in the bubbling water as the weather throws itself down on us. It's surreal; it's confusing. And why am I trying to protect my head from the rain when the rest of me is submerged?

Once the storm has passed, we light a fire and heat our cans of beans and asparagus and grill some sausages. We're lacking alcohol, but I do have some miniature bottles of Jägermeister in my tank bag, which I was saving for when we got to the Arctic Circle. Soon, as they don't even know I intend to go there, this was to be the bait with which to entice them. And as we've progressed further into the wilderness, the opportunity to replenish such a vital supply seems unlikely, so I decide to keep schtum, and we have a sober night.

Once again, with water and general dampness, the mozzies are out in force. They've been known to drive horses and cattle to distraction with their sheer mass of numbers and relentless appetites. Incidentally, we're told no one ever tethers a horse up here; it's like streaking it out on a cross. The bears will come and eat any living thing that can't run away. Being sober and possibly a little starved for conversation, DRob thanks me for all the preparation I've put into this trip and particularly the schedule, on his version of which I conveniently omitted the Arctic Circle bit. I have to admit, though, now we're back on track, it really is working out quite well. Smothered in DEET, covered in clothing and netting, and still getting bitten, I take myself off to my tent for an early night. I recall hearing a gun shot at some point, but it doesn't really disturb me.

Day 10

Whitehorse, Yukon Territory

418 miles

I think eleven hours sleep ought to be enough. I pack up my damp tent and ride over to where the others are camped. Predictably, they aren't awake, so I try to relight the fire. I only manage to make a lot of smoke, but it at least keeps the mozzies away. Turns out I missed all the fun last night. Jonathan went for an evening dip in the hot springs, and as soon as there was no one around, he opted to skinny dip then walked back in flip flops with only a towel around him. It still being light, and unaware of what the time was, he decided to wander out to the road to see if the buffalo were still there. They weren't, but there was a grizzly bear that, upon seeing him, rose up on its hind legs to look him in the eye. Apparently it was quite big, but not as big as his protective mother who also stood up to see what had attracted the attention of her cub. Forgetting all he had learnt about passive action in the event of a grizzly confrontation, he just froze and stared at it, then ran. By pure chance, a family on vacation was driving down the deserted road and stopped to photograph the bears. Relieved, Jonathan ran round the car, pulling at the door handles and trying to get in.

"Open the door; open the door!" wasn't having the desired effect. The driver and his family weren't stupid; they'd locked the doors to protect themselves from both the wild and the running scared, naked in flip flops.

Against all odds and inclinations, the bears ran off. Not surprisingly, they were somewhat freaked out—I'm talking about the voyeurs, although the bears could have been equally traumatised. Back at camp, Jonathan hysterically announced, "There are bears outside; there are bears outside!" and everyone left their camp and cooking, picked up their cameras, and rushed off to find them. The camp ground hosts, however, took the matter very seriously. Hence the gun shot I heard. The bears weren't having a good evening, and there I was with my earplugs in, dozing through it all.

To compensate for all the excitement I'd missed out on, I open my last sachet of peanut butter. Then we all go for a morning dip. As we walk the elevated path, Jonathan describes his encounter again in full detail. This near-death experience has clearly had a greater effect on him than I realise; either that or he's been reflecting on his father's condition.

As we walk towards the steaming, bubbling, thermal fury, he philosophically says, "If each of these boards was a day of your life, would you speed up as you got nearer the end?" It makes me realise that I seem to be rushing through my life, always eager to get to the next thrill, not always acknowledging that the present is actually a good place to be. If you don't acknowledge the present, you can't recall it, and then you have no memorable past. If you are always looking to the future, then your life will forever be a chase. There's a lot to be said for appreciating the moment; however, this conflicts with the schedule. Being unprepared would have us turning back like the Harley riders. No research would leave us with no available camping spots or ferry reservations. The itinerary was designed to get as much as possible out of the trip in the time available to us. It may only be North America, not Siberia, but because of its size and Western prices, it means this is quite likely a trip of a lifetime. Of course, I want to enjoy every moment, but equally, I want a lot of enjoyable moments.

I consider all this as I sit in the hot pool. It's quite a conundrum, made all the more annoying by my agonising over it. Once again, the other two seem far more relaxed and appreciative of the beauty around them than I do. One thing's for sure, I'm never going to be the organiser of a money-rich, time-poor tour again. Next time things will be different.

A herd of school kids turns up, and the tranquillity runs off into the forest. We head for the changing hut. As I'm bending down to pull up my underwear, a fellow bather asks me if this is my first time. It's a very badly timed comment, which has me, once again, hastily leaving the actual moment. I no more want total recall of this moment than I do dirt up the Dempster; he's not getting behind this.

It's another late start, and out on the road it's colder than it looks. We pass the herd of buffalo again, but don't even stop. It's remarkable how quickly we become blasé about a sight that not long ago would have brought us to a screeching halt.

The signposts now give distances to names of places, which when reached, are nothing more than a shop or fuel station. There are no other buildings or inhabitants. These places are strategically placed as dictated by necessity, so the traveller can get fuel on their way to the next place of civilisation. The land is generally becoming wilder now. There is far less evidence of human impact, and even the road turns to gravel for long stretches at times. The weather, too, seems to be less tamed. From a little elevation, we see a blackened sky ahead of us. The sun is still shining, which makes the darkness ahead even more foreboding. Putting on our waterproofs is now just a matter of course; a daily occurrence. We take the downpour in our stride. It's not so awful. With such long distances between landmarks, the crossing into the Yukon Territory is quite significant. We have been riding through British Columbia for a week.

The next town on the map is Watson Lake, a place that instantly has a white trash feel. We stop for fuel, and a staggering drunk enters the forecourt and starts screaming at a girl, who locks herself in her car. What an interesting creature the human can be! How, surrounded by hundreds of miles of unspoilt natural beauty, we're able to build a self-sustaining settlement and roads to and from it on the heaving permafrost tundra, yet within a few generations can breed out of ourselves all survival or pioneer instincts. It's evolution in reverse. Survival of the fittest? I predict a bear victory.

Apart from breeding fodder for day-time TV, Watson Lake has a "signpost forest." It seems people from all over the world bring signposts to put on the trees. From a British Rail ticket to a Cyrillic town name, it's a graveyard of stolen, redundant, and relocated signposts. I think it's physically impossible not to pass through without at least taking a photo. The weather becomes particularly unpleasant as we continue onto our destination of Teslin, and when we get there, we find nothing in the town to keep us. We look at a room in a guesthouse, and it makes the decision to move on even easier. There are clear distinctions between places to stop at and places not to. There is either something—a fuel station, shop, or campground—or absolutely nothing but impenetrable pines stretching over endless hills. So the indecision to stay or go only occurs once every couple hours. The next place which requires such a decision boasts a salmon bake. It has lake-side camping potential, but today it's holding a Gospel Music Festival.

We ride in, find a space between the motorhomes, converted school buses, pickup trucks, and various other improvised mobile accommodation, and without obligating ourselves, we tentatively take a look around. Although there has been a disproportionate amount of cloud on our way up through Canada, here we find ourselves among a transient city of people who all want to be sunbeams. A festival of brainwashed zombies with vacant smiles slapped on their faces, happily lobotomised and programmed. Give me a grizzly any fuckin' day; a bear can see reason, I'm really bloody scared here. Jonathan takes off. I wait with DRob whilst he dithers, and we don't see Jonathan again.

There's only one road, and we're only going in one direction. He can only be ahead of us. Ironically, this is the first night that we've passed our intended stopping place, so there isn't a clear and obvious meeting point anywhere up ahead. As the miles pass, we start to consider more and more unlikely scenarios. I haven't had phone reception for days. We come to a campsite, the only place of any significance since the gospel festival. A variety of campers are scattered around. They all stop what they're doing as we slowly ride through looking for a turquoise BMW.

I'm pretty sure someone would say something if they had seen another bike. They don't look very approachable. We're besieged by mozzies. Bugger this! What the hell are we going to do now? Keep on going? What else can we do?

We ride on to the town of Whitehorse—tomorrow's destination. It's big. Well, compared to what we've been through it is. Still no phone reception though. We get a room and hit the bar. A guy with his leg in plaster is singing *Blue Suede Shoes*; he's missing the absurdity. I manage to stop myself from partaking in the karaoke, but only just. I don't stop myself drinking though. It's a very sociable place; very drunk, but friendly. I meet a German guy who gives me a DVD. He has just finished the production of his film about a long-distance dog sledding competition that happens every year up here. I have great admiration for someone who has completed their project. For all my efforts to write a book, I've got little more than half a page of scribbled line. *You should write a book* is a phrase in life I've heard almost as frequently as *get ya hair cut*. And when this journey's itinerary is complete, I'm going to see what I can do about that.

It won't get dark. How the hell are you supposed to know when to stop drinking if it won't get dark? No one has the answer, and no one knows how to stop drinking, either. They don't even know when to close the bar, so they don't. This is weird. It might be 3:30AM, but I might be in a different time zone too. Who can say? There are a lot of unanswered questions this evening. Tonight. This morning. Whatever the hell it is!

Day 11

Whitehorse, Yukon Territory

20 miles

When Jonathan had taken me to pick up my Harley from the jewellery pawn shop last summer, in what appeared at the time to be a very spontaneous act, he also bought a ring with five diamonds embedded in it. When I later asked him what the hell that was all about, he nonchalantly replied that he was going to ask his girlfriend to marry him, as he wanted to knock her up. I was stunned. How incredibly romantic, calculated, and surprising! This called for an immediate drinking session. He probably reworded his intentions when he gave her the ring on some Caribbean beach, as she accepted his proposal.

The date of the planned wedding was today. Clearly, it had to be postponed, because trips such as this require far more planning and commitment. The postponement didn't seem to bother anyone involved, but Jonathan's sudden disappearance on such an auspicious day was now raising some suspicion. The fact that if I hadn't got the Harley, he wouldn't have seen the ring was all conveniently forgotten. Now I wasn't the initiator of the engagement; I was the adjourner of the wedding with my inflexible and enticing plans. Not that I felt any resentment directed at me, but I'm pretty sure it was close to the surface, ready to attack, if I ever put my foot in it. This has and continues to be a pattern in my life. When spouses get there claws in my mates, they are at best, discouraged and occasionally outright forbidden to see me. It's not unknown for ultimatums to be issued. My plans, habits, company, and lifestyle are a great threat to the women who want to domesticate and dominate my once free and wild friends. Somewhere along the courting process, balls and spine are subtly removed, possibly willingly relinquished, and many of my friends, who have 0accompanied me so far, now, opt for sofa alternatives. This was not the case with Jonathan and his fiancée; I'm just sayin.'"

Back to the moment, and I notice checkout time is only an hour away. As we're a day ahead of ourselves, I decide to pay for another night. I don't want to mention it, but I'm paying my dues for last night's socialising, and I'm really not feeling my best. Be that as it may, I have obligations to fulfil today, and the top priority is finding Jonathan. Even in this sizeable town, with a bloody great satellite dish outside my window, I still have no reception on my mobile. I call Tammara from the phone in reception. It goes to voicemail.

"Ah, right, now listen. Don't worry. I'm sure everything is just fine, but we seem to have mislaid Jonathan . . . about fourteen hours ago. I know today should have been your wedding day and everything, and I will try my hardest to find him, I just wondered if you might have heard from him."

As I hang up, I hear laughing. Some guests checking in have overheard my apologetic message. I go and get DRob; he's responsible, and I'm hungry. As we walk out onto the street there is Jonathan sitting on his bike. Apparently, he's been there for hours. He's already eaten, so I tell him he'd better go and call his fiancée, as I may have inadvertently caused a little concern. "Oh happy wedding day, by the way."

Inside the restaurant, I feel far more relaxed. There's quite a variety among the clientele—obviously there are the hungry, the workers, the locals, the hotel's guests, and those passing through—but it's the state of mind that is remarkable. Clearly, no one has the ability to cope with twenty-four hours of daylight. Drinking and working has overlapped into a chaotic mix and descended upon the service industry. A vast proportion of the restaurant is drunk; some are hung over, but with the availability of alcohol, the drinking is beginning, continuing, or restarting. It's like an international airport bar, only with a sense of community and exuberance. As we wait for our food, a very loud, drunk girl walks in talking on her phone, "I'm absolutely hammered. I've only just finished work." It's the barmaid from last night, this morning, whatever. She sits down and orders a whiskey sour. I have a strong urge to join her. After all, we do have a day off today.

Jonathan keeps having micro adventures within our journey. Clearly, my itinerary is not exciting enough for him. Having lost us, he found a bunch of locals drinking round a fire, and spent the night partying with them and provoking them into showing him their extensive knife collection. But what started with a presentation soon turned into threatening behaviour when he started chatting up their women; he's a bloody liability.

Eight years ago, I was backpacking through Laos. I stayed a few days in the jungle, camped under a mosquito net on a bamboo platform. One day, I decided to swim across the river. It was much wider than it appeared and had an incredibly strong current. I drifted downstream for some distance before making it to the far bank. When I pulled my panting body up out of the water, there on the tiny, sandy beach was a Canadian girl with an inner tube. She was suffering badly from the side effects of the malaria tablets she was taking. She was experiencing episodes of delirium and paranoia, and coming across a tattooed English hippy floating downstream wasn't helping her inner torment at all. However, we crossed back over the river, found some common ground, and travelled together for a few weeks. Thinking she would be safe in her remote location, her parting words were, "If you're ever in Whitehorse, look me up!" And here I am.

This is the pinnacle of my planning. Not only are we here, but it's at the most unlikely of times—an international band has actually scheduled this date on their unconventional world tour to play in Whitehorse. Tickets for The White Stripes had unsurprisingly sold out in an instant, but I felt optimistic. Only once have I ever failed to get into a concert, and that was for Alanis Morissette on her *Jagged Little Pill* tour. I just couldn't find a way into the small London venue she was playing. And here I am now in Alanis's homeland, once again trying to procure tickets; is that ironic?

So we all smarten ourselves up and go to visit my friend. She's married now with two kids. After a few beers on her deck, her parents join us. We must have passed the initiation test, as we're all invited to stay for dinner: a Sunday roast, with meat from a caribou that her husband recently hunted and shot up the Dempster. She says we'll never get tickets for the concert tomorrow, and we may as well not waste our time. Annoyingly, I take her advice, based on understanding just how rare it must be for Whitehorse to be a stop on any band's tour and the fact that they've chosen to play in a tiny venue. It's not that I'm a huge fan of the band, I just wanted it to work out.

It's been strange staying in the same place for so long, but socialising with locals inevitably comes with regional knowledge, and now we're excited by a remote, alternative route to Alaska that they've told us about. It's a rough road, longer, but far more scenic, and it will take us an extra day. However, if we don't stick around for the gig, we'll have a spare day to do the dirty desolate road, where we will also not see any white stripes.

Day 12

Chicken, Alaska, USA

455 miles

This respite has changed many things; our route, our sense of understanding, and now there seems to have been a role reversal too. This morning, I'm the one who's woken by an impatient knocking on my door. The others are anxious to get going. Up until Whitehorse, it was all about the riding. However, it only took a few days of staying put to get an awareness of what a place is actually like to live in. It's given the journey another dimension. Not that any of us even realised that we were missing anything along the way. But what we have discovered is that there's more to a journey than simply making the deadlines to a destination.

Feeling somewhat rushed by my oh-so-efficient and ready-to-go friends, I find myself swearing and struggling with the stupid pannier fastening locks on the Connie. A passing woman somewhat patronisingly says, "Having fun?" And that's when I realise that, yes, actually I am. And I shouldn't be cussing about something so small when I'm living this dream. "I'm going to Alaska," I say for possibly the last time.

Our breakfast waitress gives us more attitude than service, and it's once again 10AM by the time we set off. As a token gesture, we ride past the Arts Centre where The White Stripes will be playing tonight, then we head for the Klondike Highway, which will take us to Dawson. If I wasn't so rushed, if my phone had reception, if I'd checked my email, I would have got the message that, due to popular demand, Jack White and his sister have announced they will be playing a free gig in the park this afternoon. So close, yet so far. Sometimes you remember the things you miss more that the things you saw.

From inside my helmet, when we finally do get going, I reflect on the places we've been, not solely on where we're going. There is variety within my thoughts, and it confirms what I touched on at the hot springs, that if you use the present only to calculate the future, you won't have a past to reflect on. This change wasn't intentional, but it's happened, and now that I'm aware of it, I've had a bit of realisation about this whole motorcycle travel thing. It's too easy to twist the throttle and take off; the trick is to stop and take off your helmet for a while.

I'm really enjoying this part of the journey, more than any other day of the trip. I have no idea what's coming on this new and relatively spontaneous choice of routes. I, therefore, have no expectations. Plus, we're a day ahead of schedule, and it's hardly rained. We're promised again that the weather will improve in the next few days, but we've been hearing that since we entered Canada. There's a lot of dirt road, and it strikes me with both horror and humour that we are, indeed, heading for the Dempster Highway and the imminent dirt. What we have to deal with first, though, are ravenous plagues of mozzies. We get stopped at roadworks, with signs of half-hour waits between pilot car escorts. I've no idea how the roadworkers deal with the mozzies because, as soon as we stop, they swarm round us in black clouds. They even have the ability to pierce through clothing. With visors down and collars tight, we simply wait to be alerted to our next most accessible piece of flesh with yet another itchy bite.

The endless pines have in fact ended, replaced with tall scrub and a haze of purple flowers. It feels far out. It's like no landscape I have seen before; very inhospitable. How can you make shelter with no vegetation to speak of? I love it though. Now I'm getting the feeling this is what I came for. This is a wilderness that thrills with nothing more than its vast unspoilt and desolate landscape. It's the one environment that stirs something in my soul. The dormant nomad in me awakens and wonders about the possibility of a permanent existence out here. This place is everything a Tesco Club Card isn't, and the only blue and white I ever want to see again is cloud and sky.

We come to the city of Dawson, and a decision has to be made. Across the mighty Yukon River is The Top of the World Highway, notorious for its ever-changing weather conditions, which can make it impassable. There is nothing out there but a customs post as the road crosses into the most northerly of America's fifty states. Dawson is an old gold rush town. You can just tell. The main street is straight out of a Western movie, yet with a genuine working population, albeit less than a thousand. We only know enough about the Top of the World Highway to have us doubting our ability to cross it. The only information available to us here is that it takes about four hours to do the one hundred miles, and there is a 60% chance of rain. We face our decision with two 5% beers each, and before we know it, we're on the ferry crossing the river. On the other side, the road winds straight up a mountainside, which isn't a huge surprise, given the name of the road.

We look down on Dawson wistfully, anticipating the thin air and thick mud ahead of us. Top of the World, my arse! We aren't even above the timber line. It's barely 4,000 feet above sea level. Denver is higher than this. There was more snow in Whitehorse. So the scare mongering and over-hyped name amount to very little, yet there seems to be a desire to maintain the myth and make the road seem far worse than it actually is. I'm out in front. It may be dirt road, but it's graded and maintained.

I stop at a vista point to wait for the others; a bloke comes the other way on a hired motorbike. He's a lawyer and has given up his suit and put on some leathers for the week. He warns of horrendous conditions ahead and the certain death I face. When the others catch up, he recoils somewhat and carries on his way. As we carry on ours, we find there are no such conditions, and the customs post into Alaska is the easiest transition into America I have ever had. I don't even have to remove my helmet, and the customs official certainly isn't interested in what's up the Dempster.

The first town we get to in Alaska is called Chicken, named after a bird common to the area—the ptarmigan—which no one could spell, so Chicken was close enough. It has a population of just seventeen. On the outskirts, DRob goes off in search of some beer, whilst I wait for Jonathan to catch up. He takes a while, and when we ride into town, DRob is nowhere to be found. But a bar is, so we get a drink. How the hell can we lose someone in a town where we've just increased the population by fifteen per cent? Someone asks if we're looking for a motorcyclist. Apparently, he's down by the airstrip. If we had insecurity issues, we'd say he was trying to avoid us. Other than the bar-cum-liquor store, there's a souvenir shop and a fuel station; so not really that many places to hide. We ride over to the airstrip and find a few small planes, but no DRob. We decide that staying put is our best option and go back to the bar, and there's DRob. How did you . . . ?

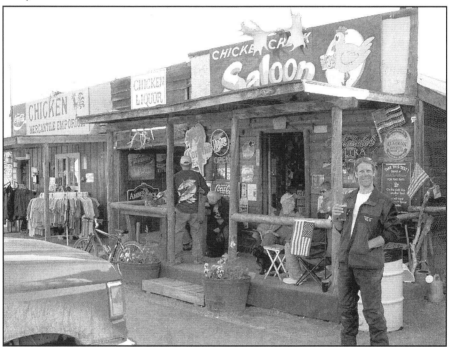

"If you fill your tanks here," the fuel station cashier tells us, "You can camp for free by that little river, where you can also pan for gold if you like." Sounds a bit labour intensive to me. There's no food to be had anywhere, so we drink Jägermeister, light a fire, and DRob chats to some gold miners.

"Where you boys heading?"

"Alaska," we say, out of habit.

"Ya in Alaska now, boys."

"Oh, yeah! Course we are," I say. "The Arctic Circle then."

"What?" says DRob.

"That reminds me, there's something I've been meaning to tell
  you."

Day 13

Arctic Circle, Alaska

505 miles

Now this is a novelty. Waking up to sunshine and then joyously rolling up a dry tent as I sip my complimentary coffee from the fuel station. Long-drop toilets and hand-pumped water under blue skies; this feels so good. The bumper stickers say, "What happens in Chicken stays in Chicken." Nothing happened, so we decide not to stay. We ride seventy miles of empty roads, warmth, and wilderness. It's unfamiliar, uplifting, and inspiring. Canada Dry is very misleading branding; today Baked Alaska seems far more appropriately named. The warmth on my waterproofs this morning made them easy to roll up tight, and I feel compact, agile, and liberated, wearing just essentials, not the usual excessive riding gear. The road is smooth, the flowers are wild and in blossom, and on the distant horizon are snow-capped mountains; this makes me feel fabulous.

We rejoin the ALCAN Highway at Tok. The motorhomes are back, along with other heavily laden vehicles and the cheap, roadside gimmicks to attract the tourists. As if created just for me, on the breakfast menu is the Grumpy Grizzly Breakfast. It comes with two reindeer sausages. I put ketchup on the ends, "Look, I've given them a red nose," I say to DRob and Jonathan. I think they preferred it when I was grumpy. They both leave me in there, Jonathan to call Tammara, who flies into Anchorage today, and DRob to go and faff around with his oil, no doubt contemplating my suggestion that today we ride all the way to the Arctic Circle in the light of the midnight sun. It's what I always envisioned doing, right from the conception of this plan. I don't mind persuading, even coercing. Fuck it; I'll tow him there if I have to, but I just don't want to hear a "no," because I want this more than anything else. It encapsulates all my passions: midsummer light, new challenging roads, and absolute wilderness combined with the destination of a principal point, albeit an invisible line around the top of the planet, where at midnight five days ago, the solstice sun never set. The promise of this enticing and enchanting land has brought me this far. My hopes and dreams are interrupted by the booming voices of brainwashed, military gung-ho kids talking about the next country they would obliterate. I liked the naivety of my Rudolph sausages, and I'm enjoying the thrill of the unknown to come, but the reality of what I'm hearing has me leaving my seat and the restaurant, because I know you can't argue with a sick mind, and I don't want their voices in my head.

Jonathan has decided to go straight to Anchorage to meet Tammara. What can I say? That's what happens. We decide on a meeting place three days from now. We swap communal essentials, and that's it. Goodbye Jonny. I feel sad. It feels wrong. I'm incomplete. The chemistry, the mood, the challenge; everything has changed. I didn't expect his departure to have this much impact on my frame of mind. It's the surprise of how I feel as much as the loss that leaves me so sullen. As DRob and I head north out of town back into the wild, I try to come to terms with this temporary transition. And then the smile comes back on my face; coming the other way, all flashing lights, white teeth, and waves, is Jonathan. He missed the only left turn, the one to Anchorage, and is doubling back, bloody idiot!

Delta Junction represents the end of the 1,422 mile-long ALCAN Highway, and we pull over to the marker post for the obligatory photo. It's a place of meetings, recounting tales from our journeys. I speak to an old man who last did this trip in '53 with three friends, and it took them three months. He tells the story with pride, but there's a sense of sadness, too, as he recalls his youth. Although I don't say it, it sounds like he did that journey in the moment, which is why he has such clear memories. It's nothing to be sad about. Do I want to be him, reliving this journey old and alone, with just my recollections for company? Yes, actually, that's exactly what I want to do. I can't think of anything I'd rather do more, unless of course, DRob and Jonathan want to come along too. I'll ask them in 2044. Annoyingly, this romantic notion is snubbed when a lady in a car shouts out something at us. Turns out she wants to moan about the speed at which we've overtaken her. She sanctimoniously and hypocritically states that she drives at exactly three miles per hour above the speed limit.

"So you admit you're breaking the law then? A slapped face and a shot to the head are both assault," DRob defuses the situation; diplomacy is what he does best. Antagonism is my usual instinctive reaction to such confrontation, and it's never helped any situation ever, but maybe one day it will.

It doesn't take long to shake off that negative little encounter. As we ride up towards Fairbanks, we see a moose on the road. It brings us to a halt for photos. Although I've let DRob take most of the photos, this is an opportunity I want to capture myself, and I get a shot of its arse as it disappears into the trees. As well as diplomacy, another of DRob's qualities is his methodical nature. It can make travelling with him infuriating, but it's also what makes him such a spectacular doctor. It doesn't help much with his spontaneous photography technique though, and by the time he has his camera ready and looks up for the shot, the moose is long gone. He then systematically replaces his camera, as I wait astride my bike ready to go. When he has it all packed away, we turn our heads to pull out, back onto the road, and there is the moose, directly behind us. I grab my camera and get an excellent shot. "I'll send you a copy, DRob. Come on, let's go!"

It was for this that I'd bought my heated suit; the journey to the Arctic Circle. I mean, it just sounds cold, but as we approach Fairbanks, I see a temperature gauge that says different. It's 78° Fahrenheit today. The first thing we see after all this wilderness, after ten days of pine trees and unspoilt nature, is a bloody great military base. It's so offensive. The impenetrable forest has been stripped and replaced by fencing topped with coiled barbed wire, watch towers, and signs saying "no stopping" and "no photos." It's so ugly. A jet takes off parallel to us. America bought this state from Russia and now, fifteen years after the Cold War, the fear of those damned Commies is yet to be replaced by the threat of Islamic fundamentalists, and those Commies lurk just across the Bering Strait. The most impressive thing about Fairbanks is how America has managed to tame and sterilise a seemingly wild and inhospitable terrain. As well as the military base, it's a big college town. We could be in any city on the mainland US with its Starbucks and shopping malls. The inhabitants seem oblivious to the land that lies beyond their city. I want to use the Internet, but I don't think I want it so badly that I have to endure some trendy coffee shop full of students drinking soy hazelnut Frappuccinos and speaking loudly on their phones. I ask if I can use a computer.

"Only if you buy a coffee."

"OK, gimme a coffee."

"What kind?"

The kind that gives me access to your computer, I feel like saying. "Black."

"For here or to go?"

"What do you think?" Actually, fuck it! Let's get out of here. The culture shock, without exception, occurs upon re-entry into civilisation. The roads are full of four-by-fours with pounding base and "support our troops" stickers, and there are more flags in the air than mozzies. In fact, where the hell *are* all the mozzies?

If everything happens for a reason, then this is all the incentive DRob needs to get back into the wild. Although he still won't commit to going all the way, we are now leaving for the Arctic Circle.

It's like the motorcycling equivalent of stomping. That's how I leave Fairbanks, reluctantly delaying my exit with the need for fuel and with a fury at a development I can't face or even begin to confront. I suppose it's a quirk of my nature that my peaks are higher and my troughs are deeper. Perhaps pills could even out the extremities, but actually, I can generally handle it and so can the people who stick with me. It could be conceived as a spoilt brat tantrum, but upon closer examination, it's sparked by something other than the need for attention. In this case, it was the shocking realisation at how civilisation has moved in and taken over without any respect for the environment. Pretentious as this may sound, I know it's how progress occurs, but I've never seen it so blatantly displayed with such disrespect. It's just hideous. And I'm sure if I ever went to the polar oil fields of Prudhoe Bay and witnessed the devastation there, I'd be absolutely inconsolable. Perhaps the naivety of ketchup noses on reindeer sausages is a self-protection mechanism; I'm not totally unaware of what's going on, but I'm not fully informed either. Now I just feel disappointment generated by what I've experienced in Fairbanks, based partly on my ignorance colliding with my awareness.

With heightened sensitivity, we leave it all behind. I lead us past a sign that says it's 118 miles to the next fuel stop. There's a place called Livengood up ahead; we'll stop there. But some kind of sensibility kicks in, and after a few miles, I turn the throttle in the opposite direction to my yearning. "Perhaps we should have topped up there," I think. On the basis that I'm communicating again, DRob agrees. We turn around. I put the nozzle in my tank, and nothing happens. I go inside the restaurant-cum-shop, where I'm told it'll be an hour before the pumps are fixed. Why is everything conspiring to prevent me from doing this journey that I so desperately want to do, the journey that brought about this entire itinerary. It has delayed weddings, brought people across oceans, and has cost hours of time in preparation that, all tolled, would amount to weeks. Don't even think about the monetary costs. Why can't we do this? Bollocks! Let's eat. I'm fatigued and frustrated. I just want to ride, and I can't.

Four men walk in wearing biking clothes. They have just come from Prudhoe Bay. They're English and have shipped their bikes over especially. They're both knowledgeable and experienced. Everything changes. They give advice, tell horror stories; we laugh, we drink, we eat, and by the time the pumps are fixed, we are informed, fed, and more ready than we'll ever be. Everything happens for a reason, particularly out here. Stop fighting it, Flid. It's written, if only you could just see that. Remember the moment? Well, fuckin' live in it!

A trucker is filling his immense tanks alongside me. He has nothing but contempt for anyone who uses this road for pleasure; it's his place of work. To make it worse, I'm a bloody foreigner. But I've also been a trucker. I say all the right things. First I get his attention, then his respect, followed by his advice—watch out for rocks—and finally, a handshake. I feel privileged. You see, I can charm, if I choose to. I just don't find the majority of people worth the effort. And now we're ready, DRob still won't commit to my destination. But that's fine; it adds to the challenge. It's 10PM; let's go!

I'm wearing fingerless gloves and sunglasses; so much for bringing the heated clothing. The Brits wave us off, and we head north into a setting sun. The feeling of exhilaration combined with apprehension is a potent potion, and I have to stop, lift up my visor, and ask DRob, "How ya feeling?"

"I'm OK at the moment;" he doesn't get why I've stopped. I've stopped because we're about to embark on, what is for me, the most anticipated ride I have taken in twenty years of motorcycling.

The thought, alone, is making me shiver with anticipation. I'm in awe. I'm ecstatic. I'm freaking the fuck out. And in reality, it's based solely on what lies ahead, because when you actually look at this road, it's just a paved black strip between some trees.

At Livengood there are no services at all. Hmm! Lucky I'd listened to whatever turned me round. The road turns to dirt. This is the Dalton Highway. We reduce our tyre pressures as we've been advised to and move forward, fuelled mainly on determination, but at midnight, we add a little Jägermeister into the mix. It's still warm, so the shudder I've just experienced must have been brought about by location. Flowers blossom under a sky that is so bright I can practically see the name of the day changing. We go through sleeping roadworks, where the excavators have wheels taller than me. I'm dwarfed by everything out here. The road is being resurfaced with football-sized rocks. We negotiate them carefully, and there are no mishaps, but we need another Jäger to ease the tension in our shoulders. The light is beautiful. Everything is beautiful. For all the colours and cloud formations, there isn't a single vapour trail in the sky. Even planes, it would seem, don't fly over here. I haven't seen a sky without an artificial additional smear since September twelfth back in 2001, when all planes in the US were grounded. We come to the Yukon River; so wide. "Colorado on steroids" is how someone described Alaska before we left. What a concise description! This state does nothing by halves. This is the most vast land I have ever seen. The bridge across the river is hard to grasp the scale of, but it seems immense. I don't want to stop, neither does DRob. We pull over to put in our linings and have another shot of Jäger. The whole time, the Alaskan pipeline has been running alongside us, but somehow it doesn't detract from the landscape. It's a marvel that only adds to the experience. When our engines aren't running, we can hear the oil slosh as it's pumped to Valdez on the Pacific coast. It's a giant vein dispensing the lifeblood of our modern planet; the precious, poisonous liquid that will likely be the death of us all.

Sand Hill is the daunting name of the incline that faces us. Have they never heard of the Cape of Good Hope naming philosophy? "Dreamy Ascent" would be so much more encouraging.

I follow DRob's dust trail hanging in the cool air. With the increased concentration and exertion, the majority of the particles get sucked into my lungs. We reach the top and are rewarded with much improved road conditions. Sixty miles to go, and the temperature and clothing combination complement each other. The dark road stretches into the colours of the ever-changing sky. It's incredible; the land so wild and barren. I stop to make coffee at 3AM as the adrenalin is wearing off. The Jäger has taken its toll, and the fatigue of the road conditions has exhausted me. This is just a break though, let's be clear, we're going on. Time is just a number out here.

Mist hangs on the tundra below our elevated vantage point, caused by the temperature of the water in the kettle lakes. Looking down onto clouds adds yet another dramatic element to this surreal experience. Owls fly over us out of the light. It is now technically dawn. Even the flora is like nothing I have seen before; white fluffy mushrooms that perhaps help to summon up the northern lights. The thought gives me a flashback to being a nomadic warrior on the edge of time, or perhaps that was a premonition. This is my calling. It's been calling me for so long. It's all so wondrous. The sun changes its position from north-west to north-east as we ride into tomorrow.

A new day in a strange land, and there at last, is the sign that announces the circle of eternal light on solstice night. It's 4AM and bright. The sign is the backdrop of our photographs. I pull the miniature Jägermeisters out of my tank bag, brought with the intention of a celebration, not a top up. How was I to know we would be chugging on a big bottle all the way here? I'm exhausted and experiencing a feeling that will only ever be generated by riding through a darkless night in a land that was never designed to see the likes of me. In another time, the quest to get to this point would have required the kind of stamina you don't get from a green bottle. But I'm fortunate, honoured, humbled, and euphoric to have made it here on a less than suitable bike. This has been the goal, the destination, the achievement. This is just what I wanted to do. We find a spot and pitch our tents on the tundra. The mozzies surround me. Inside the tent, I remove my helmet and undress, as the warmth of the sun sooths my clenched and aching body. I've just pitched my tent in the Arctic Circle; this is what I live for, and nothing else matters.

Day 14

Chena Hot Springs, Alaska

265 miles

The last thing DRob said to me before going to his tent last night was, "I won't be up 'til midday." It's 1 10:30AM when he comes calling. His tent is packed up, and he has no shelter from the rain or the mozzies. I unzip my door to see him standing there fully clothed, in gloves and helmet. I'll get up then, shall I?

I have to pack up quickly, as the mozzies are lying in wait. There's a solitary beer in my top box, and it's in the way. It seems ridiculous to transport it any further, so we share it for breakfast. So with an empty tummy and a tiny buzz, we ride in the opposite direction to the Polar Sea. I'd love to go all the way, but this is not the right bike, nor the right time. Some things need to be left unexplored to keep the wanderlust alive. Anyway, I'm still reeling from yesterday's ride. The ride now is OK, but the level of excitement doesn't quite match the level of endurance as we head south under a bright, high sun. Last night's twilight had given the land a magical quality. At the Yukon River, there's a small place for fuel and food, both of which we require in large quantities. We know we have the worst of the road ahead of us. There are a lot more trucks, too, steaming towards us, leaving clouds of dust in their wake, their numerous wheels throwing up rocks and stones. They make no effort to slow for us. I don't expect them to; I probably wouldn't either. We practically come to a halt as they approach; to skid out on the loose surface in front of one could be fatal. Besides, our visibility is dramatically reduced after they pass.

The roadworks are awake now, and we approach just as the pilot car is about to leave. It's perfect timing. The rain has started again, and there's just enough time to put on the waterproofs. Then, with nothing impatiently pushing us from behind, we follow the little procession, trying to stay in the compressed tyre tracks through the soft, muddy surface. We ride alongside the thunderous plant taking car-size bites out of the hillside and crushing the rocks effortlessly before spitting them onto a sodden surface. The plant has a brutality and an ineptitude. It manufactures function without finesse. For the working trucks servicing the oil fields, this rocky debris is a road improvement. For a couple of street bikes, it's just turned the passable into the nearly impossible. Out here, a compactor would look like a phone on vibrate. Once we're out of the mush, I think we relax a bit too much. Upon slowing for an oncoming truck, DRob puts too much pressure on his front brake, and the Sprint slides out from under him. No harm done, but it reminds us that although this road may be more populated during these hours, it doesn't make it any easier to ride. Luckily, he has me behind him to help pick it up, once I've taken the obligatory horizontal photo.

Now the destination has been reached and we're heading south again, my thoughts start wandering home and where that might be. I'd sold my house in England last year and haven't bought another one. I'd been staying with DRob when I was in the UK. I should ask him if I can stay again. Not that I plan to go back to England.

I've been working on a plan for some time. A friend of mine is doing a life sentence for murder. She woke up next to her dead baby one morning, and the charges against her made it a landmark case. Her trial made national news; it was a very high-profile and controversial case. We've been communicating for some time and talking about the possibility of me writing her story: a long, complicated, and frightening one. She may not be entirely innocent. Are any of us? But she is certainly not guilty of the murder charge, and a life sentence in the US simply means you will die in prison. Once a month, I would receive a distinctive, handwritten letter from her on yellow A4 paper. When I sold my house and moved in with DRob on his nice estate with the well-kept lawns and picket fences, I always found it amusing that in the safe urban environment, the postman would deliver his weekly medical magazine and offers from wine distribution companies along with a white airmail envelope with American stamps and California State Prison Service stamped on it in big red letters. It seemed such a paradox to the house, the estate, and the other mail we would receive. The letters screamed to be steamed open and investigated. The intrigue they created was extreme. Often, my friend would sign in with, "Sorry I've not been in touch sooner, I've been very busy," and sign out with, "I have to go now, I have a lot to do." In her defence, she was working hard on an appeal case, but how busy can you be in prison? I hope she has time to see me if I visit.

That possibility is still a long way away. I'm going to try and think about something else now. We reach the paved road with triumphant relief, but also a pang of sadness. We've just emptied the Jäger bottle. However, the journey is not even half over. I just need to have an aspiration adjustment. Remembering there is more ahead of us than behind is all it takes to bring back the thrill. We stop again at the place we met the English bikers last night. Twenty hours have passed; some of the most exhilarating hours of my life; right up there with seeing David Gilmore play the *Comfortably Numb* solo live on top of a wall, and two other things that are too incriminating to mention. I'll withhold the sex and drugs and admit only to the rock 'n' roll.

Somehow, it's become 6PM. With filled stomachs and re-inflated tyres, we head back towards Fairbanks. Traffic lights. Oh, god! I hate this. I see red. I want to be out of it again. A lady in the passenger seat of a car next to me asks how I like my flip-up lid. I flip it up, sing its virtues, and ask where I might find a jet wash. The bikes are filthy and encrusted in mud, and more worryingly, calcium chloride. It's used to reduce dust and is very corrosive. We've been warned of its debilitating qualities if left to fester for any length of time.

The boys who work the carwash hold up the cars for us to use the power washers to get right into our clogged radiator grills. Baked and congealed, it was having the effect of making our bikes run much hotter than usual. Aware we're causing a long queue, I move out of the way, but typically, the meticulous DRob is doing a full valet. Whilst I wait for him, I'm approached by a kid on a BMX; in the UK he would be called a chav. I treat him with the same disrespect. He's all gangland, hoodie, bling, and baseball cap. "What do you fuckin' want?" I think as he comes over to me.

"Make sure you guys ride carefully," he says to me.

Why's that? I'm thinking, Because your homies do drive by shootings? "I know of someone who had an accident," he continues, and that's it. It's just a bit of advice from a kid who wants to make contact. Something about what he's seen has struck a chord, and he wanted to voice it. To a degree, it's a self-protection mechanism on my part, which is why I have so few stories of getting into dangerous situations. But I might have more stories of interactions with people who look undesirable, if only I could let down my guard and curb my judgement a little.

We're now two days ahead of schedule, so we head east to some hot springs. It's a really upmarket place; a cabin for the night is nearly $300. The guy at reception is English and from the Bristol area. Bizarrely, it turns out we both went to the same primary school. That's not very likely, is it? Neither is it a big enough coincidence to get a room any cheaper, so we camp. Once again, the combination of water and wilderness makes the place very popular with the mozzies. Not that the actual hot spring pools are that natural; big, concrete oblongs they are—nothing more than a thermally heated swimming pool. But then, given where we woke up this morning, anywhere is going to seem industrialised.

Day 15

Nenana, Alaska

122 miles

I wake up cold in the night. In a statically planned manoeuvre, I exit the tent and simultaneously manage to get some clothes out of the pannier whilst having a wee. It may sound a bit gross, but I'm besieged by mozzies, who associate the sound of a zip being undone with access to the blood of an Englishman. I get back to my tent with five new bites.

In the morning, we're inquisitioned by the campsite host, who has a superiority complex. He seems to think the word *hostile* is a derivative of hospitality. They're Nazis, these people. I've seen it before. They live in their motorhomes permanently and apply to be "hosts" at various campsites and national parks for a season. They love their newfound positions of power and pedantically enforce every rule with draconian authority. I'm glad I pissed on his lawn last night. I can't be arsed to go back to the pool; the flies and mozzies are driving me insane. They were actually dive-bombing my tent during the night. I thought it must be rain, but it was just the kamikaze squadron. A moose and its calf wander through the site. I can't even take a photo; I need a shelter from pests on the wing.

So it's with several negative encounters that we gladly leave the place. Humans and mozzies spoil everything. Fairbanks is equally horrendous; and we can't seem to get service in a restaurant, oil at the auto parts shop, or photos transferred to disk at the one-hour photo stop. Neither can we get online at the Internet café, not that I'm even in the mood now to try and convey the Arctic experience in a mass email. Fairbanks takes all the fun out of everything and enjoys doing it. Our next intended town doesn't materialise, and instead, we find ourselves out on a fast, smooth road, which is actually ideal. It's the best surface we've ridden since being in Alaska: long, sweeping bends and no traffic. It's the perfect place to work off the aggression generated by a morning of annoyances and inabilities.

We come to a rest stop; "Skinny Dick's Halfway Inn." The place is full of innuendo and adult humour, with rude and nasty bumper stickers and T-shirts with slogans that turn from funny to offensive once off the hanger. It's a seedy little place, but it at least has a bar, and after a beer or two the jokes all seem funnier. We leave in a much better mood than when we arrived, returning to the high-speed twisties of the super smooth surface.

Within half an hour, we reach the town of Nenana. There's no point in going any further, as we don't meet up with Jonathan again until tomorrow. It's a dusty little one-horse town. Well, that's pure speculation; I don't even see a horse. The courthouse doubles as the laundromat and hairdresser's, so you can wash your clothes and get a haircut before going to trial; that says one-horse town to me. I feel lethargic. I don't know if I'm run down, or if this town has just sucked the life out of me. Either way, it's a lucky coincidence, as there's nothing to do here at all. The restaurant closes at 8PM, which basically means the town closes at 8PM. I wander off to look at the railway bridge that spans the river. It broke records when it was built, but has since been succeeded. Due to a complete lack of alternatives, I go to bed at 10PM.

The trip to the Arctic Circle has had a profound effect upon me. I no longer want to be around people, towns, cities, or any kind of human evidence. I wonder how long I'd have to stay in such an environment before wanting some civilisation again. The place moved me, and although the plans don't allow for it, I can feel it pulling me back.

Day 16

Denali National Park, Alaska

101 miles

The sound of white noise in my ears leaves no room for DRob's freight-train snoring. During the night, I unplugged the TV aerial and put the sizzling speaker next to my head; it drowns out the passing trains and most of DRob's inconsiderate sleeping habits. This is a writer's room. The window looks out over meandering rivers to a distant, snowy mountain range. I find it inspiring as soon as I sit down at the table with my tea. From here, I imagine myself taking excursions to the Arctic and then coming back and settling in front of this window and writing about my explorations. It's a beautiful, distraction-free environment, and if I only visited the courthouse for the sole reason of doing laundry once a week, it would be just fine by me. Writing seems to be on my mind more and more, perhaps because the main thing we have to do today is kill time.

It's only seventy miles to this afternoon's meet up point. So we ride at the speed limit. It seems as good a time as any to get a puncture, and a four-inch nail does the honours. How convenient! Unfortunately, my fix-a-flat doesn't do what the name on the can suggests it should do. I try to use my tyre-plugging kit, but that doesn't work either, so I put the nail back in the hole, put some air in the tyre, and ride on.

It looks at first as though there is white cloud forming over a distant mountain, then I realise the white is in fact a snowy mountaintop. It's massive, it must be Mount McKinley. It's the highest mountain in the world in some respects, as its base-to-summit height exceeds Mount Everest's by over 4,000 feet. Everest stands on the Tibetan Plateau, and if McKinley stood alongside, it would dwarf Everest. Statistics aside, from this distance I can just tell it's big. It stands in Denali National Park, and this is where we'll be staying for the next three nights. That's assuming I can get this puncture fixed.

I drift into a tyre place. The nail has come out, and the tyre is flat again. The tyre fitter doesn't seem to understand English nor that he works in a tyre repair and supply shop. We don't exactly hit it off. Time for some DRob diplomacy. I ride up the road to the entrance of a motorhome park, remove my wheel, and give it to DRob to go and get the service I seem incapable of. Whilst I wait for him, I do some anthropology research on the owners of motorhomes and fifth-wheel trailers. Firstly, I try to comprehend the worth of their extravagant vehicles, then I watch how they interact with each other. There seems to be a standoffishness combined with fake pleasantries; there also appears to be an underlying disdain for lesser vehicles. There are most definitely no signs of camaraderie that I can see. These boxes seem to isolate, rather than unify. Well, that's the way it looks to me as I sit by my incomplete bike. Perhaps I'm just a little jealous; I'm currently the owner of a one-wheeled vehicle and feel a bit inadequate.

DRob returns with my wheel and a dodgy-looking plug in my tubeless tyre. It's holding air though, and that has to be an improvement. We're half an hour late at the coffee shop meeting point, but a waitress figures out who we are and has a message for us. Jonathan and Tammara are running three hours late. That seems rather an excessive delay. When I booked our campsite in Denali, two months ago, I read that Mount McKinley is so big it creates its own weather, and the one it seems to favour the most is cloud and rain. The exposed view we had of it this morning was exceptional, and now the mountain's preferable shroud of cloud has rolled in. We make the most of our free time and find a photo shop to back up all our photos onto disk. The dopey girl gives me back my memory cards, saying they've been read and it's now OK to delete my photos, but she's read the same card twice. If I'd taken her advice, I'd have lost two weeks' worth of photos. DRob has much worse news. The brand new Nikon he bought especially for the trip came complete with a memory card, but a cheap-arse dodgy memory card. He has frequently been checking his photos and deleting the bad ones over the last two weeks, usually last thing at night in his tent, after a drink and with his iPod on. This was too much for his camera's generic brand memory. It has corrupted. All the photos are lost, gone forever, irretrievable. I've been letting him take the majority of the shots. All those miles—5,000 so far—all that scenery, and the only photo we have of us at the Arctic Circle is the one I took on my phone. There are words to express this situation, and most of them are spelt with stars. This is tragic.

The skies blacken, and a storm arrives along with Jonathan and Tammara. We're not in the best frame of mind, and it turns out the reason they're late is because they decided to take a scenic flight around Mount McKinley—the mountain we can't see, because we've been waiting here for them. The mountain we now have to ride through pissing rain to get to, because we wasted the good weather waiting for them. It's not the joyous reunion I was expecting.

If it wasn't for the national park, this insignificant little town wouldn't exist. It caters for the tourist trade, although only just. The only available supplies for our extended stay in the park comprise cans of stew, bagels, crisps, and of course, the obligatory Jägermeister and beer. The sky is the darkest it's been in a week, and it's nothing to do with the time of day, just the horrendous weather. The only thing keeping me going is the ecstatic enthusiasm Tammara has brought with her. We ride into the park, but there is nowhere to check in. We shelter under the information station until a ranger moves us on. I take the initiative; if there's no one to advise, we'll make our own way. The site I've booked is down thirty-five miles of dirt road, the furthest point in the park private vehicles are allowed to go. This would have been a lovely little ride three hours ago; instead, it's just dark, wet, and miserable.

The campsite does nothing to lift our spirits. The "hosts" show us to a patch between wall-to-wall motorhomes. It's claustrophobic, yet we're exposed too: overlooked by windows with fly screens. Why do campsites always do this? Denali National Park is over twice the size of Jamaica, why did ya make a site so small? The hosts say we have too many vehicles. You're allowed up to ten people on a pitch; we're only four. You can have a forty-foot motorhome or a trailer and one additional vehicle; that's a minimum of eight wheels. We have only six. But rules are rules, and despite our meagre quantities, we have violated the inflexible stipulations, and there's absolutely no room in the argument for common sense. On top of that, we're not allowed to pitch our tents on the greasy bit within our allotted site, as this is for "recreation." We have to pitch on the uneven gravel, which is fine if you're in a big, fat motorhome, but we aren't; we're sleeping on the ground. They graciously decide to let the matter of our excess motorcycle slide tonight, but first thing in the morning the matter will be at the top of the agenda, and a meeting will be held to discuss this infringement of protocol. Fuckwits!

Day 17

Denali National Park, Alaska

NOT ENOUGH MILES

Apparently in the night, Jonathan's side stand sank into the ground, and his bike fell over. Fortunately, the tent saved its fall; unfortunately, so did Jonathan. How many micro adventures does he want? With my earplugs in, I missed it all. I wish I was missing what was happening now. Under the dull, grey skies, and as unwelcome as a cricket ball through a window, the host arrives, pointing out our violations like broken glass through a dustbin bag. I turn my back on her, sort out my stuff, then go and sit at a picnic table and scrawl in my diary with paper-piercing pressure. The end result is we have to move to another campsite and pay more for the privilege. I know that look—particularly with the emphasis DRob wears it—it means, "Don't say anything, Flid, please. Nothing you say will help this situation. I'll pay you if I have to, but please, whatever you do, keep your offensive mouth shut and don't antagonise her." I hate being passive in the face of ignorant authority, but if you want to get on in America you'd better learn how to. The suppression of my imminent outburst leaves me shaking, but for the team I keep it inside. Their relief is visible. It's not about the money, it's not about the moving, it's about the principle, and principles are what keep me company when all other expectations in life let me down.

We move sites and it's 1:30PM by the time we're ready to head out. We're not allowed to ride the bikes unless we're leaving, and if we do leave, we cannot return. From this point on and into the very depths of the park, whether camping or touring, the shuttle bus is the only option. We wait at the bus stop. We don't have to wait long before one comes, and goes right past without stopping. I'm beginning to find the day's events somewhat irritating. Apparently, we need a bus pass, and we have to buy it from the site superior. If she's so bloody superior perhaps she should correct the inconsistencies in the park's booking website. I'm left to stare out at the gloom, which hangs in the air like desperation, whilst the others deal with the situation. It doesn't take long before they return, but it's because the woman with the discipline fixation will only process the request with the credit card of the person who booked the site, and it has to be rebooked and paid for again in full. I give up my card, and I'm spanked with an additional $120 fee. My mood deteriorates. While waiting for the next bus, we read of the wonders of the wildlife we'll see from the bus. My mood improves and goes up a notch.

The bus is lifeless, the journey bumpy, the scenery like Dartmoor in the rain. There is very little visibility beyond the low cloud, and the pre-boarding gusto is soon smothered by the apathy of the other passengers. The driver tries to generate enthusiasm with a commentary that has all the motivational effects of Valium. He occasionally slows the bus so we can view places where things have been seen on other days. Then with a stamp on the brakes, we're told that up on a far hill, hidden in the heather, if we look very carefully, about three miles away, is a sheep. A sheep? For fuck's sake! I was just beginning to doze off before he over-hyped the mutton. An annoyingly vivacious passenger gets out her binoculars and excitedly announces to the bus, "It looks like it's a female." Sorry, love, still not doing it for me.

When I get this low, ain't nothing gonna change it. The bus slowly fills with more obedient and indistinguishable tourists. After thirty miles of crawling down the bumpy road, we reach the Mount McKinley vista point. There is nothing to see but cloud. It seems pointless to go any further, so we disembark. This place of supposed wilderness has some steps that lead up a hillside, where a four-piece string band is playing. I'm sure it's lovely for them to come to such a place to rehearse, but it's really not going to attract the moose and bears. Could you not bleed a little to entice them? I mean, come on, we've come an awfully long way to be here.

As we wait for a return bus, a token marmot passes by. Its significance has inflated levels it could only ever have dreamt of. It's like Billy Bragg standing in for Led Zeppelin. The furry little Manx squirrel relishes the attention and poses for photos.

We get off the bus before our stop and walk back along the river, where we do at least see some moose on the other side, which redeems the day slightly. We collect some wood as we walk. Some condescending camper tells us we shouldn't do this, which is incredulous, as it's the one thing the dictatorial host said we were allowed to do. We cook our stew over the flames of our contraband wood, and then it rains on us. There is a talk going on in the amphitheatre. I can hear the peppy voice of the speaker from my tent. The rain doesn't stop her, but it stops me wanting to go out again. Occasionally, there are experiences in life that are so magnificent I dare not relive them, in case they don't live up to my memories. Well, there's no risk of that happening here.

DAY 18

EAGLE RIVER, ALASKA

264 MILES

DRob wakes me at seven for our pre-booked, six-hour bus tour. There seems little point in going when the weather remains wet and cloudy, but what else are we going to do? We put on damp clothes, eat damp food, and catch the bus, so we can look at clouds in other parts of the park. For six hours, the archaic bone rattler trundles up and back, and we see nothing, but it's not the kind of nothing that was so awe-inspiring on the way to the Arctic Circle. This is just disappointing. That's it in a word—I didn't know what to expect in the Arctic Circle or even if we'd make it; the journey had challenge, surprise, and reward. Here, we're sold promises and hope. I know no one can guarantee a grizzly encounter, or I suppose, even the weather conditions, but this place is based around one specific mountain, and the only time we saw it was when it was a hundred miles away. That does cause a little frustration. This, combined with oppressive authority, means not only is it the wrong time to be here, but I might be the wrong type of person for such a place.

We can stay another night—I had to book a minimum of three—but it's not compulsory to stay. Soon, as leaving is the one choice we actually have the freedom to make for ourselves, we pack up and head out. The host hurries out of her box to remind us that if we leave, we can't return. The look through my visor penetrates her stupidity, and she understands that I understand. Although the dirt road is wet and muddy, being back on the bike feels good. Fifty-three miles back to the park entrance and there is a moose . . . with a collar on. Well, that just about sums the place up. Another time, under different circumstances, I'd give Denali another chance, if I ever get another chance to be here.

It's about 200 miles to Anchorage, and due to my unconvincing tyre plug, I have to do it at fifty mph. I don't want the centrifugal force blowing it out. For the first half of the journey it pisses with rain; just to taunt me further, there are viewing platforms and picnic spots which boast views of Mount McKinley. Just turning my head in the direction of the signposts sends cold water down my neck and dislodges my iPod earphone. I plod on. The others pass and then pull over. I keep the pace. A wolf crosses in front of me; it's possibly something I wouldn't have seen if I'd been riding faster or in a group. As we approach Anchorage, the skies clear, and ahead is a snowy mountain range. You see, it's always the unexpected that thrills. Tammara used to work up here in Alaska as a nanny for three children. The kids are grown now. Leslie, their mother, is divorced, and it's her we're going to be staying with. Upon arriving at her townhouse, it turns out she's the hottest thing in Alaska.

Day 19

Eagle River, Alaska

13 miles

The house is a three-storey, open-plan design. The whole of the ground floor is a concrete garage, and it's where I opt to sleep. It may be peaceful, but it's not at all scenic. In fact, it's just total blackness. I have sudden and unexpected exposure from my sensory deprivation quarters when, with a whirring sound, the garage door opens, and Leslie drives her Saab in. We are equally shocked to see each other. She has just finished work. I'm glad she missed me. Coming home from a nightshift to a house and garage full of guests is not a good combination. We all get out of her place as soon as we can to let her sleep.

It's a morning of getting supplies. Most bike shops are closed today, as it's a Monday. I do find a second-hand tyre, but it's not ideal, so the search continues. It's dull and wet again, and despite my low expectations, I find a new one at a tyre shop for a reasonable price. The guy says he can fit it tomorrow. Perfect. We gather other supplies for the needs of our bikes, bellies, and blood systems. And then it's an afternoon of laundry, oil changes, and general bike maintenance, keeping quiet until Leslie has got the beauty sleep she doesn't appear to need.

Tonight we're having a barbecue. Her ex comes over; they still have an amicable relationship. He's a Native American and very much a man of the land, when not working for the telephone company, where's he's employed that is. I like him immediately. He brings round a salmon he caught this morning. I decide not to ask if he caught it fly fishing or with a landline. As well as phones and fishing, he has chef capabilities too. As he fillets, flavours, and sears the fresh pink fish, he talks to me about the state, the environment, terrain, rivers, and animals. He has passion, respect, enthusiasm, knowledge, and an unconditional love for his three daughters. If I lived up here, I'd want him to be my friend. Leslie, DRob, and I make shish-kebabs, or "kabobs" as they're called here, which just sounds silly. It's my job to go out onto the balcony to barbecue them. The cloud has thinned to reveal snow-topped mountains above the pink late evening haze. Night is returning to the north—the sun sets eight minutes earlier every day—and soon Alaskans will once again experience a night of complete, albeit brief, darkness without having to shut themselves in a garage. I'm enjoying this lone time on the balcony: the task, the tranquillity, the view, and the freshness. Even in this terrace of townhouses, the wild is just on the other side of the road, where the Eagle River runs past. I consider all I've just been told. Alaskans not only pay no tax, but the government gives them a cheque of about $1,000 every Christmas. It's basically a share in the profit, to pacify them about the annihilation of their environment in the name of oil. I wonder if I could live here, and how feasible it would be to have Leslie as my lover and her ex as my friend. Probably not very; best concentrate on the kabobs.

It's the best salmon I've ever tasted, and after tonight, I'll forever be the annoying and ungrateful recipient of any salmon dish, always comparing it to this freshly caught and expertly prepared offering. Having cooked my first kabob, however, there's probably room for improvement on the shish front. Just when I thought the evening was over, Leslie drives us to the river for mountain views, mist-covered waters, and twilight reflections. I see a bear footprint in the black sand of the river bank. It's bigger than my hand span, and the indent from the claws reminds me to play dead or be dinner if ever I come face to face. On the drive back, there's a moose at the side of the road. We're so close to it that I can see the velvet on its antlers. Leslie doesn't promise like Denali, she just delivers like Dominoes.

Day 20

Homer, Alaska

255 miles

I'm up early to go and get my tyre fitted. As I drive Leslie's Saab through the town, I visualise myself living here. Her CD is playing in the car, and it sends me off into a lovely little daydream, the heated seat adding a perverse twist to the fantasy. Leslie doesn't seem to be a morning person, so on my return, I busy myself getting my bike ready. I don't particularly like my new tyre, but when the only option is to take it or leave it, I suppose I should just be grateful I've found one that fits.

We're going on a little tour of the Kenai Peninsula. It's always been part of the plan; only now, much like our stay in Whitehorse, we now have some additional locations we've been recommended by the locals. After ten miles, we're in downtown Anchorage. Being the largest state in the union, there's no need to build up in Alaska, so the skyline consists mainly of mountains. I'm beginning to realise just what a cold climate this is. It's July, and the snow is not only reserved for the peaks, I wouldn't have to walk far to make a snowball. Despite this, I have too many layers on, and at our first vista point, I take out my linings. I get chatting to a local cynic. He's amiable enough; it's the cruise ship tourists he has utter contempt for. He says they disembark, look at the snowy mountain range, and ask what the altitude of Anchorage is. "You've just got off a ship," he tells them scornfully, "What do you think the altitude is?"

As we head south, the scenery becomes ever more spectacular. We ride alongside the sea, although at this point it's a very sheltered extremity of the North Pacific. The clouds are high and the road dry. The hills are a lush green, and water cascades off the sheer drops into fast, clear rivers. This really is a state of giant proportions. Even the fluctuations in temperature are substantial; I have to keep removing and replacing clothes repeatedly. The enthusiasm of Tammara has not wavered, possibly because she's revisiting old memories. Having her along for the ride does not make her Yoko, it's more like having a local. She recommends a place to stop for halibut and chips—halibut seems to be a big fish out here in both popularity and size—it's a good choice and tastes even better when she says it's her treat.

The Seward Highway takes us in every direction of the compass as it follows the river winding through the valleys. I have nothing pressing on my mind except the earphones from the pressure of my helmet. My thoughts wander; the first Alaskan licence plate I ever saw was on a filthy car in Denver back in '84. Even then, it had the lure and mystique of a harsh and distant land. The plates are a simple design—a solid, dull orange colour—and along the bottom they say "The Last Frontier." It's certainly more glamorous than Idaho's "Famous Potatoes." I've been thinking for a while how good one would look on a shed wall. So when we pass a scrap yard, I bring us to a halt. This is my chance. I take off my helmet, look around, see no one, but decide it would be a good idea to ask first, this being America and me about to be a trespassing thief. The people at the fuel station next door are noncommittal, and the owner is not around. I wander through the stacks of dead cars, pretending to look for Mr. Scrap but actually scanning for the perfect plate. I want one that's not too beaten up and has fasteners that will quickly unfasten. Then there is a sound of revelation in the form of a heavenly choir that only I can hear, but the sound is somewhat paradoxical and, therefore, replaced by death grunts and backwards voices. As if Satan himself has led me, I see the plate "666 CLF"—the number of the beast and the initials "Can't Live Forever." I'm convinced it's destined for my wall, but annoyingly, I just can't get it off, and this is daylight robbery. I decide to leave it and the scene of the attempted crime behind.

Anyway, I sold my walls and the roof too. That reminds me, I must get round to asking DRob if I can live with him again upon my return home, whenever that will be.

Eventually, the road takes us down the west coast of the peninsula towards Homer. The scenery gets even grander, and the sea is pierced with smoking volcanoes against a backdrop of even bigger mountains. It really is a wild land. If I stood looking out at this view on the edge of time, or indeed the beginning of all creation, I don't think it would look any different. Some environments are constant, regardless of evolution or industrialisation; nothing can tame or change this; it's nature in its most extreme and untouchable state. If I had tried to imagine what Alaska would be like, I'd have envisioned something like this. However, my imagination has limits, whereas these surroundings do not.

We approach Homer Spit. From the elevation of the road, we see the strip of land bowing into the sea in front of imposing mountains with glacial ravines of unfathomable scale.

This place must be brutal in the winter, but there's a different kind of brutality here now. It's visual. The stony beaches and parking lots are full of the motorhome crowd. Somehow, though, it doesn't matter; this place is too wild and hostile for pedantic rules, and I don't think the inhabitants of these road-clogging boxes have the courage to leave their sanctuaries. Their presence doesn't detract from the awe of this location. There is free camping on the beach, but the wind is fierce, unpredictable, and it's cold too. We find a guesthouse, and I get the room with two picture windows and a panoramic view, appreciated all the more after my recent solitary confinement sleeping quarters. Having the coolest crib, I play host, and we all drink beer and Jäger in my room before wandering out to partake in Homer's equivalent of clubbing. Opposite the guesthouse is a rowdy bar, the kind of place you would turn around and walk out of if you were sober. Luckily, we aren't. There's karaoke on the stage, and it really is an unruly place. "Homer," says the bumper stickers, "is a small drinking town with a fishing problem." It's not a boast, nor a joke; it's a statement, and we're surrounded by the evidence. It has to be said, the majority of this journey has been alcohol fuelled, and tonight we reach our zenith.

Up until this point in my life, I've safely been able to say, "I have never attempted karaoke." However, over the last three weeks and all the miles with my iPod playing in my ears, the singing in my helmet has convinced me that I can do a fabulous rendition of *All the Young Dudes*, because it doesn't have to be sung. I've devised a version where I can speak the lyrics. It's infallible.

Just before I'm due up on stage, I go to the toilet. I have an entire fantasy I want to indulge in. I imagine it's my backstage dressing room. Then I hear my name called; I swagger out and up onto the stage. I grab the mic with both hands, letting the stand become my third leg. I'm now a stable tripod. In my best Sid Vicious stance, I speak my way through the song.

There is one snag. Although I can read the lyrics on the prompt screen, I realise just a bit too late that for all these years there were certain lines in the song that I've been making up, as I never did quite understand what the actual words were. Up until tonight, it's never really mattered, but now is not the ideal time to become aware. What a drag! In my defence, the words I do know I speak very well, and the audience seems to like my authentic English accent, regardless of the bollocks I'm spouting. Anyway, I'll never see any of them again, and I've wanted to do this for years.

DAY 21

EAGLE RIVER, ALASKA

271 MILES

The sun shines through the picture windows like an interrogation lamp. It demands answers. What the hell were you doing last night? My eyes are screwed up from the light, and my forehead is wrinkled from the cringing. Outside, I can see the pub where it all happened. It's bright yellow, which wouldn't be that strange, except last night it was green. It's Independence Day, and the fire engine is outside. The whole brigade is utilising the vehicle's extensive range of elevation devices to paint the pub. I don't want this brightness, but I have no choice. It's check out time. I make a pitiful attempt to sort the debris strewn around the room into the bin and into my panniers. Then, in the same pathetic manner, I go to the restaurant. I need eggs and hash browns, but I'm told breakfast is over. Now I just need help. I'm hungry, hung over, and homeless; I don't feel very independent. Someone comes and sits next to me. It turns out to be DRob. He's shaved off the beard he's been growing for the last three weeks. Why is everything changing today?

It's been decided that we'll all do our own thing and later will meet at the Salty Dawg Saloon. I'm not capable of doing my own thing, of doing anything. I just get on my bike and ride. Luckily, being on a peninsula, the journey presents

132

little challenge. I get to the end, stop, get off, walk down to the stony beach, and collapse in a controlled way that hopefully won't attract attention or cause concern. I try to take in the vastness of what surrounds me, which is so much bigger than my hangover. I can't think of anywhere better to feel this rough. It's an extraordinary world I'm looking out on. The horizon is the most magnificent combination of preposterous extremities of scale; an inhospitable landscape.

Lost in thought and time, I don't come back to my hangover reality until long after the scheduled meet up. I notice that the more active of the peninsula's inhabitants are standing in the sea, fishing for halibut. I'm reluctant to move from my spot; however, the hardiness of the fishermen is doing nothing to improve the way I feel. Perhaps there's something in the saloon that would help. Eventually, I head over and find the others. It's another place of visual overload. The walls are adorned with dollar bills, all bearing signatures, dates, and locations. Also, like back in Watson Lake, there amongst the memorabilia is a British Rail ticket. They get everywhere. I order a Bloody Mary, the ultimate hangover cure. It has a very high vodka content; it's good, it's tasty, it's rejuvenating; and this just hours after I said I would never drink again. Lucky I didn't say it out loud.

The table we're sitting round is a large crude slab of wood with scratched and carved inscriptions. Sharing it with us are three patch club biker girls. It looks like they call themselves "Sisters of Scrotum," but I've probably read it wrong. I'm unsure if being a lesbian is a compulsory mandate to membership, but it certainly seems a popular option. A bell is rung. Apparently, some bloke at the bar has offered to buy all the ladies a drink. This has the effect of all the guys having to buy another drink whilst they wait for the ladies to have their free one. A crafty ploy. The patch club girls are more chatty when they realise we rode here too. They may look the part, but underneath their colours, they're the same as we are. Well, similar; we all have a soft spot for a girl on a bike. For one of the gang, this is a momentous day. She has just ridden her fiftieth state. She says to celebrate she'll buy a campervan. Predictably, I ask her what her favourite place has been. Her response is a name I've not heard of: Sedona, Arizona. I make a mental note. She gives me her card. She lives in California. That could be useful; I may be looking at a prolonged stay there. I have another Bloody Mary. I'm not sure how much it's helping, but at least I'm being proactive in trying to rid myself of the hangover.

The others used their lone time far more productively than I did and have stories of enticing sights. I suppose I'd better take a look around too. When I leave the bar, the events that follow make it one of those "and then ... and then ... and then" days. Some pasty, but muscular, topless youths in oilskin trousers are standing round a trough of iced water, filleting halibut. It's warm today, but there is absolutely no need for such a blatant display of flesh. This is not muscle beach, and regardless of how strenuous their task is, I can't imagine it generates the heat their exposed bodies suggest. The onlookers seem to like it though. I get a T-shirt that says "dark side of the spoon" and has a fish replacing the prism. It seemed pretty cool at the time. I pay with plastic, as I want to see the word *Homer* on my credit card bill, as well as on my T-shirt. The fish theme continues with the ultimate halibut. A guest on a fishing boat excursion has caught a record-breaking, two-hundred-pound halibut. It's hanging by its tail from a sort of gallows. It's as tall as the incredibly chuffed fisherman, although not as fat.

Even on this most touristy of dates, during its most populated time, Homer has taken a little bit of my heart. I grew up in a fishing village, not that it bears much resemblance to this place, and I'm not even a big fan of the sea, but I am a fan of awe, expanse, and the tempestuous. I want to stay another night—we all do—and we collectively consider the possibilities. Our ferry departs in two and a half days from a port that is over 1,000 miles away. It's the one inflexible deadline on this journey. We really ought to be back in Eagle River tonight, and we haven't even made a start on the journey. We all realise a prolonged stay is simply impossible and are saddened that it's beyond consideration. I'll definitely be back; that's all there is to it. I don't know of a place that has captivated me so quickly and wholly. If it's this good on its most crowded of days, the winter isolation and solitude must make it stunning.

So with a burning pang that's brought on by both an unwanted departure and the acidity of the Bloody Marys, I put on my iPod and helmet and listen to Floyd's *On The Turning Away*. I look over my shoulder for one last glance of Homer Spit as I rise up to the main road of the mainland. I settle onto my sheepskin offcut and prepare for the long, late ride back to Eagle River, knowing I've left a little part of me behind.

This is not the type of road that can be rushed. We divert to a Russian village. Other than four kids in authentic dress, it's about as memorable as a number plate; and there's one that's been on my mind. Back at the scrap yard, there's no one home again, and the fuel station is closed too. I wander in with pliers, a screwdriver, and the devil's luck, and it falls into my hands and then slides into my pannier. The job is done!

The journey continues. The daily rain comes down, and as I look through the spray for a place to stop and don the waterproofs, I see sun rays. It seems our soaking period is going to be a lot shorter than we've been used to.

Since the ALCAN Highway, nothing has announced spontaneous wildlife viewing like a badly parked car on an open bit of road. What appears ahead suggests a sight of significance. We pull over and look down the ravine across the river. There, on the far bank, is a grizzly, close enough to be stunning and far enough away to be safe. As we watch her, the cubs come out of the undergrowth. They pick at a salmon that Mum has just caught, and she stands on her hind legs and looks out protectively as they eat their snack. After they leave, the show continues when a black bear comes along to try its paw at fishing. Then an eagle swoops down to eat the remnants of the salmon the cubs left. As it starts to pick at the bones, some seagulls arrive. Outnumbered and overpowered, the eagle is bullied away from the prize. I find this quite symbolic on Independence Day—although I'm not sure who the seagulls represent—but undeniably, the symbol of freedom has just been vanquished and left to starve.

The miles are passing effortlessly, until I put too much faith in my new tyre. On a lovely, sweeping bend, the back slides out, then grips with a jolt. I'm nearly high-sided off. I slow down a bit after that. It may hold air, this new tyre, but it's not holding onto the road. Well, not with any consistency. The photo stops are frequent, but it's also conceivable that we can make it all the way back to Leslie's tonight. It's 9PM when we stop to discuss the options. I have no preference, but I'm happy to keep on riding.

This day is so stimulating, it just won't stop happening. It may be the same road in the opposite direction, but it all seems new, with glaciers and mountain views. And as an added bonus, the skies have cleared and low light enhances everything. As we approach Anchorage, it's 11:20PM. The sun dips behind a mountain, and I take off my sunglasses. There are a few July Fourth fireworks as we enter the city. Then I see a big display; people are sitting on the roofs of their cars, and the kids are wrapped up in blankets. It's way past their bedtime. The others are out in front, and I let them go. I want to see fireworks. They probably figure that out. The sky is as dark as it's going to get, and everyone seems to accept that fireworks against a twilight sky is a small price to pay in exchange for living in Alaska.

I manage to find my way back to Leslie's. No one missed me; they guessed where I was and that I just wanted to milk a last little bit of enjoyment out of the day.

Day 22

Tok, Alaska

572 miles

Waking up in Leslie's home may not be as scenic as waking up in Homer, but it means today there is less time pressure. Even so, six hours sleep will have to suffice. I stomp around noisily to wake the others; we still have a long day ahead of us. Yet somehow, three and a half hours pass before we're ready to leave, and we haven't even eaten. I think Jonathan wants one last shag before leaving Tammara. Ever the opportunist, I take advantage of her vulnerability and slip my number plate in her case.

Once again, we are three, heading out into low cloud and heavy rain. This is most definitely the turning point of the trip. We're heading back now, albeit indirectly. However, our southbound return starts with a day that will see us further north than where we started. That's Alaska for you. The Glenn Highway runs in a valley between two mountain ranges, past ice fields, and over vast rivers, promising spectacular wildlife and scenery. If I hadn't read that I'd never know because all we see is rain. The only consolation is we're given a ten per cent discount at a restaurant because "it's raining on our holiday." The cloud-censored scenery continues, and the wet starts to penetrate through my many layers. A chill sets in, and I contemplate the benefits of stopping and removing the majority of my clothes to put on my heated waistcoat. After all, I've been carrying it for the last three weeks, and it's not been out of the panniers once. As soon as I make the effort to put it on, the benefits are instant. This feels wonderful. It's not just the heat; it's the affection with which it's delivered. The glow caresses my neck, and with loving warmth, it takes the cramp out of my shoulders like a passionate massage. It radiates heat into my very core, like the first sunny day of spring. I can't believe I didn't use it earlier. I'd considered it to be a device for frost and snow, but I should have been using it daily. All that Jägermeister just to numb the pain, when all I needed to do was plug in the waistcoat. What a waste! I've just fallen in love with my fifty-dollar bankrupt stock, heated accessory, and it reciprocates unconditionally. All I had to do was turn it on. The dull, wet day had wiped the smile off my face, but this electric comfort has just brought it back. And the positivity is so strong it even clears the skies, although not until we've passed the best of the scenery.

We are all tired. On average we only do 260 miles a day, but there's far more to the days than distance alone. We may have hardened up to the road, but it's our lifestyle when we're off the bikes that's taking its toll. We come to Glennallen. The town is basically a T-junction. There's a road that leads down to Valdez, the end of the Alaskan pipeline, but it's a 230-mile roundtrip diversion. Jonathan and I are up for it, but DRob says he'll go on to Tok, get a room, and meet us there. His bike has been progressively using more and more oil, and besides, as he says, he's just knackered. Jonathan and DRob look over his Sprint whilst I strip to my underwear to rearrange my layers of damp, drying, and heated clothing. I watch a gummy old motorhome driver get himself some extremely bad service at the fuel station, due solely to his shitty, aggressive attitude. It's an interesting observation.

As soon as Jonathan and I get on the road to Valdez, we see a moose on the road, which we see as a sign that we've made the right decision. However, the next eighty miles drag a bit. I can't keep my eyes open. It's not that the road is dull, like the A14 in England, it's just Alaskan dull. The snow-capped mountains aren't high enough, the moose not frequent enough, the empty roads not stimulating enough. So when a glacier comes into view, we get overexcited. We seem to be heading straight for it. It's like a living thing coming down the valley to devour the road. Its blue, icy claws reach out to us. We stop right in front, it calls to be climbed on. The colours are hypnotic, with a cyan blue that is as hard to capture as a rainbow. Its pull is magnetic, and the impossible shades draw me to them in a trance-like state. It's only when I decide I want to take a photo that I realise my camera is in the tank bag of my out-of-sight and unattended bike, along with about $5,000 in cash, my passport, phone, and other quite important things. This irresponsible action is out of character for me, particularly when I'm sober; such is the attraction of the glacier.

The experience wakes me up, and the road keeps me awake. We ride past waterfalls, and then there is a long, winding descent down into Valdez, a town that's more about the journey than the destination. Although this marks the end of the pipeline, fuel is expensive. But we fill up anyway, turn around, and embark on the 240 miles to meet DRob in Tok. We have one and a quarter hours until the meeting time, and as usual, no reception on our phones. The sun is out and the air is warm, dandelion spores hang in the air, and the deadline drops out of sight. When we get back to the Glenn Highway, it's already 10PM. With a slice of pizza for sustenance, we continue the last 140 miles. I'm plugged into my iPod and my waistcoat, and it's so comfortable I don't bother to stop for fuel. *I'll stop at the next one* is a phrase I should have abandoned long ago. It has no place up here. My fuel gauge touches the red, and the population count drops to zero. I turn off the heated waistcoat to stop the extra strain on the alternator. I slow my speed. But I know I'm not going to make it to Tok on what's left in the tank. The needle drops below the red; the bike is going to splutter to a halt at any moment. I see a light ahead. Perhaps I can ask where I can find fuel. Wait a minute; it is a fuel station! There's a pump. It's open. It's alive. That was lucky!

With twenty miles to go, I'm now riding at eighty mph again. Jonathan trails behind. I'm wondering how we're going to find DRob. A car comes towards us. It's a cop. I brake hard. But it's too late; he's clocked us. I see his brake lights in my mirror. His lights go on, and he does a U-turn. I slow down, but I don't stop. In my mirrors, I see him pull Jonathan over. I keep riding, then turn off my ignition and lights, glide into Tok, and hide my bike in the carwash of the fuel station. It's midnight, and they're just closing. They have a note from DRob. I wait for Jonathan. He's been fined $82. The cop said he could tell Jonathan was gaining on me, therefore, going faster. He told the cop that was because I was braking harder.

"Did you notice how short his forks looked?" he'd asked the cop.

It's generally accepted the rider in front gets the ticket. I was taking that risk, and Jonathan was letting me, so I don't feel guilty that he got what was destined for me. We find DRob, wake him up, drink his beer, and watch his TV until 1:30AM. He's so welcoming and hospitable. Well, that's the impression I got.

DAY 23

SKAGWAY, ALASKA

515 MILES

DRob brings me round some postcards that he bought yesterday. When am I ever going to find time to write them? There hasn't been a spare minute since we left. There has always been something to do. Even in dull Denali there was some important sulking at the top of the agenda. Maybe on the ferry I'll get a chance. It leaves in twenty-one hours and we're 500 miles away. When we left Denver, twenty-three days ago, it was six and a half thousand miles away. It's looking like we might catch it.

I've got a microwave in my room and leftover pizza in my pannier. That's breakfast sorted. No need to revisit that restaurant for the Grumpy Grizzly Breakfast. Anyway, I'm not grumpy. The sun is shining, and although we're back on the ALCAN Highway along with the convoy of motorhomes, the blue skies make for happy miles. It's been a journey of blocked sun as opposed to sun block, so we're all the more appreciative of this rare weather condition. After our first eighty-mile stint, we stop at a small, abandoned town. Out of habit we're all overdressed, and we happily remove clothes and liners.

This sun has enhanced the riding conditions, comfort, and scenery, so the mood is upbeat too. We haven't worn this little in weeks. Where are we going to put all the discarded clothes? This beer is taking up a lot of space too. It's a team decision, reluctantly, we have to get rid of the cans. Anyway, we wouldn't want to get caught importing them into Canada. DRob puts so much pressure on his left-hand pannier trying to close it that he pushes his bike over. That's the third time it's been down. It's incredulous that someone with such advanced medical skills can have so little mechanical finesse. The front brake lever has bent in a semicircle now, but it's still intact. So it is with beer on our breath and happy smiles that we cross back into Canada—an effortless transition—and we'll be out again later today. There are lots of roadworks and dirt roads. I'm convinced my rear tyre is flat, but the problem isn't its pressure, just its incompatibility with the front one.

Due to our alternative route north from Whitehorse, this road is all new to us—big snowy mountains, large lakes, and distant horizons. Our progress today appears to be good until we realise it's 5PM and that we still have 300 miles to go. It's not a hardship or even frustrating how long it's taking us, it's just that I can't see where all the time goes. In fact, these are the last 300 miles we'll be riding together, and I don't really want them to end. With this realisation, a shadow of sadness is cast over the day. It's been looming for a while; on the return from the Arctic Circle then again leaving Anchorage. After today, Jonathan will be riding alone, directly back to Denver.

However, what we have ahead of us is the journey's grand finale. We cross a tundra of wild flowers and lakes with rocky islands. We leapfrog each other as various sites have us stopping for photos. All the highlights of this trip seem to be condensed into an encore as we ride down the Klondike Highway. The wildlife begins with foxes and a porcupine, and the landscape gets wilder as the road leads us to higher altitude, where we look down on lakes that resemble inland seas. Around every corner is another range of rocky, snow-capped mountains. Some inconsiderate fool has left a bin bag at the side of the road. How could they in such a pristine environment? As I get closer, it starts to blow into the road. I slow down a bit. Shit; it's a bear!

He seems a bit dopey and more interested in foraging in the undergrowth than he is in the traffic. He's big enough to ruin my day if he wanted, but after our recent grizzly encounter, this brown bear doesn't seem nearly as threatening. His presence brings us to a standstill; engines running, cameras zoomed, we watch him do what bears do when they don't care who's watching them. I'm still reeling from the experience when fifteen minutes later we come across another one romping down the road towards us. They're like buses in this place.

The road rises to over 4,000 feet, and we ride into cloud. With thinner air and steeper inclines, my engine labours. Without sympathy or remorse, I've switched on everything that produces heat. It could be the straw that blows a twenty-five-amp fuse. It's cold enough to snow. In fact, as we climb higher there's fresh snow on the ground. This relatively short highway has the most incredible diversity in terrain. It could have saved us two weeks of touring had we known. We cross back out of Canada and stop in no man's land for a shot of Jäger. With numb fingers, I take a photo by the Alaska sign. The wind is fierce and icy, and now that I've discovered my heated clothing, I'm keen to plug myself back in and move on. Its electric warmth has more appeal than medicinal Jägermeister. We cross back into the US with alcohol breath and wind down into Skagway, where our ferry leaves in eight hours.

We see a pizza place, cruise the town, find nothing better, and return to find it shut. So we go to a bar and have chicken wings. DRob scouts for a room, but we have to be up at 5AM. I'll just rough it somewhere. A cop comes into the bar and tells us we can sleep in the park if we leave now.

"You're not going to wake us up in the night, shining your flashlight in our eyes, are you? Because I hate being woken up that way."

He says he wouldn't have to use a flashlight, as it doesn't get dark. It's a valid point. With my stupid comment and a tableful of shot glasses, it's pretty obvious we've all been drinking and are about to ride our bikes. So to fool him we walk . . . to the other bar. This one is very lively. It's full of locals, Skaggies. It's heaving. I know I've got to get up soon, so after a quick whiskey, we head for the park. I sleep by the side of my bike. It's not even worth putting up the tent; I just light a mosquito coil.

The sky is quite dark now. It's two weeks since the solstice, and we're much further south. I miss the midnight light. Mozzies buzz in my ears, and my phone keeps bleeping, because the battery is nearly flat. The four hours pass with barely any sleep, but at least I didn't pay for a room.

Day 24

Ferry to Ketchikan, Alaska

2 miles

I must have fallen asleep, as the others get the rare but gratifying task of waking me at 5AM. I find a toilet block, which is not only open but has hot water too. Oh, joy! I'm cold, and I was bitten in the night. I look in the mirror. From my appearance, it's obvious that itchy cool park is where I've been. We ride to the ferry terminal. We're early, but our tickets are ready, and we're beckoned straight onto the waiting boat. This is it; nothing else matters. Well, not to me. From this point on, I have utter independence—no commitments, no obligations, no connections, no job, no house, no woman. Even our printed itinerary runs out in three days. I've been keeping my little post-trip plan to myself, as the few times I've mentioned it I haven't liked the response I've got.

The last part of the preparation and research is about to be implemented. Fastenings; I read that the ferry doesn't provide tie downs for motorcycles, so we all brought our own with us. I also read that passengers without cabins are allowed to pitch their tents on the viewing deck at the back of the ferry. Obviously, tent pegs don't go into steel, so we brought duct tape to stick the guide ropes to the floor. It works pretty well, and with that last predicament prepared for, my work here is done. DRob decides he's going to get a cabin.

When I booked the ferry, I put his title as Dr., which he was briefly annoyed about. When he checked in the purser said to him, "Would it be OK doc, to call on you in the event of an emergency?" This is precisely why DRob doesn't like to be called Doctor Rob. Of course, he agrees to be on call; there's no question. It's his vocation, even if he is on vacation. This verbal contract is sealed with an instant upgrade. Not so annoyed now then, eh Doc?

Its only 6 AM. I'm so tired. I go to the restaurant and have breakfast thrown at me. I try my tent out. It's in direct sunlight and uncomfortably hot inside. Then leaving port, a noisy seagull squawks next to me; and pulling out, the breeze is so strong the tent bows. When the ferry finally gets going, my pitch is sheltered and shaded, but three loud Americans stand right outside having a chat. I'm not going to get any sleep. Besides, the scenery on the way out of the port is too good to miss. It's strange not having anything to do; no urgency, no deadlines.

I go to the viewing lounge to listen to a talk. Jonathan joins me. Then we wander the ferry aimlessly. We've been so driven to get here, and now we've arrived, the transition from rider to passenger is not sitting comfortably. We go and bang on the door of DRob's penthouse suite. No response. With absolutely nothing else to do, we continue to knock. Eventually he answers, but it's not a nice answer.

"What?"

"Do you want to come out to play?"

"No!"

"Can we come in then?"

"Must you?"

"The purser said if it was an emergency, it was OK to call on you. I heard him ask, and you said it was."

"So?"

"It's an emergency; we're really bored!"

In the afternoon, we dock at Juneau. We have some shore leave and try to hitch the thirteen miles to the centre. We get a lift, but not very far. And then we have to try and catch a bus, but nothing stops for us. In the end, I get us a taxi, and once again, we have deadlines. Upon my request, the taxi takes us to a crab shack. It's a weird little town; totally isolated. No one can drive to and from Juneau; all cars come via the sea. Despite this, it's the most populated city in Alaska. It's the capital. We sit in the shadow of a cruise ship. The mountains on the far shore are hidden by it, these things are so immense. They moor up right outside a town so that the passengers can shuffle down the ramp and into a staged and condensed miniature version of everything they have missed between here and the last port of call. The shops sell souvenirs and memorabilia of all the things they haven't seen, and the restaurants serve up local food at inflated prices. It's fake and lacks integrity, but being the capital it's where the government resides, so perhaps it's quite apt. It occurs to me that up until this point, Alaska hasn't had to over-hype or promote anything; it's a genuine and authentic state. There's no need for the "world's largest ball of thread" or any other gimmicks. Denali may have failed to live up to my expectations, but not in a way that a lukewarm and overpriced latte in the world's biggest coffee shop would.

I decide as a kind of last supper that I'm going to treat us all to Alaskan snow crab legs. I should have known better; cruise ship ports are not the place for exquisite, genuine, and good value food. It's little more than a beachside burger bar selling shite in a bucket. The others make appreciative noises, but served with a cardboard bun and microwaved melted butter in a plastic pot, the only credibility the meal has is the smell it leaves on our fingers. When your bikes and all other possessions are on a boat that will leave before you can walk to it, the taxi drivers can charge whatever they want to. And the fuckers do! So that's been a laboured little insight into what dependent travel is like.

DRob is tired, Jonathan says he's hung over, so I sit in a chair with my iPod on and work out a route back. Well, out of Canada at least. I miss my bike. I wish I could go and see it, but it's off limits, down in the bowels of the ship. I go to another talk. Apparently, there might be whales later. The bar is expensive, but the barmaid is pretty. She too talks of whale sightings. It certainly seems to be a popular topic. News comes in that one has been spotted off the starboard side. I assume that's the side where everyone is standing. I go and bang on DRob's door again. It's not that I don't want him to miss the whales, it's just that he has a door and I don't, so banging on it is sort of fun.

I go off whale watching; a few tails are breaking the water. As the sun goes down, the whole sky becomes a dramatic spectrum of colour. It's our first sunset in two weeks, and it goes on for hours. Whales breech beside the ship, silhouetted against a sky of fire, tails rising out of the sea and water cascading off with the picturesque qualities of a greeting card in a pretentious shop. In the wake of the ship are sea lions, and dolphins too. The show goes on and on. The captain speaks over the tannoy to tell us that this unique and spectacular combination of light and sea life is such a rare occurrence he has slowed the speed to prolong the experience. No shit! Well, there you go.

Twenty one consecutive days of riding in rain, a mountain we never saw, a national park of disappointment, and all we were denied in Denali; at last here is our reward, our prize. Right place, right time. The sky fades to a pale pink haze, and all the time the light has been reflecting off the snowy mountaintops that surround the horizon. Now this is an impressive grand finale; an evening of sky, sea, land, and nature complementing each other in the most extravagant of displays. I've seen a lot of sunsets, but I will never forget tonight. Thank you, Alaska.

Day 25

Ferry to Prince Rupert, British Columbia, Canada

13 miles

In the night I heard rain on my tent, and then I could feel my sleeping bag getting wet, so I went into the kids' play area and slept by the ball pool, looking like a monster slug with a lion's mane. This action could be misconstrued and frowned upon, so by 9AM, after a few awkward disturbances, I get up. I'm glad to see my tent is still there. With only wet tape holding it down and no weight inside, I half expect to see it shredded and flapping by the only guide rope that's tied to the railing.

There are puddles of water in it, so I can't put my sleeping bag back in. Like the homeless person I am, I take it with me to the restaurant. The place is warm but uninviting. Another pile of shite is slung on a plate and thrust in my direction. Then a large quantity of money is demanded for the "service."

DRob turns up. I give him a brief and violently passionate description of my breakfast experience. He considers my review and opts to take my stuff to his room. I go and peel my tent off the deck and empty out as much water as I can. Back in his penthouse cabin, I dry it off with his lush, fluffy towels. Then I take a shower. Hmm! Probably should have done that the other way round. I do feel slightly fresher, although still sleep deprived.

At Ketchikan, the ferry docks. I'm reunited with my bike and load my stuff back on. Jonathan's bike is staying put all the way to Washington State. So he jumps on the back of mine for one last meal together. It's dull and rainy. This place is another stop on the cruise ship circuit and equally bloody awful. Ketchikan is also an isolated island. The question is, does Ketchikan exist because the cruise ships come here, or do the cruise ships come here because Ketchikan exists? Either way, I dislike the place for several reasons, and the miserable weather reflects the way I feel. We are simply prolonging the goodbye. The place is as touristy as hell. It lacks identity and conviction; the shops provide no service other than those a cruise ship passenger may require. Thankfully, having our own transport, we're able to ride inland, away from the promenade façade and find a diner full of locals.

After the meal, I go the bathroom, which is out the back by the kitchen. Overdressed and struggling with my tank bag and helmet, this confined space requires nimble and agile skills, neither of which I possess. I open the door to leave, simultaneously flicking off the light switch. The door opens inwards, hits my boot, and slams shut, leaving me in darkness. I fumble for the handle and pull it open again. As I go to leave, the latch catches on my trousers and pulls me back in. On my third attempt, dragging my tank bag by the shoulder harness, I manage to exit successfully. The manoeuvre, it has to be said, lacked grace. I squint as I walk into the light. A grey and toothless cook is sitting on a stool having a cigarette break. He's witnessed the struggle. We make eye contact, he exhales a lungful of smoke, and with a poker face, he just says, "Fuckin' doors!" I couldn't have said it better myself.

It's time. I take Jonathan back to the dock. The ferry is ready to depart. I give Jonathan a hug, but I don't say anything, because I know my voice would crack if I did. I'm glad it's raining now. As though in a sepia-toned movie scene, we wave him aboard the boat and continue to wave from the shore as he departs. From the dock, we look up at him, now beginning to feel a little self-conscious from the constant waving. Ships don't depart very swiftly, so to draw it to a close with a flash of inspiration, Jonathan, standing on the stern and surrounded by passengers he'll spend the next two days with, turns round, drops his trousers and moons us. A naked, male bottom has never evoked this much emotion in me. I can't get behind that!

And then there were two. I turn to DRob. We don't need words; we need a bar. It's as empty and lifeless as I feel inside. I try to write those damn postcards, but I couldn't have picked a worse time. There's nothing to do, nothing I want to do. I don't have my drinking head on, and the weather outside doesn't encourage riding or exploring. I'm not hungry, and the souvenir and gift shops depress me further. I find an Internet café, but I'm not inspired to write a mass email. It's ridiculous; we have several thousand miles left to go, undiscovered roads and scenery; we have plenty of time too. We still have a significant slice of Canada to ride through before we get to the "lower forty-eight." Yet, somehow I can't shake off this end-of-trip feeling. Jonathan was an integral part of the trip. I suppose we all are. There's nothing to do but kill time and adjust to this new and reduced chemistry. The time had constantly flown past when we'd been riding, but now it drags like leg irons. We're captive and dependent on our connecting ferry. I can't find a distraction to take my thoughts away from this miserable town and everything it represents. We're joined on the dock by a couple of other motorcyclists. They aren't like us. They tell us how tomorrow morning when we dock, they're going to "hit it hard and corner fast" due to the high-endurance, 400-mile day they have planned. I don't say anything.

At 8PM, we board our ferry. I find a sun chair under a sheltered viewing deck and blag it with my sleeping bag. "Dis vill do nicely." We share a solitary beer, standing at the stern as the ferry departs. Now we are leaving Alaska. How very different it is to last night's experience.

DAY 26

TERRACE, BRITISH COLUMBIA

190 MILES

At 4AM, a voice over the tannoy announces something I don't want to hear. It's nothing dramatic, like hitting an iceberg, just that we will be docking shortly. If you're getting off in Prince Rupert, you'd better be ready. We are, and I'm not! But I only have a sleeping bag to roll up, so for the time being, I'll stay in it. The morning is grey, cloudy, and damp. I stay on my lounger until the ferry docks and then stand around waiting for the elevator doors to open up and take us to the car deck. I'm surrounded by motorhome drivers with an inane conversation that's too loud and intrusive for my delicate morning mood. I take the stairs, load the bike, put on waterproofs, and we ride off the ferry to clear customs back into Canada for the third time in two weeks.

Prince Rupert has nothing to offer in the dullness of an early Monday morning. So we ride straight out of town, up into the hills, and towards a horizon that promises brighter weather, but doesn't deliver. I see two lights in my mirror. It's the motorcyclists from last night. They catch us up with their engines screaming just as we come to a bendy stretch of road, then they drop right back. Even with my dodgy rear tyre and no real destination or deadline, we out-corner them. I'd instantly summed them up last night. I feel a warm, smug comfort based on the accuracy of my contemptuous judgement. After ninety miles, we ride into a town called Terrace. I feel so tired. For the last three nights I've only been getting four hours of disturbed sleep, and it's taking its toll. A lardy, carbohydrate breakfast is doing nothing to help the situation. It's not even 9AM. DRob is equally tired. We've been driven for weeks. Since the day we left, we've had a deadline and a destination. Now we have neither, and we don't have Jonathan either. The mental and physical exhaustion, along with over three debauched weeks of challenging riding, has left us shattered. We really have been hitting it hard. All we've been running on has run out. We discuss the possibility of getting a room and having a long, relaxing day. Next door to the restaurant is a hotel. I explain to the Asian owner how all we want is a peaceful place to rest.

"Then you leave tonight?" he asks.

"No, we'll leave tomorrow."

"You want room now for tonight?"

"Yes, all day and all night. Is that possible?"

"Yes, possible. Sixty dollars per room."

And that's it. That's our riding day. The morning rush hour, insignificant thought it is, hasn't even finished, and we've called it a day. I go straight to bed.

It's hard to make good decisions when you're tired and emotional. When I wake up at lunchtime, my instinct is to ride, but we've paid and committed to being here until tomorrow. I really feel like we've done more than enough sitting around and waiting in the last few days. Yet, we seem to have volunteered ourselves to do some more.

The couple who told us we'd get dirt up the Dempster were from Kitimat and spoke highly of the place. It has a smelting plant; why the hell that would make anyone want to go, I don't know. But the skies have cleared, we're feeling a bit fidgety, and it's only sixty miles from here. So we take a ride out. Not a term we've used much, but this being a little jaunt means we can ride without panniers, which, although liberating in some respects, also leaves us naked and vulnerable. In those boxes we carry our independence. It's an OK ride. It might even have us waxing lyrical, if we hadn't just experienced the last 6,000 plus miles. The smelting plant is where what the North Americans call "aluminum" foil is made. One of the more popular brands is called "Alcan." It never occurred to me before, but having now ridden the ALCAN Highway, I've just made the connection. The same thing happened with a bottle of Scotch once in Scotland. So now I can say I've seen where America's most popular kitchen foil is made. I don't know when I'll ever be in a position to say it, but if I do I can hand on heart back up my boastful claim. Although, we do decide to pass on the guided tour.

On the way back, we stop by some hot springs, which have all the design initiative and imagination of a Travelodge room. The water smells of chlorine rather than sulphur, and the café diners look out over the concrete pool, which blocks the mountain view and makes the whole bathing experience about as relaxing as testifying in court. DRob voices some very strong opinions, which is quite uncharacteristic. Still, it's really amusing to see him so animated. Perhaps he's been in my company too much. I'm not sure cynicism suits him. Pessimism is what he usually does best; his reason being that having low expectations means he's rarely disappointed. I'm not sure what that says about our friendship.

I'm concerned about my bike. I gave the tyre the benefit of the doubt, thinking its terrible handling may have been due to the weight I was carrying, but today without luggage, I can only put its lack of road holding down to the inadequate and incompatible rear tyre.

Back at the hotel, I'm happily surprised that after so long in each other's company we still have plenty to talk and laugh about. But then we always did when we shared a house, so there's no reason why on the road things should be any different. I wonder what DRob expected.

DAY 27

BEDNESTI, BRITISH COLUMBIA

358 MILES

Right, let's get this thing moving again. Enough of this drowsy dithering. Our twenty-seven-hour residency is over, and we're given a healthy bagel and yoghurt breakfast to help us on our way. I leave my unused petrol can at the hotel. I've been carrying it the entire trip. I don't need it anymore. I didn't need it at all.

We ride out of the snow-capped mountain landscape we've become so used to. It is replaced by pine-covered rolling hills and rising temperatures. The pines are gradually being wiped out by a pesky bug. The trees appear to have autumn colours, but pines aren't deciduous. These trees are just dead or dying. It goes on for hundreds of miles.

We stop at a Chinese restaurant in Houston for lunch. I have a problem. The waitress asks if I want lemonade.

"No thanks, just water."

"What?"

"Water? You have water?"

"No."

"OK, forget it. I won't have a drink."

"Do you just want some water?"

"Oh yeah, good idea. Thanks."

What they lack in beverage request comprehension, they make up for with a beef noodle soup that is incredibly authentic and tasty. I've been constantly disappointed with said soup since the day I sat on a tiny, wooden stool on the pavement, eating from a chipped, china bowl handed to me from a street vendor in Hanoi, proving that the most memorable and enjoyable food comes from the preparation, not the package it's presented in. The steaming, fresh soup was accompanied with an array of herbs and spices to vary the taste as I pleased. Until today, I've had no success in repeating that experience. It was on that same trip in Southeast Asia that I met an American on a train. He had a streaming cold, and I was trapped in his contagious company. I was in my late twenties, and he was much older. He said he travelled mainly on his stomach these days. He wasn't fat or even a connoisseur of fine cuisine, he just had an appreciation for good local food. I think that comes as you get older. It's a great substitute when other tasty pleasures become less available.

DRob is due to get new tyres fitted in Prince George, but we've lost our ability to "hit it hard" and stop a few hours short of the city. It's a pretty, low-key little resort, and we find a secluded place to pitch the tents, overlooking a lake. We decide we should do a beer run; however, we're quite isolated here. It's a premature and spontaneous stop, so we're not fully prepared. A car comes up the dirt track, driven by a young couple hoping for some privacy to have a smoke. The girl is about to start work here as a live-in maid; her boyfriend has driven her down and is about to say goodbye. He passes the joint to me. I take a single hit, just to be social, I feel my forehead tighten and my mind wander. It's almost instant. I'm high, God, I'm high. I haven't felt like this for ages. I spent my twenties in this state. No wonder I never got anything done, and if I did, I don't remember.

We ride ten miles south, looking for a place that might sell alcohol. There's nothing; just trees. Much like the majority of Canada. Why would we think that an off-licence would miraculously appear in the sprawling wilderness? Because we're stoned, that's why. We turn around and ride back into the setting sun, pleasantly wasted, warm, and slowly moving towards a sky that was made specifically for a rider who is righteously stoned. I pretend I'm riding back up to the Arctic Circle again. It's the perfect road: straight, empty, and undulating. An easy ride; twenty unfruitful miles that don't matter at all.

DRob wants to eat. We go into a restaurant-cum-bar that's an awful place of blaring TVs. I order nothing and leave. DRob gets his food to go. We attract a weirdo: a young girl who is really fucked up. She reminds me of a troublesome girlfriend I once had, and for that reason alone, I'm wary of her. She wants some DEET because she's getting bitten. I tell her it's industrial strength and not to put it on her face, "It'll melt ya skin." She puts it on her face, and unsurprisingly, it burns. I light a fire from sticks and leaves I've gathered from the forest floor. I'm still stoned, but focused and functioning. She says I look exactly like someone she knows, but he only speaks French. Probably not me then. Turns out she's only eighteen; too young to buy alcohol, and she wants me to buy her whiskey from the restaurant. I think she doesn't need it. She repeatedly asks where we're from. She just can't grasp that we're from another country.

"So, Alaska," she says, "Isn't it supposed to be cold there?"

She wants a ride on my bike. I'm disinclined to acquiesce her request. In fact, she's getting annoying, perhaps because she's making a happy man feel very old. She's a pretty little thing; naive, vulnerable, and hopeless. She'll probably live and die here. I suppose you don't need to be streetwise if there are no streets. After everything I've gathered has burnt, she wanders off. Probably for the best.

DAY 28

Lac la Hache, British Columbia

238 miles

DRob snores so loudly in the night that I have to get up and move my tent. I angrily up stakes whilst shouting insults and abuse in his direction. All of which he is oblivious to; his infuriating rumblings not missing a beat as his selfish sleeping habits reverberate through the night.

We wake to blue skies. This has never happened to us in Canada before. The locals say it does, the picture postcards imply it does, but it's not something we've witnessed until today. I thought this weather condition was about as likely as DRob considerately getting up and moving his tent during the night.

We ride on to Prince George. I lead us to the place where his Triumph is booked in for new tyres. We were going to use the time to have a late breakfast, but my Connie won't start. I spend the next two hours in the bike shop parking area, going through the electrical system. I don't diagnose the fault, but I must have disturbed some dodgy connection, because the starter button eventually does what its name suggests, and the engine fires up. They charge DRob $700 for supplying and fitting two new tyres. Thieving bastards! Still, now he can once again corner with confidence. I take the lead, and he follows me the wrong way down a one-way street. When a car comes towards us, with panic and realisation,

157

I swerve into a side road and straight into the car park of a Mexican restaurant. Perfect, we haven't had breakfast, and it's already lunchtime.

Maybe we should try and do some miles now. There's little reason not to. In this heat, though, it makes for a tough and tiring ride. The rain was shit, but at least we were used to it. We could get our heads down and do the distance. But this is stifling. We pass a lake with a beach; it's very inviting. There are girls lying around in bikinis. DRob puts on his Speedos to go swimming. I sit in the shade of a tree and cringe. Friends should not let friends wear Speedos. There's no reason to, and I have no excuse for my shortcomings. I failed him, and it's unforgivable, even more so given the beach's occupants. I am forever rueful when I recall this day.

Once he's had his dip, dried, and changed, I take off my T-shirt, walk to the lake, and soak it, then put it back on. That's how hot it is today, I actually want to ride in wet clothing. This isn't the kind of riding we've had much experience in on this trip, and we're both finding it a bit of a handicap. This cloudless, blue sky has me considering the possibility of going back to Banff and Jasper, just a few hundred miles to the east of us. Then I remember the procession of motorhomes and decide these less popular roads might be the better choice. We have to keep stopping to find shade and cool off. This must be how you deal with summer if you come from Yorkshire. We feel a little lost without an itinerary or deadlines anymore. DRob's flight is in two weeks, and Denver is only 1,600 miles away.

As afternoon turns to evening; we find a pub. It's a bit posh looking; and the food is overpriced, over-prepared; and overrated. In the toilets, today's horoscopes are stuck above the urinals. Mine is so awful I rip it down and throw it in the bin. I don't need to read this shit. Let's stick to the facts: you will be a victim of mild extortion due to an unfortunate purchase of an inadequate, but pretentious attempt at gourmet food.

We speak to a Harley rider. The usually stuff, "How ya doin'? Where ya been? Where ya goin'?" His surprise by our answers makes us realise that, actually, on these bikes it's quite an achievement to have ridden where we have. It also makes me miss the tundra and wilderness even more. Here the land is farmed and inhabited, and it gets dark at night too. I also have money concerns again. It's a constant in my life, but for four wonderful weeks I've been parting with it like I own the printer. It came to me relatively easily and with perfect timing, and I've enjoyed doing all that's been on offer to me, but now the time has come to be a bit more responsible again. It hasn't just been a journey into the unknown, it's been a holiday from being on a budget, which for me, is also a bit like a journey into the unknown.

We continue south, hoping to make a few more miles in this cooler evening air. However, there's smoke on the horizon, and we're passed by emergency vehicles. Eventually, we come to a road block, where we are told the route will be closed for the rest of the evening. Great, one hot day, and the bloody country catches fire. There are no alternative routes, so we turn around and find a campsite by a lake, which would probably be very beautiful if I hadn't been spoilt with such dramatic scenery over the last month. They don't serve alcohol, and once again, we have none on us. This just wouldn't happen if Jonathan was here. I have an early night. If it's too hot to ride and too hard to get a drink, then we may as well be sensible and formulate a plan. We decide to get up early and ride the cool dawn light. Slowly, we're returning to a familiar reality; dark nights and early to bed. Now I remember what saving money feels like; my old friends, Dreary and Thrifty, are back.

Day 29

Hope, British Columbia

237 miles

My alarm sounds its wake-up call at 5AM; time to go. I'm feeling OK. I unzip my tent and look out into a fresh, inviting morning. Across the campground, I see DRob packing up. He's heard my zipper and is looking my way. Strange that he's so much quieter once he's awake. I wave good morning and then go about silently rolling up my dry tent. It's so easy, plus now I have a well-rehearsed packing system. I go to the showers, but you have to put in a dollar to get water, and I can't get behind that. I finish packing up. It's really quite chilly. I put on my thermal top and opt for my big gloves, put in my earphones, wrap a scarf around my neck. and push on my helmet. DRob sticks his thumb up, I nod. and we break the silence, start our bikes. and ride out of the site.

We'd said we wanted to be on the road by 5:30AM. We weren't specific as to what road, but we're on the path out of the campsite and it's exactly 5:30AM. The sun is yet to rise above the hills. The chill of the morning may only be temporary, but it's very real. The road blocks are gone, but a smoky haze still hangs in the air. Even with music in my ears and an engine between my legs, I can sense a peace and solitude. We are the only ones up and about. As my heated grips slowly warm up, I reduce the pressure I'm holding them with. We pass the cause of last night's emergency: the burnt out remains of a barn. It's still burning, although the flames are not going to spread. Just as well, really, as all the firemen have vacated the site.

On we ride through some small towns that are just coming to life as the sun makes an appearance and starts to warm the air. The hills turn to mountains, and again there is snow visible on the highest peaks. The other side of this mountain range to the east is Banff National Park. The landscape is becoming a lot more vertical, and we find ourselves winding into a canyon. The road runs alongside a river, as is usually the case in a canyon. I think canyon riding is one of my favourite terrains. It seems to incorporate most of what I enjoy. There's the grand scale, twisting roads, the chill of the wild, white water, and the warmth of the reflected sun. This particular river we're following has train tracks running on either side of it. It looks like a very realistic model railway. Occasionally, we see long freight trains constricted and barely moving. As they climb up the canyon, they look like mercury rising in a twisted thermometer. DRob is happily leading the way, scrubbing in his new tyres, and I instinctively follow his lines.

After two hours, we stop at a breakfast place. We pull up side by side, take off our helmets, look at each other, and simultaneously say "good morning," and then both burst out laughing. After such a beautiful ride, with so many miles behind us, on some level we'd been communicating, but these are our first two spoken words of the day, and when they're followed by laughter, it's about as good a start to a day as any motorcyclist could ask for. We eat on a deck overlooking the river. The temperature is perfect now. Humming birds hover by feeders, and the water thunders beneath us. It's an altogether stunning morning, location, and experience. Those pre-breakfast miles always seem like the most progressive ones of the day. That effortless momentum never lasts; as the day becomes more populated and the hour more social, an element of stamina is required. Although it's not necessary today, as we're already nearly halfway to the place where we'll spend our last night together.

It's still only midmorning when we arrive in Hope, a place of mountainous beauty, easy jokes, and movie fame. *Rambo: First Blood* was filmed here. I've never seen it, but like *Star Wars*, I am, of course, aware of it. We find some Swiss chalets to stay in.

I pay on my plastic, as I'm out of Canadian dollars. DRob dozes, and I busy myself doing laundry and reading about the Rambo Walking Tour. It sounds unmissable, unlike the movie. For us, the tour starts in a bar. It isn't the first stop on the suggested itinerary, but it's not written in blood. DRob explains the plot to me with excruciating detail. I think I remember once seeing the motorbike chase scene. Our attempt at finding the settings of certain scenes fails miserably, and even when we do succeed, it doesn't mean anything to me. We decide to get the bikes and travel to some of the more remote locations in the film. We find the level crossing Rambo jumped his bike over. This is all a bit like washing up the plates for a meal I never ate. I'm sure it was great; I can see the evidence, but I'm missing something quite significant. We take a walk by a river and through some abandoned train tunnels. I watch salmon jump as they try to swim upstream. This may not have been in the movie, but it's real, and it's happening now; therefore, it's quite satisfying. Eagles fly overhead, and I think this town is selling itself short, living off the reputation of a twenty-five-year-old blockbuster.

It's our final night together. There have been a lot of goodbyes lately, and I'm not sad. A new solo chapter of my journey will begin tomorrow, and although it'll be a lot quieter, I'm not close to wanting this trip to end. I think there are more highs to come, and despite this being my last night in Canada, like the people of this town I'm leaving behind, I too live in hope.

Day 30

Centralia, Washington, USA

265 miles

Once again, the skies are overcast. It seems to be the standard weather condition for meetings and departures. Despite the low cloud, the town still has appeal, and if I had more Canadian dollars, I may consider staying another night. I have enough money for breakfast, although I've just about had enough of fried diner food. There are probably healthier options on the menu, but out of habit I order eggs and hash browns. It's getting very windy outside; clouds are blowing down the mountains, and it feels quite ominous. A couple in the restaurant say they pity us being exposed to the looming storm. This is nothing; at least it's dry. DRob wants to get some postcards, so we go to the visitors' centre. Then he wants to write them too. "Come on," I'm thinking. I'm anxious to get out of here before whatever is blowing in arrives. But having written them, he wants to find a post office so they have a Canadian postmark on them. I use this frustrating delay to check over my bike. I notice the rear brake pads are now down to the metal; probably should have checked them earlier. They seemed fine last time I looked at them in Alaska.

It really is blowing a gale now. Branches have snapped off trees and are tumbling down the street. The lake has white caps on it, and the gusts have the kind of force that could blow a bike over. It's highway all the way to the border of the US. The wind subsides, but its starts to rain, and the spray is blinding. It's the most densely populated road we have seen the entire trip. We hope to ride on through to clearer weather ahead and don't make a waterproof stop. Besides, a fast road like this with reduced visibility is not the ideal place to pull over.

The spray and traffic stop as we approach the US border. The soaking continues though, and now with added sweat, we push our bikes in the stop-start queue. With the slow progress we're able to remove layers of clothing in an attempt to reduce the discomfort. I replace my Canadian map with the one I have for the US west coast. It takes an hour to get to the barrier, but the immigration process is easy. Instantly, the landscape changes. Pretty little farm communities are spread out across the plains, and the road is dead straight and flat, ideal for someone with reduced braking ability. We come to Billingham, the place where Jonathan docked and disembarked three days ago. I got a text from him this morning; he's back home in Denver now.

We find a Walmart. DRob gets oil to refill his engine, and I find a cartridge to refill my pen. The documenting of all these miles and new experiences has used up a lot of ink. It's lucky I don't remember all that occurs when we drink, or my ramblings would be the thickness of *The Milepost* guidebook that we happily discarded this morning. I don't care if it does have souvenir qualities, I'd rather have smuggled in dirt from the Dempster; it would have more sentimentality attached to it than that phonebook-sized magazine of adverts. It had its uses, but it's just not very motorcycle-friendly in volume, weight, and content. Like a *Lonely Planet* guide, you can use it defensively to discover what places would appeal to and be frequented by irritants, then go elsewhere.

We find a bar for a goodbye drink. A couple of pints of Alaskan Amber. The waitress asks where we have ridden from. We tell her Alaska.

"Oh," she replies, "Did you come through Canada?"

We're back among the geographically ignorant residents of the "lower forty-eight." What the hell does a school geography lesson consist of here that they don't even know their own country? I once stayed in a place in Denver, where I witnessed the homework of a twelve-year-old. Geography that week consisted of learning the state flower of Indiana. Apparently, that's far more important than knowing the countries that border your own. Although in the waitress's defence, she did know the names of all sixteen draught beers behind the bar, which will probably help her chosen career more than knowing how to get to her forty-ninth state.

We ride together down Interstate 5. I see a Kawasaki dealership and indicate off the highway. DRob follows me up the slip road, but at the lights, he stays in the lane to rejoin the highway. He puts out his hand to touch goodbye, but I have my clutch held in and can't select neutral. His light turns green, his lane moves forward, and then he's gone down the entry ramp and back onto the highway. That's the last I see of him. After four weeks and 8,000 miles, now it's just me. Alone at a junction on a Washington highway, and as has been the theme of the journey, I have alcohol on my breath; the spirit of adventure.

I have brake pads to focus on; the purchase and the fitment is effortless, unlike the highway I rejoin. It's 5PM on a Friday evening. Oh, joy, the traffic is thick and slow. It's illegal to filter, but it's infuriating to sit and swelter in the stagnant queue. So I go down the middle of the stationary cars, which is really dangerous, as no one is expecting this, but at least I make progress. People hoot and flash their lights, but fuck 'em! Land of the free, right? Well, watch this you conforming cowards. This is what freedom looks like. For the next two and a half hours, I weave through the static traffic down to Seattle, playing Nirvana and Hole in my helmet.

My engine runs hot, and with the concentration and my protective clothing, I'm panting with fatigue. I stop at a town called Federal Way for fuel and a wee. It's a very dodgy area. I'm in the 'hood. The transition is horrid: cars, traffic, cities, people, and dodgy dealings. The day will continue until I make it stop, so at 8:30PM, I pull off the highway, find a motel, haggle the price down, and lock myself in my room. This is not the kind of solitude that the Arctic offered; this is man-made isolation: enclosed, not exposed, in a harsh environment as opposed to a wilderness. These are the trappings of the transient in the confines of society. How can this be freedom, where there is nowhere left to lose yourself?

Day 31

Reedsport, Oregon

285 miles

My room includes a free breakfast, which consists of a croissant; one of many that sit in a plastic tub on the reception desk. Being a rebel without any cream cheese, I take a second one. I'm so bad. It's not an early start, and I only have myself to blame. I've been checking out the prison website, and it turns out visiting is only allowed at the weekends, which is a little inconvenient, as I'll arrive on Monday.

Out on the road, I'm just another motorcycle tourer. There was, on some level, a mutual respect, if not a camaraderie, amongst the travellers of the ALCAN Highway. My plates may say I'm out of state, but I'm no longer out of this world.

I head south towards Oregon. There's a cone-shaped mountain on the horizon, just like the one around Seattle; Mount Rainier it's called. This one looks just the same; like a giant solitary limpet on the landscape. But it can't be the same one. I'm sure I've travelled further than that. Regardless of which one it is, it will have to suffice, as it's the only one around, and I really miss my snowy mountain landscapes. You'd think I'd have had enough of them, but I can never seem to get enough of vast, snowy mountain ranges. I'm sure I was never meant to have been born in Essex.

Sometimes I wonder if there was a mix up. I think there might be some yeti in my blood; it would explain a lot. However, mine was a home birth, and so it's unlikely I was placed in the wrong crib.

Oh, dear. You see; it's started already. I don't have to spend long in my own company before I start to have the kind of thoughts that makes company avoid me, or in this case, attracts unwanted company. As I sit in the heated resentment of the crawling city traffic, quietly sweating and minding my own business, I feel someone approach out the corner of my eye. A ranting black woman comes up to me, and whilst I sit there baking and captive, she tells me how she's just got a court injunction on her ex, and if he comes near her again, she'll have him thrown in jail. It was obviously a very exciting time for her, judging solely by her unmissable erect nipples. She walks backwards into the traffic, still ranting at me. I shrug at the driver next to me and say, "I don't even get off the bike and I attract 'em. How do I do it?" I long for the deserted tundra and the open space for my mind to wander, not restricted by the confines of this traffic and consumed by the anticipation of a manoeuvre that could be hazardous to my health.

After an air-conditioned lunch stop, the day feels even hotter, so I ride without my jacket for comfort; a comfort that could instantly disappear if I hit the tarmac. As I head for the coast and the legendary Highway 101, the thick sea mist has me not only putting my jacket back on, but also reaching for my scarf and big gloves. I can't listen to my Christina Aguilera album anymore. It's been a popular choice this ride, but I need the dexterity that my fingerless gloves provide to turn the volume down when she hits the high notes, to prevent my ears from bleeding.

This highway is overrated. There's so much traffic, the sea mist takes away the view, it has ridiculously low speed limits, and the road surface itself is badly maintained. I'm giving it a second chance, but it's just not living up to its romanticism, hype, and all the songs about it. I don't like the places I'm going through. I'm not getting a good vibe. Usually, I'd just keep going, but I recall a passage in *Jupiter's Travels*, and my thoughts, instincts, and actions are not my own. The day has passed, or maybe I've passed through it; nothing particularly lovely has occurred, other than the daydreams of other places. I make a stop and get a shitty room in a smelly town; swapping the adjectives around wouldn't improve anything. I spend the evening looking at my map and plotting an indirect route to California. I don't want to kill the time I have; I want to spend it wisely. I just have to figure out where it will have the most value.

DAY 32

SANTA ROSA, CALIFORNIA

511 MILES

My alarm goes off at 5AM. I'm surprised to see it's still dark. I'm less surprised to see it's because of low cloud and rain. My thoughts of unhindered progress, dawn escapes, and sunrise roads are instantly replaced with the immediately more pleasurable pursuit of staying in bed. Then I go back to the initial idea as three loud MG drivers decide to have a conversation right outside my room. As I load my bike, they try to impress me with their bilingual skills and drop words like "jumper" and "bollock" into their patronising conversation. Admittedly, there is such a thing as a bollock, but they're generally referred to in pairs, and in this case, I'm getting it in triplicate. I put on my waterproofs, and the first 130 miles are done in heavy rain, but the rain is warm, and I stay dry. Eventually, the day is bright enough to encourage me to stop for a Pacific photo, but it's barely worth the effort, and then the bike won't start again. This is becoming a more frequent occurrence, and if it continues, it'll have me double thinking every stop I make, and that's no way to ride.

I stop at a Mexican restaurant in Eureka. My soggy sheepskin seat cover is currently on the back seat drying. The waitress asks if my dog would like a bowl of water.

"It's not a dog, it's a sheep."

"Do you want to wake it up and bring it in?"

"It's not asleep; it's dead. I'm trying to dry it out."

"So it doesn't need water?"

"No, it'll just make it wetter."

I'm not sure she fully understands me. I don't try to be strange, but sometimes my innocent actions are so misconstrued. The rest of the meal is straightforward, even if served with underlying accusations of animal cruelty, but that just could be in my head. I should have ordered a vegetarian dish.

As I go to leave, a guy on a KLR 650 pulls up. He, too, has just ridden down from Alaska. He bought his bike in Eagle River. I tell him that's where my back tyre came from, but the coincidence doesn't seem to impress him. Our other common bond is how we're struggling with losing our "special" status. At least he has an Alaskan plate on his bike, which is far more noticeable than an Alaskan-purchased tyre.

I carry on south on a fast dual carriageway. Ahead is a pickup truck towing a trailer. On the trailer is a large, black, plastic water storage tank. It's so flimsy it can barely keep its form, especially from the force of the wind. As I get closer, I see strips of black coming off the trailer. My first thought is that the tyre is shredding, but that thought doesn't last very long. It's soon followed by a far more accurate diagnosis; the rubber is, in fact, bungee cords snapping. This is confirmed as the tank takes flight. If it were to land directly over me it would cover me. But I don't expect such precision. I brake hard. It lands in front of me and bounces. With split second reactions—like a goalie judging the direction of a penalty kick ball—I half guess, half anticipate, and wholly hope its direction. I go right. It lands on my left, and I pass it. Still braking, I look in my mirrors. There's chaos behind me, as the traffic swerves and brakes. The driver of the pickup pulls over. My adrenalin is pumping so hard, I don't even stop. I regain a little composure, select the correct gear, a suitable lane, and shake from the exhilaration. A car pulls level with me. The lady in the passenger seat is looking my way. I pound my heart with my left fist, and she laughs. Yeah, it's funny now. But that's how it happens. Without warning, my last living thought could have been distinguishing the difference between a rubber bungee cord and a rubber tyre. I follow a steady driver until I've calmed down to a level of control.

I've ridden into an area of redwoods, and I see a sign for "Avenue of Giants"; the day's highlights begin. The skies clear, and the sun filters through the towering foliage. It's got the same unfathomable scale that Alaska had. Somehow, riding through a tree with a tunnel carved in it seems so normal. It's hard to judge just how big these redwoods are when there are no other trees around.

I divert to Highway 1 via a phenomenal road that twists through a forest. There is no other traffic, and even with my dodgy tyre, I rev high and lean low. I know it's about to end when I get to the coastal sea mist, but I don't slow the pace. Focused on the traffic, I maintain the empty road momentum, because the cars seem to be perfectly placed for overtaking without having to slow down for oncoming traffic. I feel the thrill of the Pacific Coast Highway at last. It gets even better as I become aware that I've left the mist behind, and the redwoods are back too. It turns out that this is because I've taken a wrong turn. I seem to be on Highway 128. The big clue is that I'm no longer on the coast. Actually, it's not wrong, it's spectacular, just unintended.

At about sevenish, I see a bar and stop for a beer. This is most out of character for me when I'm riding alone, but something pulls me in. There's the obligatory drunk at the bar; loud and obnoxious. The road calls me back even louder. It's far more inviting. I need a place to stay. Windsor is too posh, and finding somewhere within budget becomes a chore. For all America's empty spaces, there is nearly always a fence and a prohibitive signpost. Wild camping is more than taking an opportunity, it's trespassing, and the penalty is not worth the saving. If they're so brave, how come they all carry guns. I'm not carrying one. Surely, it's braver to go unarmed into a place that is protected by the right-to-shoot laws.

Day 33

Modesto, California

209 miles

I glance out of my window at 5AM to see the first light of dawn. A palm tree is silhouetted against brightening colours, and the view has a balmy passion. After snowy mountains, a landscape with a palm tree is probably my second most favourite place to be. Despite the inviting view, I stay in bed for another four hours. This being California, I have to ride across the road to buy a banana for breakfast. A wonderful paradox of risk and indolence in the pursuit of health. Another trait of California is the traffic, and my lie in has got me on the road just in time for the worst of the Monday morning rush. It's fast, erratic, and coming at me from every direction. In spite of the attention it requires, I'm still able to spot a dealership and head off to see if they might have the tyres I need. They don't, so I continue south towards the low cloud that covers San Francisco. I cross the red oxide bridge, the uprights disappearing into the mist, but it doesn't stop me from taking photos of myself with them in the background, my jacket half unzipped and the *h* of my Motorhead T-shirt visible beneath my bandana. It's a brilliant shot. I ride on into the city. It's quite exciting to be in a familiar town. I recognise street names. There is so much to look at; stimulation all around taking my attention from the road.

There are hundreds of hotels. Maybe I should have carried on and stayed here last night. Maybe I should stop now. Maybe I should actually make a decision. I opt for an Internet café. In an email, my mum says I've won a £50 premium bond. I consider treating myself, but every day's a treat. How could I distinguish the difference? The city dwellers are suited and fashion conscious. I'm not blending in at all. Not that a Motorhead T-shirt ever goes out of fashion. I order some fish tacos for lunch, and from that point on, my day turns into a self-inflicted, stop-start mess of unsuccessful and half-hearted attempts at fulfilling my needs. I can't get the tyres I want, or the tools, or the book I want to read. I go to a suburb where an old friend lives. I know his address by heart, as I've written it on so many postcards over the seventeen years since I last saw him. That visit had been less than a year after the "big quake," and he'd recounted firsthand stories of the event; the most memorable being at 5AM, when everyone was standing in the street with no power and no idea if the earthquake was over. The beer was getting warm in the fridges, and so they all started drinking. That's the kind of neighbourhood he lives in. I ride the streets of his little hilltop community, but I can't find the place I'm looking for, and unannounced and with only a vague and fading acquaintanceship, I don't get to see my old California Deadhead friend with his enviable '65 panhead.

I annoy myself with my distracted plans and lack of conviction, wrong roads and time wasting. So I do what I've been doing for a while and head south. But I go too far and miss my turn off. I try to stay on Highway 84, but it keeps doing lefts and rights, joining highways and creeping off down slip roads. The traffic is slow and dense. I filter between trucks that seem to be inadvertently causing a rolling road block. Then the road heads east across the plains, and I experience the worst wind I have ever ridden in. There is no constancy to it, and the gusts are so violent their strength has me fighting to keep in lane. Then without warning, as I'm overtaking a truck, I'm sideswiped across the highway. I slow my pace, but it's impossible to take evasive actions against an invisible and sporadic force.

Again, I seem to have found an area that is void of campsites, not that I could pitch in this wind anyway. I wind down into the ugly city of Modesto, which really has nothing to boast about. I find a strip of three motels in an industrial area and get a cheap room. It takes a bit longer than it should have to realise there's a lot of business taking place here. There are big black pimps and girls of various sizes, appeal, colour, and levels of dress. Well, I'm here now. I walk to a little shack and buy some beer, then sit in my room and watch the customers come and go. Cars pull up all night, money changing hands, and skinny, tattooed, heroin-zombie girls have screeching catfights with busty black mamas. As the light fades, the profiles outside my window are dawn-and-dusk different to this morning's palm silhouette sunrise.

Sex, drugs, and violence. The cops pull up, leave again, and business carries on as usual. By accident, I seem to be acclimatising myself from the wilderness to the wrong side of the law as my prison visit draws closer. I consider my £50 premium bond win and a little treat, something beautiful, something rough, something wild, something uninhibited. Yeah, I know what I'm gagging for; what pleasures I want to indulge in with my windfall. I think I'll spend a few days in Yosemite National Park.

Day 34

Yosemite National Park
California

194 miles

White noise from my unplugged TV drowns out most of the sounds of white trash outside my room. I couldn't sleep with these girls, even if I wanted to. They never sleep. When I open my curtains, they're still out touting for business. So are the cops. I watch them interrogate two young women. It seems like a game to me. Maybe that's why it's called "being on the game," because everyone knows what's happening here. This police intervention is just a token gesture, and they play on it.

I've got a busy day. I've got to get tyres and go to prison. I load my bike under the watchful and suspicious eye of a loitering sheriff. I ride right past him, go the wrong way, and have to come back past him again. Bugger. In my tank bag, I have the motorcycle dealership section ripped out of the yellow pages that's in my room. I ride into Modesto to try and find one. I pass a BMW dealer and decide it might be worth a try. The bimbo receptionist asks what model I have.

"It's not a BMW, I just want tyres."

"We only do BMW tyres."

I manage to speak to an older guy with a ponytail, and things progress. He can have my tyres by Friday. I can take off the wheels myself to save on labour, and the cost of supply and fitting will be $300. Perfect, I'll take 'em. Then he shows me a map and a good route to take to Yosemite. It's not relevant, though, as I don't tell him I'm going via a prison.

Chowchilla is another name I know from frequently writing the address. It's where my friend is imprisoned. I ride a hot highway full of trucks heading to Los Angeles. I pass the town and see a sign for the Valley State Prison for Women. So that's what the VSPW that I've written on every envelope stands for. I've never been to a working prison before, not voluntarily nor by force. I've seen *Porridge* and *The Shawshank Redemption* as well as other darker portrayals. I've read several books too, as the concept intrigues me. It frightens me too; not the fear of being imprisoned so much as the fear of being wrongly imprisoned. Thinking about it, I have been inside several prisons: a sightseeing trip to Alcatraz, the gaol where Ned Kelly was hanged in Australia, and the Tuol Sleng security prison and genocide museum in Cambodia. However, those visits were very different to the reality of having a friend locked up in a functioning maximum security prison.

I instinctively head for the visitor's centre, but not for postcards or souvenirs. I speak to an officer who fetches a sergeant. He's very helpful, explains the visiting procedure, and gives me good advice. He knows my friend, as she used to do clerical work for him. He says the visit will be behind glass, as being from overseas they cannot run a check on—not that it would do me any favours if they could. Visiting protocol is so strict they even have a booklet of dos and don'ts. I will study it in the freedom of the Yosemite National Park. The visiting lieutenant will be back on duty this Friday. It's suggested I speak to him as well.

I'm not exactly sure why, but when I leave I have an incredible feeling of wellbeing. Is it that I've procured my tyres? That I'll be able to visit my friend at last after talking about it for so long? Or my ability to be free to walk out of a prison? Perhaps it's just that a plan is coming to fruition. California is a long way to come to visit an incarcerated friend, especially as I went via Alaska. But I'm so close now, and I've even met someone who actually knows her name. I feel confident and content in my own company again. American society is a long way from the freedom they love to sing about, but I've just seen the alternative. What it must be like to have all liberty stripped from you. Riding into the heat haze on a baking, flat road once again feels like the privilege that it is. It's just that after the previous 9,000 miles, without a reminder, the daily distances could almost be seen as a duty.

I pass fig and olive trees and the sweltering communities that make a living from these crops. Some of the properties have sprawling yards, with trailers and mobile homes on them. I consider the possibility of renting one out if I do end up staying here to write the story of my friend's downfall. Although several people who know more of the story than I do have warned me of the danger of getting involved. This has only heightened my intrigue and determination. From over a year's worth of correspondence and knowing people who were at the trial, I've got a reasonable understanding of the course of events. However, whether via a reversed charge call from prison or a letter, I know every word is officially examined. One-sided, agenda-driven, or censored, the whole truth is an elusive factor. It's not that I'm solely motivated to clear her name; it's just that the facts of the case are astonishing. She was prosecuted on evidence, the proof of which was found on exhibits that were "lost" before the trial began. There was no evidence for a murder conviction, but the State of California got one anyway.

As I ride the parched, but irrigated plains, the heat is on me, although the promise of cooler, more entertaining roads lies in the hazy hills ahead, and slowly I climb to greener, fresher landscapes. My national park card allows me free entry. The money saved I waste by not taking supplies with me and having to pay the inflated prices reserved for the captive visitors to Yosemite.

I find a campsite that is typically cramped and with no privacy. I don't have the correct money to put in the envelope and post in the camp collection box. I ask a fellow camper for change. and the conversation that follows involves him telling me that Alaska is half day and half night. Why tell me about a place I've been to and you haven't? And anyway, you're bloody wrong. He proceeds to inform me that Paul McCartney is a Cockney, and after his bombardment of bollocks, he doesn't even have any change. I put up my tent anyway, then read the inmate visiting regulations. It's definitely not *Prisoner Cell Block H*. I have a little doze, until a barking dog wakes me up. It goes on and on. As politely as I can, I enquire if the owners will let this go on all night. Apparently, this is a dog-friendly campground, so I'm clearly in the wrong place. I pack up my tent and look for somewhere more tranquil and less dog-friendly. After all, what my tent lacks in soundproofing, it makes up for in impermanence. I don't need an estate agent to help me move. I go to a vista point for the sunset. The other visitors are whooping and hollering at the grandeur of the natural beauty. The sun turns red, the sky pink, and the main attraction—the Half Dome rock—turns orange. But there is no golden silence, just an annoying need to howl appreciation. I suppose they've just come to see it, but I want to feel it.

When it's almost dark, I look for a place to fly camp. I can't find anywhere suitable, so go back to the campsite. No way, fuck this place! It gives me the incentive to try harder. I leave the road and get the bike stuck. It's a strain to get it moving again. I don't want my lights on, but they come on with the ignition. At this point I'm more concerned about authority than wildlife. Eventually, I find a flat spot and hide my bike behind a rock. I cover my tyre tracks, put up my tent. and check it can't be seen by passing cars. I'm hidden. I'm free. I'm taking the initiative and being a fugitive from the confines of the campsite. The stars are bright and infinite, and the silence is vast. There are things out there I know nothing about, from outer space to the out-of-sight beyond the trees. My food is locked inside my top box, and that's stashed some distance away. I've found my own little piece of wild in this sanitised nature. It may not be safe or even sensible, but it's secluded and solitary, if not necessarily secure.

DAY 35

ABOVE SILHOUETTE FALLS, YOSEMITE CALIFORNIA

184 MILES

It isn't the best sleep. At some point, I look out of my tent to see a herd of deer staring at me, their amber eyes reflecting the light I shine in their direction. At 4AM, I wake with a start, but my search beam reveals nothing except my paranoia. There's a hint of dawn in the east, although I'm surrounded by darkness. I pack up my tent, fetch my top box, and with relief I get my bike back onto the road. I'm innocent again, now I've come out from behind my rock. I could have ridden to this point from anywhere. I ride back to the place I was at last night. The parking area is still and dark, and there's something moving by the toilet block. A large shadow: it's a bear.

I watch it go through the trash cans. This seems to be his dawn routine. I follow from a distance as he scavenges for his breakfast. I try to photograph him, but it's too dark. He heads towards the tourist trail, where I'd also intended to go, and cautiously, I continue in his tracks. I decide to sing, so he knows I'm there. There's always a song playing in my head, always, but just when I need some lyrics, there's nothing in my repertoire. I dig deep, scrape the barrel, and come up with *Teddy*

Bears' Picnic. I'm singing this for my own safety. I'd never have thought when I learnt this children's song that I'd one day be using it in such a scenario. Now he knows I'm in the vicinity, and he's not bothered at all. We both go about our business. He continues his morning forage, and I find a viewing point where I can get a photo of him and fully appreciate the silence of a wilderness sunrise. It's spectacular. The sun comes up directly behind Half Dome, shooting rays all around it. The bear climbs over some railings and wanders out of sight. Yosemite is not awake yet, and I enjoy the solitude. Everything is better for it.

I once had a girlfriend whose supportive sister came to her defence when we split up, saying I'd die sad and lonely. Sticks and stones, darling! Her sister had never been alone, ever. From parents to boyfriend to marriage to children. Don't knock what you've never had. Probably, her few moments of isolation were so alien to her, loneliness was the overpowering first sensation. She never got to experience the joy her own company could be. Actually, I never enjoyed her company either, but I'm sure she had the capacity to. Clearly, dying sad and alone was her deepest fear. I'm rarely unhappy in my solitude. It frequently enhances many situations, particularly out in the wilds to witness what nature has to offer. This scenery has far more impact without the company of the terminally oblivious.

By 9:00AM the sun is well and truly up, as are the not-so-early risers. The sound of chatter is raising. I go back to where I left my bike to ride to a less popular and populated place. My top box catches my eye. Has someone spat on it? No, but there is slobber. And there are paw marks in the dirt, plus claw scratches too. A bear has tried to get into my pic-a-nic box to take my bagels. The big question is, did this happen whilst the bike was parked here or last night when the top box was hidden thirty feet from my tent? That sure is a big surprise!

I ride to a quiet spot and make some breakfast. I love being this independent; sitting in the sunshine of a new day, surrounded by pines, and perched on a rock with a cup of steaming chai and a bear bait bagel. I brace myself for a ride into the valley to view El Capitan, one of the park's most famous monoliths. It's hard to decide which one it is, everything around me is on such a magnificent scale. I park up the bike and find a sandy river bank in the shade of a weeping willow, and there I doze for a few hours. Down here, the campsites are even more cramped. I just don't get it. They live in a vast country, you hardly ever see a row of terraced houses, everyone seems to have a garden around their detached property. Yet, they seem to willingly let themselves be crammed into a crowded campground as soon as they leave the confines of their homes to go into the "great outdoors." I do a second lap to make sure it really is as bad as it appears. It is, so I head off.

I ride round the park. I'm not riding hard, as I'm low on fuel, but every car I catch up with courteously pulls over as soon as it can. I ride to the town of Oakhurst just as I go onto reserve. It's only the third time this trip that it's happened. If only I'd managed my alcohol consumption as well. Although it's been seriously reduced since the others left. They were such a bad influence on me. I find the barbecue place that I smelt yesterday. With a full tummy, tank, and replenished supplies, I head back to the park.

I apply for a free wilderness camping permit, which involves lying about my bear-proof food carrier. It's a white lie. I could drag my proven bear-proof top box with me into the back country. I'd probably be the only trekker with a Givi suitcase: the biker-hiker. I ride to the trail head and prepare for my overnighter as best I can. I have a shoulder bag to put my water and emergency bagel in, I carry my tent and Therm-a-Rest under my arm, and the rest I leave locked on the bike.

As the path starts to climb, I change my plan and head down to the waterfalls. It's a long walk. All I really want is a small, flat area with a bit of a view, but it seems too much to ask for. The scrub undergrowth and steepness means there is nowhere to pitch a tent. The river that the falls flow into comes into view down in the canyon. I climb some rocks and see an inviting cave, inviting if I was a bear, that is. So I continue on some distance until I find a Therm-a-Rest sized area and make camp. It's perfect. I'm just above the falls, I can look over the cliff edge, if I dare, and see the river a thousand feet below. I'm on the other side of Half Dome; the quiet side, the dark side, the Silhouette Falls side. As the light fades, I decide to eat my bagel, as I don't want it attracting a resident of the cave. The camp space I have is uneven and on a slope, so I sleep half off my Therm-a-Rest to compensate. It's not ideal; it's actually much better than that.

Day 36

Modesto, California

222 miles

I don't want to miss the sunrise, but I don't want to get up yet either. This results in me periodically sticking my head out of the tent to check the sky. It's not unlike the actions of a cuckoo in a Swiss clock, only with more frequency. It's a futile technique that not only keeps me from sleeping, but also deprives me of the changing sky. Being on the morning side of Half Dome, the sun hits it directly. I'm the only person on the planet this morning with this view, and even though it wouldn't disturb anyone, I still don't feel the need to audibly express my appreciation. The textures of the granite dome in this low light are so pronounced it looks like it's been wrapped in a film of translucent veiny skin with pigmentation issues. I can see now why it's been pictured on a coin. Although a twenty-five-cent view seems to undervalue it a bit. Technically, it's only half a dome, but even so, it's worth more than a quarter.

I wander to the river that flows to the waterfall. The level has dropped, probably due to the thaw being stemmed by the cold night. The temperature of the water is much warmer than the chill in the air, and I soak myself more than I intend to. My Therm-a-Rest has got a puncture. I'm not surprised it's gone down, though, and now it's the only flat surface around here. With no food, but plenty of water, I find the path to start my hike back. I hear my first whoop of the day. Why do they feel the need to do this? Is the sound of the waterfall and the breeze in the pine trees not enough? I must be looking a bit wild now, as I don't get much response from them when we cross paths, but this is exactly what I want. The sun is up and on me now, but it's not a stifling heat, just enough to warm my bones. I still sweat with exertion as I climb, though. I stop for another water break. A solo hiker comes down towards me, followed by three deer. We both agree that hiking alone is far more rewarding and immediately go back to our solitary status. The deer can't quite gather the courage to pass me. They're only eight feet away, but standing their ground. We have to pass each other, so I sit silently, as unthreateningly as I can, and hope they will come by. More noisy hikers come down the path, and the buck runs past me only feet away, but the does are too nervous and jump into the undergrowth. As diplomatically as I can, I tell the hikers if they were quieter they would see what I have seen.

I continue up the path the last two and half miles to where my Connie is waiting for me. I have a wonderful sense of achievement as I slowly organise the luggage on my bike. I stop at the same place I did yesterday, for the same breakfast, and then head back to the valley. It's full of smoke. The park is on fire; how exciting. I ride down into it. I can see the flames; there are fire crews and lights and sirens. I'm thinking that this must be a really big deal, until I see a sign that says "controlled burn." I'm not sure how controlled it is; I bet they just put the sign there to prevent panic and to cover up their out-of-control burn. I head out to the north. The road is uneventful, and I see people stopping to take photos of unimpressive mountains. If they think these are good, it doesn't say much for what I'm riding into. I see another refugee-style camp ground. I'm the first to admit that I'm not the most social of creatures, but I still fail to see the attraction of such high-density living, when surely the point is to get away from it. Still, I'm not going to waste any more time thinking about it.

I continue on and stop for a brief smoke-filled valley view, but when I'm ready to leave, the bike won't start. I do the usual, but it's unresponsive. I pull off the tank and seat to get to the wiring. I dismantle the clutch safety switch. All this time, bikes are passing the lay-by I'm in. There must have been fifty Harleys in the hour and a half I spent tracing wires. They're so quick to wave on the road, but not one of the motherfuckers uses his waving hand to pull in his clutch and come to my assistance. Whilst I go about diagnosing and repairing, I lose all faith in the brotherhood of biking.

I've known for a while what the new breed of Harley riders is like. I don't even need confirmation. But I'd hoped that behind their blind patriotism and fashion brand obsession there might just also be an inkling of two-wheeled solidarity. OK, you magpies, you've shown your true colours, and clearly if it's not shiny, you're not interested! When I get my bike started, I leave the park, dropping in altitude and rising in attitude. Oh, yes. They all wave again now. I don't lift my hand, although my middle finger is twitching. The temperature rises, and my blood boils. I tried to help those piss-pot helmet tossers on the ALCAN Highway, and they were above it. Overconfident and underprepared, they turned back. They are beneath my contempt. I abhor their ill-conceived ideas of what motorcycling is about. Their minds and vision are narrow, their judgement as inaccurate as the personas they impersonate. They aren't bad, they're just a bad interpretation of what they think they are. At least their unimaginative ways keep them saddled to one brand, easy to spot and easy to judge. God forbid they dilute themselves across the entire genre of motorcycling.

The heat of the plains distracts me from my downward spiral, but does nothing for my concentration. My irritability is soon replaced with fatigue. I find myself going past the BMW shop, so I stop in. It's the right decision; my assumptions and accusations are put to rest, and my faith once again restored. I'm told my tyres will be in tomorrow, and I'm recommended a hotel close by; inexpensive, with a swimming pool, and no hos.

You can't blame a company like Harley-Davidson for wanting to be successful, especially after their turbulent history. You can't blame people for buying into good marketing. Attractive branding makes for an expanding clientele. Harley sells a dream, but without direction or understanding. It's interpreted with Marlon Brando imagery and played out by posers. I shouldn't mind, and I if I give up all hope I wouldn't, but I suppose I romanticise about the past with *Easyrider Magazine* imagery from my impressionable youth. It was a time when those two wheels, powered by a once iconic V-twin, united and liberated. The engine was the heart of a beast that evoked passion and desire. These days, it's suffocated, emission conforming, and noise regulation compliant, electronically managed, and suppressed. No longer wild and unpredictable, the engine has become as regulated and manipulated as the riders. I suppose it's representative of what's happening to society in general, and I long for the way things were. It's easy to take the piss as I do, but I'd stop for any biker in need. How ironic that today's disillusionment has led me to a BMW shop, where my faith has been restored.

Chowchilla, California

133 miles

It's got to the point now where I just don't know if my bike is going to start when I press the starter button. It's not a good feeling. This morning it does, and the next time I stop is outside a shop where I buy electrical contact cleaner spray. I haven't located the fault, so all I can do at this stage is eliminate suspects. The next stop is the BMW shop. I'm really not sure what the role of the receptionist is; she is without a clue. I have to assume she was employed on her looks alone, and even they aren't that impressive. And trust me, after this long on the road, my standards have dropped dramatically. My tyres haven't arrived, so I decide to try and find a Walmart, but before I leave, another rider turns up. He's an older guy. He's interesting and informed, and I soon lose track of time, deep in conversation. It's only when a big, brown UPS truck rolls up that I realise this must be the lunchtime tyre delivery. I park my bike by the side of the workshop in the shade on the pavement and start to remove the wheels. I do it with skill and speed. I know this bike pretty well now. With pit stop efficiency, I hand over the back wheel as the front one is returned to me with sexy new rubber on it. The mechanics make fun of my filthy, stripped Kawasaki outside their upmarket shop. I tell them it gives them credibility, they should encourage such things. They don't know if I'm joking or not. Neither do I. They work into their lunch break for me and let me clean up in their washroom. With tip and taxes I'm out of there for $375 and a reinstated faith in the motorcycle fraternity.

Tomorrow is visiting day, and I have to prepare. I can't find a Walmart, so I head straight to the town of Chowchilla, which is down seventy miles of baking concrete highway, so I start work on flattening out the beautiful curved profile of my tyres immediately. There are only two motels in town: a shitty one and a Days Inn. I'm going to be here at least two nights, and my stuff will be left in my room unattended, so I opt for the better of the two. Although I prefer the palm-lined main street of the town, I decide the security of the indistinguishable motel chain is a better option. My bike is right outside my room, and across the parking area is a swimming pool.

I go back to the prison. The lieutenant I wanted to see isn't there, but I speak to another sergeant who assures me I will get in tomorrow. He says it's best to arrive early, as my processing could take longer than the other visitors.

The dress code protocol is strict, and nothing I have meets the criteria. Only certain colours are allowed: no blue jeans, no orange, no stripes, or suits with arrows on, and no combats or jewellery. So I head off to my favourite tailor and get a white, Walmart short-sleeved shirt, and whilst I'm at it, I pick up some food, baking products, and a file. It's quite a strange concept to think I'll be staying in the same room for two nights. I do my laundry and the kind of things that my "passing through" status doesn't normally allow me to do, like having perishables in the fridge. I still don't know if I'll be staying here long term. I get the feeling I won't, but I'll make a decision after the visit. I spend the afternoon by the pool, and in the evening, I remove all my friendship bracelets and earrings. I even have to take off a toe ring I have worn since I bought it in India eleven years ago. I can't even wear a ponytail tie. I don't question it; I just accept it. I think that's the attitude you have to adopt if you want to get on in prison.

Day 38

Chowchilla, California

27 miles

I'm ready to start my day at 5AM. I'm hoping the Connie will be ready to start shortly after. It's just getting light. I make some tea and rush it in anticipation of what will happen when I press the starter button. It's responsive, and I head for the highway. It's fresh, but not cold; I can just about get away with fingerless gloves. After about five miles, I pull off the highway and head east towards the first light over the Sierra Nevada Mountains. The beauty of the dawn clashes with the ominous brutality of the prison; and the brutality wins. The previously inconspicuous institution is now a glow of security lights illuminating the desert sky. As I approach, I can see the guards in the watch towers. There is no subtlety here. This is a blatant blot on the landscape. I ride into the parking area, where there is already a crowd gathered. They all watch as I ride past and park the bike. I'm glad I've been here before and have been informed as to the procedure.

I wander over to the small group of about a dozen people. Colene comes over and introduces herself to me. She got here at 9:00AM and is second in line. She's wearing a T-shirt that says "Concrete Shoes, One Size Fits All—Organised Crime." Nicely understated I think. I wonder if it meets the dress code. She introduces me to some of the others. They're all here to visit murderers and

187

are far more friendly than I expected. When they pick up on my accent, they all become even more interested and genial. After a while, a guard comes out and escorts us to the door of the visitors' centre. I'm already feeling a bit institutionalised. I would never want to be led in this direction against my will. We walk up in the order we arrived to collect our numbers. I'm given number thirteen. "I'm not a number; I'm a free man," I think to myself. Having been allotted our positions, we all have a couple of hours to kill before visiting starts. Colene says they all go to Starbucks and invites me along. I'm sure it could be very interesting, but I opt to meet them back here later.

Back in my room, I make some breakfast and double-check that my body and clothing have met the protocol. The time soon passes. When I go to leave again, several other of the hotel guests are also heading the same way. Quite lucrative it is to have a hotel so close to a prison.

Back in the parking area the word has spread, and I have a little crowd around me. They all seem to know who I am now. There is a friendly vibe here. Everyone introduces themselves to me, and they chatter and joke amongst themselves. They meet here regularly. One person announces, "I don't wanna have to do this every weekend."

"Well, you shouldn't befriend murderers then," comes the reply. At 8 AM, we're marched into the visitors' centre. As predicted, my processing takes a while. It's not looking good. There are a lot of forms for me to fill in, followed by frowning faces in front of computer screens as my details are logged and processed. I have a warrant for my arrest in Utah, an actual arrest in Sturgis, and my UK record has a few blemishes too. My hands are shaking, and I can feel a sweat coming on. I'm not a fugitive in California; the circumstances of my unresolved situation in Utah is not a federal issue. I can't be arrested here, can I? My lifestyle has never fitted into the option boxes on a form, but I remain firm, polite, gracious, and insistent. I meet the lieutenant I'd come to see yesterday. I'm able to drop the names of the other sergeants I've spoken to over the last week. He says if he had a record of me sent direct to him from my embassy, things would be easier. He needs to see proof of travel. Well, I'm here, aren't I? Last week, I couldn't prove it, as I wasn't here. Next week, my possible absence will support the case that I haven't travelled here. But today the evidence is standing right in front of you. Ta-da! Of course, I don't say that.

He offers me a two-hour visit behind glass. I haggle it up to four hours. I've come a long way, but as he points out, not specifically for this visit. It's been a bit of a vacation. I've been in the US for two and a half months. If I could prove I came to this country just to see my friend, my visiting privileges would reflect that. I don't want to push my luck. I've already done quite well to negotiate my time in prison to double the initial offer. There are more forms to fill in. It would have helped if I'd managed to spell my friend's last name correctly. I'm one of the last visitors to be processed. I even have to take my motel plastic card key out of my pocket and put it in a locker. I only have my passport with me as identification and thirteen one-dollar bills, with which I'm allowed to buy food. The highlight of any visit for the inmate is that they can eat from the cafeteria with the visitor, instead of from the usual trough.

I pass through a metal detector, and then I'm checked again. A sliding door in front of me opens, and I'm instructed to walk through it. It closes behind me. In front is another door. Above me is a watch tower. I'm in-between towering fences topped with coiled, barbed wire. It's a bit like entering the Glastonbury Festival since "the fence" went up. The second door opens, and I'm free to walk into the prison grounds. I'm unescorted and only have a vague understanding of where I have to go. I walk slowly, aware I'm being watched. What a paradox. I'm free to wander inside a prison, a place I may be breaking the law by being in. A trustee girl is tending to a flower bed. She doesn't look up. Really? I've got a new shirt on and everything, and I can't get the attention of a deprived jailbird, how humiliating.

I'm in awe of where I am. This place may not give me respect for the law, but it certainly gives me a fear of being convicted for breaking it. I walk towards the building I think is the visiting area. It appears, as I get further into the depths of the prison, that the guards become more stupid. The next one I come across sits at a desk and takes my passport. He opens it up and writes down the details of . . . my Chinese visa. I'm directed to the visiting area. When I walk in, I'm told by one of my new friends to go to the podium, where another guard sits looking over the hall. I hand him my piece of paper. He nearly overlooks the "N/C" written on it. If I'd known, I could have covered it up better. He catches it at the last minute, and instead of assigning me a table, I'm shown to a booth with a window and a phone for my "NO CONTACT" visit.

There is no one the other side of the glass. She's probably busy again. It feels intrusive to turn around and watch the other visitors in conversation at the tables, but equally staring into an empty booth seems unnatural too. I look at the reflection and watch what is going on behind me. Colene comes over and introduces me to her friend. She smiles and says, "Hi." All these so-called lowlifes and not one chav. What lovely murderers they all are, so friendly.

I'm quick to put America down for its shortcomings, but this is a major plus. They certainly have mastered a classless society. Regardless of what these people have been through, come from, or are accused of, they remain unassuming and pleasant. These are not life's winners; they have every reason to be mistrusting and angry. I'm not sure what lies beneath the surface, but in this environment the affable exterior is very reassuring. Time is passing, and I'm getting impatient. The people I met outside are telling me to go and complain. I decide to give it a little longer. She must know I'm here. Someone yells out "Tesco break"; everyone gets up and the line of women stretches behind my chair. They give me advice on what to say and do, offer me food and water and assure me she'll be here soon. It turns out they aren't going to Tescos; it's a "restroom break." Easy mistake. No worries; I wasn't allowed to bring my clubcard in anyway.

After a forty-five minute wait, she arrives, wearing a blue cotton top and trousers, her blonde hair in a bun and looking much as I remember her; maybe a little thinner. She looks healthy enough. Her complexion could use some sun, but other than that, I can't see any ill effects. Most importantly, she's upbeat. She hasn't been broken. She's still cocky and assertive. There is none of that "hands touching either side of the glass," which I was half-expecting from the prison scenes in the movies. I'm glad there isn't. She doesn't do superficial. She just sits down, picks up the phone, and so begins four hours of nonstop chatter.

I can see why my earrings had to be removed. The volume on the phone is not loud enough, and with all the background noise from the contact visits behind me, I have to put a lot of pressure on the earpiece. It would have embedded my earrings into my skull. It's even worse whenever there's a "Tesco break," as the chattering is directly behind me.

It's her attitude that is getting her through this. She says she was told by a wise lifer when she first arrived not to divulge details with other inmates. The less they know, the less power they have over you. She always was very streetwise. She's also very angry. She says "motherfucker" a lot; even more than I do when I'm drunk. There are some intrinsic things I didn't know about her case. My ignorance makes me feel embarrassed and ashamed that I hadn't done all the homework I could have.

She says it's her little TV that keeps her sane. She doesn't mingle, and she doesn't get picked on, she just remains her own uncompromising person. She has a strong sense of right and wrong. I'm not sure I agree with all she says, but I'm not here to argue. She's coping with this far better than I could. It's not for me to give advice. I'll keep my opinions to myself. She has a good lawyer and an exit strategy. It sounds realistic. She says if I choose to take this story on, her lawyer can give me a lot of background and get me the transcripts from the trials, appeals, and retrials. It makes sense, but it's a daunting task. I'd hoped to just interview her and get the story that way.

She's so certain she will be released that her concerns are more about how she will cope with re-entry into society. I tell stories of readjusting to western life after being in India, and Fairbanks after the wilderness. On some level, I can relate. It's just a pep talk, really. If she can adjust to this, she can adjust to anything.

She unravels her hair. It's long, healthy, and beautiful. She's aging gracefully. I get the obligatory "You haven't changed a bit, Flid." She talks about her experiences with the other lifers and her friend who is on death row; how these people have nothing to lose and what the guards do to try to intimidate them.

"You're going to lose 120 days 'credits,'" they warn.

"What, ya gonna keep me here another 120 days after I'm dead, motherfucker?"

She says the guards all have women issues. Why would a man want a job where he locks up women all day? She tells me how they brew alcohol in pillowcases with sugar and yeast. It seems most things are available in here. One girl had a mobile phone and got away with it for a while, until she took the ringer off silent, then the whole place got locked down. I look at the clock on the wall behind me in the reflection of the glass to see how much longer I have. Annoyingly, because it's a no contact visit, I'm not allowed to buy her food, and it seems wrong to eat in front of her. I sent her a goody bag some time ago. It was a hell of a procedure, as I had to fill in the products she wanted online, and then the site wouldn't accept my overseas credit card. Her allocated provisions are too limited for her long hair, and this brings us to the topic of hair care products, and another half an hour flies past.

She describes the irony of her refusing to engage with their drug programme, but they want her to take drugs for her depression. The girl in front of me is not depressed, she just has her ups and downs. I say, "We all do; it's called life. Oh, I don't mean a life sentence. Shit, sorry!" We both laugh. Nothing is said forthright about the book. No empty promises. I suppose she avoids them, having been let down so many times before. But she's keen, and that's as much as I get. It's as much as she wants to give. Eventually, I'm tapped on the shoulder. I've done better than I expected. It was a simple, honest, and unemotional goodbye. She has survived so far and will continue to.

It's easier to get out of the prison than it was to get in. I exit into the 44° Celsius heat. I ride straight to a diner and order the cold beer she craves so badly. I lift it to my mouth, and before taking a sip, I toast her under my breath. This is the single saddest moment of the day.

So now what? I don't think I could get another visit, and even if I do, it's not going to advance the story. I can get the transcripts and read them anywhere. There's no point in staying in California. The plan has faltered. I suppose I'll head back to Denver now. Too much bloody freedom, that's my problem. I call Jonathan and speak to DRob too. He flies home in two days. I won't; don't want to make it back that quick. I suppose the journey has begun again. Where next?

DAY 39

LAS VEGAS, NEVADA

509 MILES

I wake at dawn to slamming doors. The prison visitors are leaving. I look out of the window. Yep, that's beautiful. Then I go straight back to bed. Next time I wake up, I go outside and jump into the pool. I feel guilty about every decision I'm free to make, after what I witnessed yesterday. I'm leaving. I feel guilty for that too. For so long, I've been entertaining the prospect of staying around here, writing all week and visiting at weekends. It's such a challenge to get into the prison, and pretty daunting to work on the story without visits. There's always been an element of uncertainty, but equally now the plan is, if not aborted, at least postponed. I seem to be a little lost.

There is only one thing I can think of to do, and that is to ride. The Connie seems to be in full agreement. I'm in California; its sunny, I have some money, no plans, no commitments, and no one is expecting me to be anywhere. I head out onto the burning highway. Marillion plays in my ears. I clutch at my throttle and head south. No one can get hold of me now. The riding day starts with one long, straight hit, but after a hundred miles, I'm no longer able to resist the temptation of the hilly terrain to the east, so I take a left towards it. I pass vines hanging heavy with red grapes, but the land beyond the irrigation is parched and barren. As I approach the hills, the road starts to twist and turn, and at last, I get to scrub in my new tyres. I can scrape my side stand on lefthanders, but I can't seem to get it as low on the other side. I don't wind the engine up the rev range often, but when I do, it gives a screaming, responsive roar, and the bike transforms into something quite thrilling.

I decide I'll try and find the Sequoia National Forest that's on my map. It's a half-hearted decision. I know I'm on the wrong road, but I don't really mind. It's fun, and I'm out in the boonies now. There's so little traffic even the car drivers wave. Well, the ones whose hands aren't webbed do at least. The road continues to twist until I really don't know which direction I'm heading. I ride into a canyon. What a pleasing little bonus. I've decided my favourite aspect of motorcycle travel is the unexpected scenery. It's like finding money on the ground. I'm going this way anyway, and now my day just got better. It's hot in the canyon, but it's fun. I'm lost, I suppose, but I have time and petrol and nothing to worry about. Finally, I'm spat out onto Highway 58, which takes me into the Mojave Desert. It's late July, 4PM, baking hot, and so very dry.

Now it's my turn to whoop out loud. I have just ridden my 10,000th mile this trip! I find a town which is far less significant than my celebration. I buy a big, fat, cold beer. They tell me in the shop that it's a nice day for a motorcycle ride—hmm! 46° Celsius, rising to 49°. I take my beer to the entrance ramp of the highway and gulp it down. I feel the elation of my achievement blend with the sensation of my cold beverage and the heat of my deserted surroundings. This morning I felt lost, this afternoon I got lost, and now, with no real plan or place, I've come across that elusive feeling of satisfaction. Today, I can thoroughly recommend being me.

IPod and helmet go back on, and I head off. I think I may be going crazy from the heat, or perhaps the beer. The needle of my little stick-on temperature gauge has gone past the highest figure of 120° Fahrenheit and has hit the stop. I'm rocking out to the music. I don't even feel hot with my jacket on. It keeps me cooler than having flesh exposed to the sun. Although, where my sleeves have ridden up, my forearms are burnt. I reach Barstow as the light fades, but the heat remains. I join the Interstate that will take me to Vegas. Feeling wild and hardcore, with my ten-thousandth mile behind me, tonight this feels like a place that is just right. The black night radiates its cloak of concealment. Alone on the fast road, I wonder if I'm the only living being on the planet: lawless and nomadic. From the Arctic Circle to the high desert; this may be nothing like the Dalton Highway was, but there are similarities. These are the different natures of the journey and my reactions to them. Instead of heading through wondrous landscapes towards the hidden treasure of the polar oil fields, this road has a more easily reached, but equally reckless horizon. But although the temptations of Las Vegas's riches may entice, they rarely deliver.

The city starts to sparkle, and like so many people before me, I'm drawn towards it. The only way I win in Vegas is not to gamble. I know where the cheap hotels are, and that's the way that pays in this town. Having checked in, I have an unexplainable urge to cruise the strip. I take a shower and an accidental three-hour doze. This city never sleeps. It's early, and I could go out and play. I'm hungry too, but I decide to stay home. I still don't know where I'm going tomorrow. The thought of returning to fitting kitchens and bathrooms is not a pleasant one. I'd intended to write; that was the second part of this trip, to document the story of unfair incarceration, drugs, deaths, and injustices. Opportunities appear every now and again, but they still have to be acted on. To ghost write my friend's story may be a daunting task, but the thought of going back to plumbing in toilets on all fours on someone else's bathroom floor is a demoralising one. Leaning over any toilet, be it due to work or too much pleasure, is never a desirable position to find oneself in.

Day 40

Springdale, Utah

174 miles

It's rained in the night, how unlikely; it's not cooled anything off, just brought about high levels of humidity. Now I get to ride the strip, but in the hot light of day Vegas can't hide it's tackiness behind an illumination of illusion. At a red light, a Harley rider says he wants to ride with me, but I'm not going his way. I asked him first which way was his, as mine was always going to be the other way. In the last ten days so much has happened, and the transformation to lone rider status has become very appealing. I have no wish to change it. I take a familiar highway in a familiar direction to a very familiar place. This will be my tenth visit to Zion National Park. I ride through a storm, but the rain is warm, and nothing seems to be bothering me lately, whether intense heat or soaking rain. The bike hasn't cut out once since I bought that can of contact spray, and I'm yet to take the lid off. I stay at a place I've stayed before, and when the afternoon turns to evening, I ride without a helmet to the park's visitor centre and take the shuttle bus into the canyon.

Once again, my lone status is rewarded as I walk through the canyon along the side of the river. I'm surprised how quiet the place is. I wade in the river and find a rock to sit on, where I can just gaze around me. It's overcast and humid;

not that it matters to me. My pace has slowed so much this last week, and my appreciation has risen too. It was humbling to visit the prison. These timeless surroundings have been inhabited for eight thousand years, and the formation started 150 million years ago. I don't think I could have found a more extreme place to contemplate a life sentence.

Walking on quietly, I pass deer without disturbing them. Foxes stop in their tracks and stare like they've been caught red-handed; lizards are on the move as the rocks cool down, and frogs start their evening chorus.

Not for the first time, I picture myself living here. Sometimes I forget what time of year it is. I've been through so many weather conditions in the last six weeks, from Alaskan October-like suspense and the Canadian constant rains to the off-the-scale heat of the desert. I send a text to DRob. He's just boarding the plane home. The English spring I left will be autumn when I return. Back in my little room, I get out the map and try to find a road back to Denver that I haven't ridden before. It's a bit tricky.

DAY 41

FLAGSTAFF, ARIZONA

386 MILES

There have been days, many of them, when the alarm would wake me, and I'd go straight to the window and stare out into the darkness to see if rain was falling through the orange beams of the street lights. This would determine how I dressed for the ride to work. Those were the hungry years; no heating, boil-in-the-bag curry, and a copy of *Kerrang!* on a Wednesday as my only treat. It's raining outside my window this morning, so I shelter under the duvet for another two hours, enjoying the luxury of later life as the storm passes by. When I do leave my room, directly outside is a giant cliff face. I just can't imagine how living here you could ever wake up depressed. Surely this magnificent backdrop to the day must stimulate every sense, regardless of your faith or philosophy. The imposing scale of magnitude and time has to keep life's inconveniences in perspective. We are all so insignificant in the great scheme of things.

When a graph on a computer screen triggers a black day on the stock markets, I often think that those people in suits who throw themselves out of the windows of their high-rise offices should take a trip to Zion to help them see how we're all nothing but a blip in time. Life is only about food and shelter; everything else is a bonus.

I check out of my shelter and walk to the restaurant. It's so full I can't get breakfast, so I ignore basic needs and go straight to the bonuses. I get fuel and ride without a helmet into the park and up towards the tunnel. It's warm and sunny now. I'm not really taking pictures; I know it's impossible to capture this place. It's best just to take it all in and enjoy the moment through my own eyes, instead of a lens.

Exiting Zion is like leaving a buffet dinner. I've feasted well. I can't take in anymore, but I know that once I've digested this visual overload, I'll be hungry for it all over again. I head south out of the park, as I still have time and no desire at all to stop this journey.

Sometimes, not liking the extremely popular can come with its own credibility, as long as it's possible to articulately explain your reasons. The movie, *Titanic*, and the band, U2, are a couple of examples that are almost as acceptable to dislike as they are to be fans of. There are other things, though, where it's best to just play along with the general consensus. I know from experience that dissing the Grand Canyon just makes me sound like I'm being contrary for the sake of it. I first saw it when I was twenty-one, and my immediate reaction was disappointment. It has to be the most over-hyped hole in the ground ever. Perhaps it's just too big for my mind to comprehend, or maybe it's just shit. It's definitely very big. I absolutely love canyons, but standing on a vista point looking across a chasm of time and space leaves me feeling like I'm missing something. I know of people who have taken ten-day raft trips down the Colorado River, which flows through the canyon, and they've said it's been the highlight of their lives. I don't doubt it, and I'm sure being down there, looking up, is a very different sensation to just standing looking out over it. However, I feel it deserves a second chance, so, with much lower expectations, I ride down to the north rim for a different perspective.

There are storms on the horizon, but they're isolated, and against the big sky they really don't look that threatening. I do manage to ride into one, though. It turns out to be very heavy, and the rain puddles in the folds of my jacket, then overflows into my crotch. Never much of a joy enhancer, that one. The bad visibility has the tourist traffic slowing, and that means the rain drops on me and doesn't bounce off my fairing with the force of momentum. When I get out the other side of the rainclouds, I stretch my legs beyond my fairing and start the drying process, as I wind down the road to the view point. Predictably, it's quite a popular area; all chalets and souvenirs, campervans and crowds. I walk down the concrete path that winds around the outer rim. I find a secluded rock out of sight, but not, unfortunately, out of earshot. I sit for half an hour and look out over the canyon stretching down below me. Yeah, that's enough. It's OK, I suppose, but it still doesn't really do it for me.

I head back to Highway 89 and continue south. See, this is loads better, the road follows a long, red reef of rock, and there are vast open spaces. I think it could be considered a lucky coincidence that I don't like the popular and the populated, because if it were only one of the two, life could be quite frustrating. Still feeling somewhat indecisive as to direction and destination, I decide to visit Sedona. It's the place that the patch club girl I met in Homer, Alaska, said was her favourite place in all of the fifty states that she'd visited. I expect Arizona to be like a furnace; it does have that reputation. I've met construction workers from Phoenix who have relocated to Denver with all their tools and an excessive amount of work lights. The reason for this is they work the night hours, as it's just too hot to do anything during the day. Even in Denver in summer, I've picked up tools left in the sun and burnt my hand on them. But now I'm saved from a scorching, due to some cloud cover, although I'm still at altitude, so that could all change.

I decide to call it a night in Flagstaff. It's not as late as I thought, as I've crossed a time zone, but I also come across a street of motels, all competing on price. I find a particularly squalid room at a very low price. It smells a bit, so I sit outside on the porch with the door open, having a beer and trying to air the room in the process. Technically, its 8PM, but it's dark, so I take myself off to bed and try not to think of all the previous activity the mattress has seen.

Day 42

Cortez, Colorado

372 miles

At 2AM, I get a text from DRob. He's got jet lag. It takes me an hour to get back to sleep. He's four and a half thousand miles away, and he still wakes me in the night. In the morning, it's pissing down. It's not an exciting storm; it's just rain. I head out onto Route 66, another iconic American attraction that draws people away from the more remote beauty of the land. This journey has been full of kicks, and the only way Route 66 will give me more is if I get off on wall-to-wall motels and souvenir shops. There are hundreds of them, although I think I managed to find the worst one of them all. Sedona is OK, but not exactly in the wow category. It's touristy and closed. Of the three restaurants I try, not one is open. I think the attraction of the place is based on the experience you have here, more than the location itself. I don't see a low sun shining onto red sandstone formations; I just see rain. I also think I'm full now. What else can I possibly see that will wow me? I have to turn around and go back the way I came, which is exactly what I did at the Arctic Circle. Although now it doesn't quite have the same excitement of uncertainty attached to it.

There's a lot of spray from the traffic. I can't find anywhere to eat, and it's turning into one of those horrible rides where I can't seem to stop and I don't particularly want to keep going. I end up eating a pre-packed roast beef sandwich in a wet car park. It's a wholly unsatisfying experience. I do notice there appears to be some sunshine ahead of me, though, and as I head towards Tuba City, the cloud lifts and the land clears. I'm back in grand scale territory, but with the bonus of it being unexpected. There are some stunning cloud formations across the panoramic sky, and as I head north towards Monument Valley, the mushrooming clouds frequently bring me to a stop just to try and capture their uniqueness. In the centre of the big sky is a grey storm with sheets of water like pillars holding up the low cloud. The road twists left and right, but ultimately heads right for it.

I ride towards the lightning, the teeming rain bouncing off the road. I can count down the seconds before I hit it. It's instantly blinding and bruising. The intensity has me keeping momentum to deflect it off the fairing, but the visibility is ... well, it's gone. There's a flash of lightning to my right, but I barely hear the crack of thunder, as the rain is hammering so loudly onto my helmet. I've ridden into an incredibly violent and powerful weather tantrum. I wonder if I should have stayed behind this. The rain is a solid wall, and the road is swamped. I have to slow down, although I just want to break on through to the other side.

There is no other traffic; not that I can see anything. It feels like riding through a paintball battle; the impact is hurting me through my jacket. Then there is a simultaneous crack and flash ten feet to my left, and I feel a tingle in my fingers. It strikes me that the rain is so intense and dense that the lightning has conducted through it. I've felt the shock. It energises me. I start shouting, "Is that it? Is that the best you can do? Come on motherfucker, call yourself a storm? This is just drizzle. Missed me again. Gimme some more lightning!" And then I'm out the other side. It ends as quickly as it started. The road is dry, and I can see for miles again. But I could be dead, and this might be what the journey towards the bright light is like. When I stop for fuel, tumbleweed blows across the station forecourt. This could be the afterlife, but then the cashier takes my money, so I think that I'm still of this earth. Just when I thought I couldn't be wowed any more, I was, if not struck, I at least made a connection with a lightning bolt. I can tick that one off the list now, as the proverb suggests it's unlikely to happen again.

The wind gets up. I think the storm is chasing me. I shouldn't have taunted it. I'm not giving it a second chance. As though it's something personal, I speed out of the fuel station, riding from the storm. I think the strike has affected me; that and this wide open space. I don't want to be the man with the cloud over his head. I ride into the wild, blue yonder.

The unmistakable formations of Monument Valley protrude from the flat land; like a police car in my mirror, I can't stop looking at them. This lasts until the Utah border, then I can't stop looking for police cars. I run the gauntlet, well the fingerless glove at least, and cross back into the state my licence plate inaccurately says I'm from. Tired, hungry, and badly dehydrated, once again I opt for a hotel. There are plenty of bikers staying here. Most have out-of-state plates. My plate says I'm local, which is really quite deceitful. I almost want to say where I've been; almost, but actually smug silence and a six pack seem more appealing.

DAY 43

DENVER, COLORADO

479 MILES

I wake while it's still dark and can't get back to sleep. So I tell myself if it's gone 5AM, I'm going to get up. It is, and so I do. I walk outside to judge the temperature. Yes, there's definitely an adequate amount. I select from my limited wardrobe, based on comfort, as colour is yet to feature in the day. I don't need to be on the road this early, but that's the great advantage of lone travel. I don't need to wait for someone else to stop sleeping. When the skies lighten, it coincides with my entry onto the Million Dollar highway—a cliff-hugging road, which rises to 11,000 feet before dropping into the town of Ouray. Although glamorous in name and location, a million dollars would only pay for the construction of 440 feet of the M25. Still, both roads do have a ring to them.

"Colorado on steroids," the phrase comes back to me. Alaska may be the last frontier, but once again, I'm riding past snow-capped mountains, through deep gorges, past waterfalls, and zigzagging up mountain passes. After the expansive landscapes the roads of this trip have taken me through, it's a credit to Colorado that it still has the ability to seem awesome.

When I was nine years old and first met Jonathan in the school playground, he told me how he would spend his summer holidays with family in Colorado, where the Rocky Mountains were. With primary school imagination, I visualised a log cabin among pine trees, set against sheer grey cliffs and snowy peaks. I'm seeing that reality now. This is the *Rocky Mountain High* that John Denver sang about on the records and that Jonathan's dad played when I would stay over at their house. Another popular song of my childhood was Supertramp's *Breakfast in America*, which is just what I need now. For the first time since I split company with DRob, I order eggs. They leave a funny taste in my mouth that I can't get rid of.

I start down a dirt road shortcut. It looks like a challenge I don't need to face, so I turn back to the tarmac and enjoy the sweeping curves of the smooth surface instead. I'm riding hard, the engine howls, and the tyres handle it perfectly. This style of riding makes the bike very thirsty, and I stop to fill up in Gunnison. I put so much fuel in that I'm entitled to a free car wash, but I think I'd like to stay dry today; on the outside at least. I've still got some beers in my top box, and that horrible taste lingers in my mouth. The solution seems obvious.

In the middle of doing the washing up one day, the doorbell rings. With soapy hands, I leave the sink wearing my novelty, red-tinted John Lennon glasses.

"What are you wearing those for?" my friend asks.

"Because it makes the colour of the dishes different."

"You have to ring every last ounce of pleasure out of everything, don't you?" she says.

I pull down a side road and stop by a river to have a top-box-temperature Corona. As I sip it, I realise I've stopped in this lay-by before. It's at the end of a winding road, where I once caught my breath and rejoiced at the skinny credibility strips on the edges of my worn tyres. This road seems like the perfect last hurrah, one final pleasurable ride in the trip. When I go to start the Connie, nothing happens. "Oh, come on." It hasn't done this for a week. I probably won't have to press that button again today. But the thought is all it takes; the engine fires up. The road is not how I remember it, or perhaps in this direction it doesn't deliver. It's an unsatisfactory hundred-mile detour. I ride across the San Luis Valley. It's basically a dip. The land is flat, and the mountain ranges on either side are so far away that progress seems slow, and surreptitiously, the needle on the speedometer rises. This is why it's notorious for speed traps, and, sure enough, I see a cop coming towards me, and I do my last hard braking of the trip, with the final destination signposted and in sight, I think again about the story I've been wanting to tell.

Where am I now? I'm not home; I'm still homeless. I'm not away; I've been coming here for twenty-five years. I'm not transient; I've got this address on my documents. I'm not resident; my visa runs out in a month. 11,575 miles; it seems momentous, but I've only been to another state. I'm not sure where this leaves me. A completed circuit, but an incomplete plan; an achievement with an element of failure. It shows the infinite void between wanting to write a story and finishing the last chapter, discovering that my ambitions far exceed my ability. There is little glory in my return; it only emphasises my failures, and now there is nothing else to distract me.

Jonathan and Tammara aren't home. I stand my camera on the dustbin, open the top box, get out my last beer, and toast the journey's end on self-timer. The house is unlocked, but the confines suffocate me. I instantly feel the cabin fever. I spend the evening sitting outside in the driveway, looking at the bike. It's a kind of decompression stop. My ears ring; it's like an echo of the running engine. I watch the clouds pass; they're moving, and I'm not. I realise how slowly they cross the sky; how slowly time passes when you're anchored down.

Eighteen months later, my friend is released from the Valley State Prison for Women. Six months after that, I ride the Connie back to California (having bought a second-hand CDI for it and curing the starting issue). For two intense weeks, I interview her and document twenty years of significant moments in her life—before, during, and after her incarceration. The easiest bits to write are the periods of her life in which I've had a walk-on part. A spark of realisation occurs. As we progress, I become aware that if I'm going to ghost write her prison story, she has to be as dedicated in getting me to the end sentence as she was in getting to the end of hers. I don't have the imagination to write fiction. Facts, truth, and sincerity are my objectives. It's a fascinating story, but my peripheral view is all I'm prepared to tell. It's a part of my trip; these are the experiences I've had on and off the bike. It's my story; what I've seen, what I've experienced, what I've thought. I wouldn't expect anyone to tell it like I can. I don't think I can tell anyone else's story like they could.

DRob's Triumph, it turns out, had been running on two cylinders for a lot of the journey, because the idiots who did the 24,000-mile service hadn't fitted the coil on the spark plug properly. That lack of spark and unburnt fuel "washed" the cylinder, and that's why it used so much oil. Jonathan's dad continued to fire on all cylinders for some time to come and lived to hear the tales of future bike trips. Whilst researching and recalling this trip, I discovered the statistics below. I'm embarrassed by how anal it makes me look, but it also shows how, at the time, it was the biggest thing I'd ever done.

I wonder if, like the old man on the ALCAN Highway, we'll do the trip all over again in 2044.

STATISTICS:

43 days on the road

11,575 miles

65 fuel stops

1,050 litres

$985 on fuel

12 US states

3 Canadian provinces

0 bike drops/fall offs

3 near misses (car U-turn in front of me/water tank/lightning)

1 puncture

0 speeding tickets (he, he!)

0 times wearing heated trousers

3 times wearing heated vest

0 plasters/band aids used

58 hours sleep lost due to snorers

1 wild animal attack (wasp sting)

1,000s of photos and even more smiles

Total spent on the road = $6,215

SOLITUDE AND WAVES

"I don't want a pickle, just want to ride on my motorcycle."
Arlo Guthrie

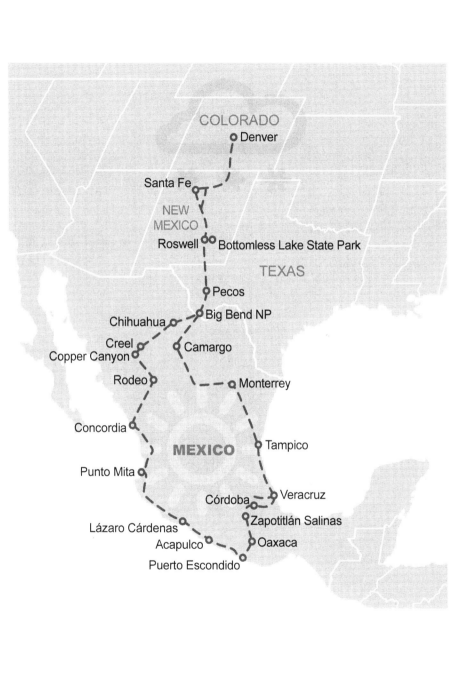

COLORADO
o Denver

Santa Fe o

NEW
MEXICO

Roswell oo Bottomless Lake State Park

TEXAS

o Pecos

o Big Bend NP

Chihuahua o

Creel o
Copper Canyon o
o Camargo

Rodeo o

o Monterrey

Concordia o

MEXICO

o Tampico

Punto Mita o

o Veracruz
Córdoba o
o Zapotitlán Salinas

Lázaro Cárdenas o
o Oaxaca
Acapulco o

Puerto Escondido o

NOVEMBER 2012

DRob is now married. Jonathan is a father. And me? Well, my lifestyle is much the same; only the sex is more sporadic, the drugs are medicinal, and the rock 'n' roll is considered classic. Initially by circumstance, but now by preference, I'm more of a solo rider. I discovered this during my trip to Mongolia two years ago.

I'd recently been invited onto a stand for the nine-day Motorcycle Live Show at the NEC in Birmingham. It felt exciting and glamorous. Walking in with my laminated pass past the hoards waiting at the gates is the closest I've ever been to experiencing "backstage" priority. My hair was brushed and my clothes smart, and I fantasised that I had VIP status. Security would open doors for me that said "no entry to public," and privileged and proud, I'd be granted entry into the hushed exhibition halls of gleaming bikes and Lycra clad models. This would never happen at B&Q. I loved the illusion, but the reality was shattering, both physically and mentally.

I am there to basically "cold sell" my book, *In Search of Greener Grass*, at the time my only book, handing out leaflets to the passing throng and trying to persuade them to part with their money by buying a book all about me. "Read about me. Look what I've done. Me, me, me. It's all about me." When my self-esteem was low, at least that's what it felt like I was saying. But on the good days, I would exclaim, "Read this, be inspired, encouraged, informed, entertained." But it only took one arsehole to knock that confidence out of me. I can't do sales. I can ride motorbikes. I can ride them far, and I'm quite good at writing about it all too.

But sales; that's not my gig. I ride alone. I write alone. I live alone. And no aspect of that lifestyle had prepared me to approach passing strangers in an environment of competitive commerce. Some people were receptive; some were just plain rude. That's cold selling for you. God, I'm only handing out flyers! You'd think by the reaction of some of the miserable gits that I was giving out parking tickets. Yes, of course I wrote the book myself. Yes, it is good. That's why I'm standing here plugging my product. It's not some faceless, Hooray Henry gap-year blog converted to an e-book and slapped on Amazon for forty-nine pence. Luckily for me, I had the master, Mr. Manicom, as a mentor, without whom I'd still be working like a waitress in a cocktail bar.

When I left the bike show bubble, I noticed that outside it was Christmas. In the kitchen and bathroom fitting trade, Christmas can mean a rush job before the rellies arrive for the festive revelling, but sometimes it's just dead. And this year it was definitely the latter. There was a lull in the fitting world that I sometimes fit in. I instinctively called a letting agent. Within three days, my house was rented, within four days, I was on a flight to Denver, and within six days, I had a bike to ride.

I've never coped well with the seven-hour time difference,, and in my dark Denver basement beneath Jonathan's family home at four in the morning, I would slowly become conscious of where I was and what I was supposed to be doing. Bike purchasing came to the forefront of my mind, and then there was no getting back to sleep.

I'm not staying here. I'm not going to exchange a British winter for a sub-zero, high-altitude Colorado one. I'm going to take advantage of the bike-unfriendly weather and my cash buyer status to prey on the desperate seller. Another thing in my favour is that it's been well-documented and hyped that the world is going to end soon. On the 21st of December, the Mayan calendar will run out, and I want be at a pyramid party in Mexico when it does. I've had deadlines before, but this one is quite significant. I haven't got a long trip planned; more a long break. Well, that's assuming the world doesn't end. Somewhere between prolonged life presumptions and planetary fatality, one way or another, I'll be resting, but first I need a ride.

There was an absolute bargain, fully-kitted-out KLR. It was out of my price range, but it wanted for nothing. The ad even says, "Ride to Mexico tomorrow." It was calling my name. In fact, it's almost too lovely, with its Jesse bags, up-rated 685cc engine, and quality accessories; all useful bling that I could just about justify; call it excessive necessities, practically practical. I'm riding into Mexico alone though. I didn't have any problems the last time, but I wasn't Mr. Flash then, and I wasn't riding alone either. At least not at first. It doesn't have to be a KLR. I look at a KTM 640 too. It's a bit beaten up; the seller had been to Alaska and back on it. Having seen what Alaska can do to a vehicle, I knew I should never buy a bike that has seen dirt up the Dempster.

Then a three-year-old KLR comes up on Craigslist. It hadn't been ridden very well; dropped on both sides resulting in a lot of broken plastic, bent levers, and road scars. In its 11,000-mile life, it had definitely seen some horizontal travel. It had no crash bars, and the pristine hand guards were clearly an afterthought. However, it came with some soft panniers and was worth some hard bargaining. In the concrete underground of a downtown car park beneath an apartment block, I looked it over with noncommittal observations. Neither the owner nor I know if I really want it. He tells me someone else is coming to take a look later. If this tactic was supposed to make me grab it, it actually had the reverse effect. There were plenty of defects to point out and I bid low.

"This evening's viewer has already offered $3,000," he tells me.

"Take that then," I said. "It's not worth any more than $2,800 to me. I've got another one to look at. Call me if he doesn't buy it." I know he's lying. He assumes I'm not.

For £1,750, I have just bought the newest bike I have ever owned. For an extra £500, I could have bought the loveliest, accessorised and attractive. The problem with attractive is other people covet it too. I don't want to be put in a position where I'm fighting a thief's dishonesty any more than I want to be fighting for a woman's honour. Frankly, I'd rather not give a damn. Bling is a thing I can do without, I tell myself, but I still wish I had it. My next dilemma and wrong decision results in my buying the cheapest tyres available. I know Mefos are superior, but I get myself a pair of Kendas. Not a nice surprise; neither is how long they take to arrive. America is big, and next-day delivery is not an automatic option. The delay brings on a severe case of procrastination, and I can't seem to get motivated. I want to be in Mexico in time for the end of the world. The end is drawing nigh, and I'm still in Denver; my ammunition of excuses not to leave far from being exhausted. The panniers are next to useless, and the zips are broken. I can't find an alternative. It's freezing in the garage, and preparation and packing are a chore I keep putting off. I wish I'd just spent the extra to get the other bike, so I could have been in Mexico yesterday.

I don't really expect adventure; I did the same trip last year. This isn't aimless wandering; I know exactly where I'm going. There's no company; this is just me escaping a winter and planning a spring, whilst someone else pays my mortgage for me. I'm downplaying it to myself, but the reality remains. I'm riding off across international borders on a bike; fun and sun are probably going to be unavoidable.

Five days after I order them, the tyres arrive, along with the forecasted blizzard. I fit them with numb fingers and split my taut and brittle skin. Snow blows in under the garage door and heaps up outside it. I'm trapped. The end of the world will just have to happen without me. I sleep on the couch by the fire. A transition is taking place. I've moved from duvet to sleeping bag. A Wednesday evening alone in the house, and I feel myself mentally preparing for the road to my Mexican rest, and the big chill that precedes it.

Day 1

Santa Fe, New Mexico

386 miles

It's hard to put my finger on any specific part of the transformation. Possibly it's the sleeping on the couch by the embers in the log burner. Perhaps it's the realisation that the snow is actually easier to deal with than the threat of snow. In the thirty years I've been visiting Denver, every impending storm has been sensationalised, every snowfall exaggerated, and the predicted low temperature overestimated. The facts are outside the window, and at first light, I know I'm leaving today. Or at least I'm going to try and leave today.

I have the place to myself and have had for two days. Food supplies are low and all alcohol expended. I've got to head out into the snow regardless; imminent starvation forces my departure.

I haven't ridden the bike at all since putting the tyres on, and my loading technique errs on the clumsy side of creative. I have a big, plastic tool box bolted to the rear rack. The throw-over panniers are cable-tied shut where the zip has broken. And to give myself more carrying capacity, I find a smaller pair of panniers, which I have thrown over the tank like obese tank saddlebags. It's cumbersome; the contents unorganised. Sitting on it in the garage, my system could be seen as functional, the reality will come with the riding, but ultimately it's cost nothing.

This is a test ride, and if I or nothing else falls off, then this is also where the journey begins. It's a bright, sunny morning, although the temperature is yet to rise above freezing. Outside the garage door, snow has blown eight inches deep and drifted across the steep and winding driveway.

This is baptism by ice for my virgin, dual-sport tyres. Though I'm not sure the thought of winter sports were built into the design. With feet out, I leave a tri-track trail as I slither down to the dirt road. I know already that I'm committed. I now have two choices: leave the bike where it is until the spring thaw or keep going, because there's no way I can get back up the snaking, snow- covered, and tyre-compacted drive. OK, so here I go then! It's a decision made due to lack of options. I'm going to Mexico, via an ice packed dirt road that leads to a slush covered valley road. The next seven miles, although ploughed, are also snow covered, the surface a combination of drift and traffic compression. I'm not anticipating the journey to come. There are no wandering thoughts of destinations, just extreme concentration all the way to the fuel station. The first fill up and my boots are already encrusted with snow. I can see the questions in the eyes of the cashier, but he knows better than to ask, and I have nothing but intentions to tell. When I reach the main road, I stop at the first town for some last minute supplies; a puncture repair kit and a bicycle pump. I lumber into the shop, not even bothering to remove my tank bag of valuables, passport, money, and a big, fat, easy-to-steal camera. It's too cold to be wary; too frozen to thieve.

I get onto Interstate 25 south; lots of southness is needed. The warmth of the highway traffic has a thawing effect on the road that creates a dirty spray with blackout qualities. I'm constantly having to wipe my visor before it dries to a coating that would provoke the uninspired yet irresistible comment of "clean me" if it were on the back of a transit. Luckily, the spray doesn't last long, because the snow returns. It, too, has blinding effects as blackout turns to whiteout. I feel no benefit from my heated grips, as my left hand is passing in front of my face with such frequency it looks like I'm waving off a cruise ship.

As the miles continue, the snowy, white plains turn to their pre-precipitation brown until only the Rocky Mountains on my right show any signs of winter. "Well, that was easy," I think to myself. Perhaps too soon.

The temperature drops again as I approach the town of Trinidad, a name that suggests I should at least be able to feel my toes, if not touch them. I need a warm up. I ask the filling attendant to recommend a restaurant, which she does, and I reluctantly take the recommended route down the authentic cobblestoned main street. It's slick with packed snow, and I have little traction as I slide past Christmas attractions, lights, and seasonal shop windows. The restaurant sign says, "Open daily from 7 until 9, seven days a week." The snow covered parking lot is unspoilt by tyre tracks; they say, "Except today." I end up in a designer café where yummy mummies coo over babies and don't bat an eye at the price of the pretentious food. The shiver of my ride turns to a hollow shudder. Chalked on the blackboard and displayed behind glass is a choice of pastries with something organic and inadequate wrapped inside. They're all given multi-syllable names and multi-figure prices. I settle for a four dollar hot chocolate. It's as disappointing as a mother half my age. I take off my boots and massage my cramped toes, whilst babies cry and mothers soothe them. A wide-rimmed receptacle is brought to my table. It resembles a saucer with a handle and is as shallow as the clientele. A blob of synthetic cream floats around the brown puddle in my so-called cup like scrunched up toilet paper. The excessive surface area means the sorrowful contents cool and congeal before I get to the bottom of my regretful purchase. Unseen and unthawed, I take my bitterness back to my bike. Let's try more of that southness. At the next junction is a Mexican restaurant. If I couldn't speak the language I wouldn't have asked the filling attendant's recommendation and gone into town, and I'd be in there now. But I'm not stopping again.

I head into New Mexico, hoping for a drop in altitude, but I'd need to bear left for that to happen. I don't want diversions; I want fast distance and a direct route. I stay on the highway, but annoyingly, the stupid southbound highway turns. I start riding into the sunset, and then the red sky is on my left. What the fuck? I look at the map in my tank bag, but I still have my shades on and my hands are too cold to remove them. I gain altitude and begin to lose temperature. My heated waistcoat and grips have been doing their thing all day, allowing me to do mine and ride all day. Now, with the loss of light and a sense of heading back to the frozen north, I'm feeling the coldness as though fully exposed. I will the highway to turn left through the next gap in the ridge that hides the last of the evening light from me. When it eventually does, it's too late. I'm frozen to the point of pain. Santa Fe is an hour beyond my extended discomfort zone. I pull off the highway, and at the first red light, I unclamp my frozen fist from my left grip, remove my glove, lift my visor, which has misted up from my short, shivering breaths, and take off my shades. Now I can see how dark it is. The light has turned to green. The last two miles to a motel are not a pleasant delayed gratification, but an agony of endurance.

It would be so much easier if I could be given a ground floor room and a key card that actually unlocks the door. The second trip to reception does nothing to warm me up. "That's frustrating," observes a bystander, whose innocence is questionable. Even the sprint up and down the stairs with filthy, frozen panniers doesn't get the blood flowing. It's not a damp cold, not an in-your-bones crippling cold, just a blasting, freeze-dried kind of cold. It doesn't last long once I close the door on the night and let the heater rumble its way to thaw. My toes are still cramped from the curling—an instinctive, but physically impossible and futile attempt to retract them into my feet—to escape the freezing air that turned the wind chill in my Alpinestars to below bearable. They weren't stars of this alpine environment.

Twelve days ago, Santa Fe recorded their coldest day of the year. This evening it has warmed up to -8° Fahrenheit. Whilst I'm suffering this journey, a crazy Dutchman I know is breaking records riding his R1 across the frozen polar sea on the north Alaskan coast. There is always someone who has it harder and that's what keeps me going.

Day 2

Pecos, Texas

362 MILES

My toes still hurt, but it's down to strain rather than frostbite. Yesterday's cold had them curled up like cringing. It's early. I wonder if light will warm the day up. I scurry down to get a coffee, glad to see the bike is still there, but less thrilled to see the frozen, white saddle.

Looking at the map, I can see how I should have borne left last night. The highway does some annoyingly unnecessary zigzagging on its way to Santa Fe; unnecessary to me. It's one thing to endure the freeze, but to have to do it needlessly really is infuriating. No, I didn't check the map. I assumed a southbound highway would do just that.

I may as well go and fill up the tank while the bike is naked. There doesn't seem to be much oil through the viewing glass when I check; perhaps it's a frozen lump in the sump. I can't pull the clutch in; it's as if the clutch plates are frozen together. And the engine turns over like a mattress in molasses. The battery drains as the starter strains, and eventually the coil kicks out a flicker of a spark, but it's enough to ignite the fuel in a choked and flooded cylinder. The exhaust pops and the crank revolves with flywheel momentum, and with the last trickle of charge, the piston reaches compression again. The bike fires up. I

219

rock the throttle and twist the choke lever like I'm feeding fuel to a newborn. Within a few seconds, the engine can fend for itself, and with a high and hearty tick over, white water vapour fills the frosty air. Phew! I think I'll let it run for a while. The tank takes far more fuel than I expected, but I'll give it the benefit of the doubt and put it down to the conditions.

The day isn't going to warm up. Nothing is. I have to keep going. As I pack up, I listen to BBC radio on my laptop. The last song of the afternoon show is Slade's *Merry Christmas*. What would I be doing if I were home? Sitting in the cold and dark, no doubt. Well, at least it's light here.

I have to go back the way I came, heading south on the northbound highway to a proper road that has a sense of direction and purpose. There are lots of thoughts going through my head, and they're all accompanied by a catchy Christmas song. The miles are long; the road is straight and empty; the snow blows across the windswept plains and under my tyres. The cloudless sky lets the sun shine on a million glistening crystals. They pierce the scratched polarisation of my Oakleys, which were forced uncaringly into a pocket last night at a red light.

The serenity, the scenery, and the song in my head remain the same until I reach Roswell. I don't have the slightest interest in UFOs, and I've seen before what this place has to offer. You can't walk into a bank without passing an alien with bulging eyes, and that's just the security guard. I'm not a green-ist, ask anyone. I love Kermit, but this place does nothing but give the cynic more reasons to be cynical. I remember how the "free" museum has a crafty way of robbing the visitor; the extortion being the only part of the entire exhibition that was out of this world.

I take the truck route to avoid downtown and any more red lights and green men. This is the shortest day of the year, quite possibly the last day ever. Clearly, I'm not going to get to the big party in Chichen Itza. I'm not even going to get to Mexico. It would at least be a consolation to see the end of all eternity from my tent. This southness is having its desired effect, but over land the changes in climate without altitude are slow. Carlsbad offers nothing but a reason to keep going. With a blood red sunset, the temperature rises, and I cross into Texas. I can switch off my waistcoat. I can even stop for photos, but I'm not going to camp. Not tonight. The land comes alive with nodding pump jacks sucking the oil out of the ground, and flame stacks burn the darkening sky. Nature is an excavation, and camping is a prefab hut. The occasional noxious cow grazes behind a barbed wire reserve, and telegraph poles and storage tanks push into a sky of toxic flavours. It's a novel horizon, but *oil* beef *hooked* if I'm going to camp here. Not really my scene.

One more night of luxury. Well, for the price I pay I'd have expected it, but all I get is sleaze.

I walk to a truck stop, a once familiar part of my life. Impatient big diesels tick over in line for the fuel pumps. I scurry between them like a rat around wheelie bins and into the fluorescent shop for heat-lamp dehydrated chicken wings of battery descent.

This motel never sleeps. Doors bang all night, cars honk their affirmation that they are remotely locked, and loud voices move too slowly past my door. It never seemingly ceases. This Motel 6 is like a Texas whorehouse . . . probably.

I do it again. I should know better. Purely for opening times and facilities, I research my preferred border crossing into Mexico, and that's when the bombardment of horror stories start up, usually penned by people who have never done it. I let the scaremongering influence my firsthand experience and judgement, and it does nothing to help ease my mind. My dreams are distressing and unstable, exes and attractions I thought I'd forgotten about. It seems the file still exists, accessible in a subconscious sleep-deprived night: alluring and dangerous.

Day 3

Big Bend National Park, Texas

210 miles

That wasn't sleep. Sixty-seven dollars? For that? Grumpily, I stomp to reception for my complimentary coffee. "Ask me how I slept. Go on, I dare you." I'm sure it's in their training not to. You have to have strong restraint to work in such a nasty place. Much like the return spring on the door, it resists my efforts to leave the cold reception. The top of my coffee falls out of the polystyrene cup, it replaces itself with another top, but this one is lower.

Every exit door opens outwards in America, that's all you have to know. The easy way to remember this is to know the reason why they do. I was told that there was once a fire in a department store in New York, resulting in a stampede to the exit door. The door opened inwards and there was such a crush of people pushing that it couldn't be opened and no one could get out. Based on this tragedy, exit doors across the country now all open outwards. The story comes back to me as I scald my wrist and stain the door mat.

A new day, a new beginning. The next solstice is half a year away. I wonder what I missed out on last night, apart from sleep? Other than birthdays, I'll party when I choose to, not when the calendar tells me to. I'm obstinate like that, but it avoids the crowds.

I list the morning's chores while waiting for the temperature to rise. I'm sure it's a busy day for mystics around the world as they calculate another apocalypse. I order my Mexican bike insurance online and walk to Walmart to print it out. They don't have a printer, but in the electronics aisle a pretty shopper momentarily charms me by asking what she should use to clean the heads of her father's cassette player. The magnetism is turned off when she adds that I look to be in the age group of someone who might know. I don't mind being the age I am, as long as it's not pointed out to me. "I recommend you format them to MP4, baby," I think of saying later, after I've had nostalgic and satisfying thoughts of albums squeezed carefully onto one side of a C90 with a short song like *Paranoid* added to fill in the space before the runoff; a fulfilling sensation that a pert little twenty-three-year-old will never experience, any more than I will ever experience a pert little twenty-three-year-old again. Bollocks. Back at my hovel, the receptionist prints the insurance out for me effortlessly. I should have checked here first.

As I take another load to my bike, a fellow biker asks of my destination. He has a Russian "girl pal" with him, and she wants him to ride with her in Siberia. "Have you ever?" Well, actually . . . He doesn't initially believe me, but the mention of Ulan Ude to his pillion and a map in a conveniently handy copy of my book soon removes all doubt. I can't help it; I haven't mentioned it for nearly two days. Well, I'll never see them again.

Mexican cleaners stand by their trolleys outside my door. It turns out I passed through a time zone, and I'm an hour later than I thought. I'll be off then. I head out onto a lonely road that leads to the international border. After 800 miles, I can now revert to fingerless gloves. I stop at the side of the silent road to readjust my multiple layers of clothing. I've entered southness. I don't stand and shiver, huddled and contorted, my core warms, and something inside me opens like a spring flower. My posture improves; I adopt a more relaxed manner, and my pace slows. I take in my surroundings, then notice the bike. It's coated in a layer of salt. The luggage that was thrown on and stuffed with numb fingers can be adjusted and organised now; well, soon.

In the middle of nowhere is a nasty little town of overpriced fuel and shitty attitude. The greedy cashier may get away with it simply because there's no other choice, but she'll never get away from here. The place is called Marathon. I expect it will be changing to Snickers sometime in the future. I head on to Big Bend National Park, named after the shape of its border with Mexico. Now that I've reached the warmth I've been aiming for, I can slow down. I have to get back into road mode: enjoy the journey, forget the destination, live in the moment, feel the immersion, take it all in. A ten dollar entry fee and I'm a tourist again. So I'd better go to the visitors' centre, I suppose, get the lay of the land. As I pull into the car park, so does another bike. It's Bob. Bob says he's been riding this park every winter for nineteen years. He marks my map with the best off-road trails and camping grounds, and with that, the transformation occurs. I'm synchronised again: back in the rhythm of the road. It's only taken three days and 1,000 miles, which is actually very quick.

As I apply for my back country camping permit, I'm told I only have an hour and forty minutes of daylight left. Where the hell did the day go? As is often the case at international borders, I meet a bloke from Reigate who invites me to the lodge for dinner, but I need to find my camping ground before dark. My relaxed manner is short-lived. Instead, I get a frozen burrito from the fuel station. I don't have my glasses, so how long do I put it in the microwave for? Long enough to buy a tin of ravioli, a packet of Kettle Chips, and some water. Another healthy dinner awaits.

The park is big, and I've done thirty miles before I find the four-wheel drive track. The evening is getting warmer, the dirt road harder. I even have to stuff my scarf into my pocket. When the surface allows, I feel behind me to check my water bottle hasn't fallen off. I ride between the rocks and around hills and up an incline that looks out over miles of nothing. I think I'll be living down there somewhere. The descent brings me to a wooden marker, and I leave the track to find my individual desert camping spot. It's perfect. The only indication it's here at all is a circle of stones. Solitary, silent, and best of all, legitimate. I have a sunset to myself. Did the ranger who booked my back country permit read me? Who I was? My desired location? Or did he just want me out of the way, like a hostess seating me in a roadside restaurant? I don't care, this is just what I'm looking for. With joyous exhilaration, I throw off my clothes and run round my stone circle like a demented druid. Having marked my territory and assessed the situation, I erect my tent in the centre.

When the distant desert dusk fades behind the highest of the far off mountains, a half moon casts me a shadow, and now I'm ready; ready to stop. I think I'll have a nice cup of tea. My camping stove hasn't been used in eleven months, but it still has fuel in it. Impressively, it still has pressure too. I've forgotten the knack of lighting it, and the hairs on the back of my hand singe with a sickening smell. I take my chai up a nearby hillock, where I question my free will. Why did I walk up this hill? Is it my choice? How long will I stay? It's cheap here and beautiful and warm. I have no deadlines, just phone reception. The human mark is minimal. In a 360-degree view, only a single light some thirty miles away is visible. Actually, it's becoming quite annoying. Bloody inconsiderate neighbours. I may have to go and have a word tomorrow.

Now I know why I rented out my house. So few people experience this silence and solitude, and even less appreciate it. I absolutely love it. I feel I'm the luckiest person here. I'm the only person here. The anti-social, light sleeper in the silence of the desert.

I'm in my sleeping bag at 6:45 on a Saturday night. But I don't care. There's no credibility here to lose. Time and days are irrelevant out here. I just wonder what I'll do for the twelve hours of darkness. Sleep is what I do; delicious, undisturbed sleep.

BIG BEND NATIONAL PARK, TEXAS

88 MILES

Through the open flap of my tent, first light spans the horizon like a shallow rainbow, just where I anticipated it would appear. It's hard to get a perspective on it. It could be a headlight or the top of an illuminated dome. But it's just dawn, just the first evidence of a new day, and it's very exciting, too new to miss and too vast to view from my tent. It's cold. I put on my thermals and run up the hill to take it all in. I'm spinning round like the dawn is picking on me. Every direction I look in is simply stunning. Only the brightest stars can compete against the crimson, rippled texture of passing morning cloud. The tops of the Chisos Mountains that the sun hid behind last night, catch the first rays with red radiation.

At any moment, the sun will appear over the ridge. I watch the shadows cross the desert floor, and the highest points of the undulating terrain catch the beams. A receding tide of non-colour sweeps towards me; I hold my breath like it's going to physically hit me. Then simultaneously I start to cast a shadow, as I feel a warmth through my thinning hair. At fucking last—finally an advantage to my advancing years! A shaggy, younger me wouldn't have felt that sun on his thick mane. Morning has broken. How exciting and how rewarding to be in awe of an event that happens every day; an event that defines day. I feel an exhilaration spawned by the most basic and fundamental laws of our revolving planet. I want to do this again. Same time tomorrow?

When the sun and hot chai have taken the chill away; blood, ink, and thoughts flow more freely. I don't even need my glasses; the light is not simulated or diffracted; it's bright, pure, and feels like it has rejuvenating qualities. As I write my diary, I hear the rush of wind and look up to see it comes from the wings of an inquisitive crow as it glides over my head. It's really quite loud, and then it's replaced by the sound of silence. No crickets, no wind, no distant traffic, not even planes overhead. Utter silence, just the sound of my pulse pumping blood in my ear vessels. Such a rare sound—well, I assume it always pumps, I just don't necessarily notice. They say when you're deprived of one sense your others are heightened. I'm just deprived of senseless sounds. This is a still land, and it can still be found. I don't think I want to leave it for a while.

There is no urgency to the day. It's free of time constraints, which feels so liberating. I eat my last bagel, and a degree of urgency returns. With my depleted supplies comes compromised liberty.

I wander around my desert. Everything is positioned perfectly, from the flora to the fossilised rocks. It's all so idyllic, so wondrous. I find a pile of gathered rocks, dilapidated dwellings surrounded by rusty cans as opposed to litter. History: embossed dates from the last century can still be made out. Miners? Prospectors? Pioneers? It just adds to the mystique.

I find my bike keys on the ground. I didn't even know I'd lost them. Maybe I hadn't. I hadn't been manically opening drawers or looking in pockets. Such pursuits only happen in man-made environments. This is simplicity:

minimalism. You couldn't create desert like this in your themed garden with cactus and succulents, tumbleweed, and the odd trace of a past civilisation. Your B&Q sand would lap up to conifers or an interwoven fence, not infinite distance and daunting mountains of red rock. Nothing is as authentic as nature.

The other thing that is genuine and a fact I have to face, is that I need more supplies.

The bike that I so sloppily packed with cold apathy is now stripped, and I lay everything out on my poncho and totally unpack and repack my panniers. This methodical and meticulous reorganisation will make for far greater efficiency, if I can just remember where I put everything. My attempts to remove the now sun-baked salt layer are ineffective. This will require a power washer.

Right, it's time for a ride then. What a great morning I'm having! I decide an unattended tent in this deserted area is safe, but not secure, so I leave the non-valuables and the water too. I'm going to ride the back trails, but I'll find water at some point, and I want to build up my provisions, not take them out with me.

Bob's recommended trail is horrendous, and I'm moving further away from any kind of help. My electronics take a pounding; laptops and DSLRs weren't designed for this battering, but better broken in my possession than taken in full working order in my absence. After twenty-six miles of uninhabited, deserted dirt road, I run along the side of a ridge. I take photos but can't capture the feeling or scale. I'm riding slowly, but it's too fast to feel and too slow for change. I don't need to do this track again, but I'm also reassured that I have the best camping spot. Reaching the paved road is a relief, but inevitably, it leads to the tourist sites. I suppose I'd better have a look. People, lots of people, noisy people. I have the need for something healthy and fill up at the all-you-can-eat salad bar. Although my ravioli is becoming more appealing, and the calling to my silent wilderness is deafening. I happily leave humanity behind. I deliberately ride past my turnoff, and when I stop for fuel and more water from the "village store," I discover they have showers. I'm not ready for spontaneous decisions; I'll think about it. This is where the big motorhomes stay. I'll never understand them, but they can't get to my campsite, and that's all I need to know.

I have a strong urge to go back "home" to my tent, my domain, my sanctuary. From an incline, I look through my zoomed lens and locate my tent. I really am out there. Once back, I have time to deliberate the indecisions of the stationary road warrior. Do I want this ravioli now? No. Do I want to carry it tomorrow? No.

Do I have an answer? No. The ravioli remains, and the light fades. I suppose I could stay another night.

This isolation and tranquillity is so stimulating. If I had demons, they would surely come out to play in a place like this. But I don't, and nothing too bad seems to be surfacing. Well, save for the occasional embarrassing memory or recollection, released from suppression as the song in my head gets spontaneously sung out loud to repress the cringeworthy reminiscing.

I make tea and take it up to my hillock to watch the sunset. I stand tall, I stretch, I reach out to the space around me. It's tai chi with chai tea. They say a man should know his limitations. I can't find mine out here.

Before 7PM, the chill takes me to my sleeping bag for a night of wild dreams, alluring and precarious. Is this exorcising, opening up, or drying out? I haven't had a drink since I left Denver. Despite this, nature calls, and I leave the tent under moonlight. Again, under starlight, and next time I open my eyes it's new light.

Day 5

Big Bend National Park, Texas

152 miles

I miss first light, but I'm up for seconds. Up to my hillock for more dawn. I'm worryingly happy. Is it OK to be this content and this alone? What is normal? Living in a motorhome so close to this experience, but isolated and oblivious to it? Having said that, I suppose I'd better see what I am missing. Is there somewhere better I could be? How can this satisfaction stay if I don't prove to myself I've found the best of the desert? I ride out to the hot springs. Yuk, lots of that people species again. I don't like them at all. I go off in search of the Gravel Pit Campground along the river, the Rio Grande that separates the United States from Mexico.

I see a couple walking down the dirt track. They tell me they're parked up at Gravel Pit and the other two spots are vacant. It's a sneaky little track that takes me there, and it's right on the river. Yeah, I'll have some of this. This means I have to go to the ranger station to have my allotted site changed. It's dead on twelve, and they've just closed for an hour. I go the "village shop" to charge some batteries and get Wi-Fi access. The recreational area has a line of washing machines against the wall. They have burnt-out bearings, and their mechanical complaining is a painful screech, as is the squawk of old motorhome owners who frequent the area. Accompanied by a bunch of screaming children being dragged to the shower block, it's a horrific environment.

I send a few quick emails and resist Facebook, or at least resist posting on it. Abstaining from it is as easy as abstaining from alcohol, I just have to exercise a little will power. After an hour, I'm semi-charged and fully pissed off. I go back to the ranger station and book myself into Gravel Pit. I discover the park has won an award—the darkest place in mainland USA. Curiously, it's quite a bright trophy. On a more useful note, I'm told it's safe to bathe in the river, so I'll forego the dollar-sucking showers. Once again, I ride back to my camp. It takes ages to pack up, but it doesn't matter. I've got all day. I'm beginning to realise I don't need to leave this park at all. I've got everything I need here. I don't even have to go to Mexico if I don't want to.

I run out of room before the camp is clear, and the bike resembles a Christmas tree hanging with gifts of cold-weather clothes. It's not a pretty sight. I need to work on this. Bloody low-capacity soft panniers! They're shit, and there's no option to strap stuff on top of them. It's all bungees and bollocks. Again, I wish I'd bought the fully accessorised KLR. It's torturous to keep considering it; I know I could have made my money back selling the accessories alone.

Back to the river camping spot, dump my stuff, and go and bathe in the river. I could swim to Mexico from here. It's ludicrous that further west there are impenetrable fences, drones, and helicopters with searchlights, watch towers and 4x4 patrols. Here I could wade across without even getting my back wet.

This evening, unexpectedly, the bond with my bike begins. I wasn't even aware there was anything missing in our relationship. I'm sure I've said that before. We ride up to nearly 6,000 feet. It's cold, but the west side of the park, I discover, is the most popular for a reason. It's by far the most scenic. With low light, the shadows bring new dimensions to the formations of rock, and they pose with a timeless posture. I race around the road that takes me to the dark side of the view. The park is so vast and the scenery so stimulating that the distances disappear in a constant stream of thoughts and sights. Something fist-size crawls across the road in front of me. The hairy fist doesn't have fingers, it has legs, eight of them. It's a tarantula. I stop, turn around, and photograph it; the low sun makes its shadow longer than its legs. Despite the zoom, I get close, it's only later I find out they are capable of jumping three feet. I was closer than that. Miles go unnoticed, but still they pass, and soon I have to fill my tank again. I take the opportunity to purchase another frozen burrito. The cashier wishes me a merry Christmas. I wish he hadn't. The light is going, and it's a long way back. Well, forty miles, and I'm sure I'll feel every one of them now that the temperature has dropped. However, it turns out to be one of those rare occasions when I warm up as I ride. I drop 4,000 feet under a pink sky, the formations now silhouetted against the end of the day. I have no luggage, and the road is smooth and empty. The wind is warm, as are the road and the tyres. I lean the bike more than I've had the opportunity to before, it's quite possibly the best Christmas Eve ride ever. I sing a Bruce Dickinson song out loud, the one I save for the best rides. Even my voice sounds good this evening.

I meet the neighbours again. They live in their camper full time. They invite me for some Christmas Eve hors d'oeuvres. I put up my tent by moonlight, waiting for the appropriate time to activate my verbal invitation. It's good to have a little company; keeps the weirdness away. Well, I try my hardest. Their 4x4 camper looks very expensive. We pick at the food and drink iced tea. They have, they tell me, four levels of protection: air horn, car alarm, mace, and level four is a machete. I consider mine: a Swiss army knife with multiple torturing devices, from toothpick to corkscrew. Never underestimate the pain of tweaking tweezers. Yeah, be afraid! Ya better run on home to ya Mama if ya know what's good for ya! I probably talk too much. I say nothing I haven't said before, and therefore I hear nothing I've not heard before.

They are new to the road. I was once too. It makes me sound immodest, when all I am is more experienced. That makes me sound condescending, when all I want is acceptance. We chat until 10:30, a late night in this environment. As I walk back to my tent, their horn honks affirmation that they're securely locked inside their box, unaware that their solar-charged light shines through the night and my tent like a gleaming trophy. The ravioli lives to see another day, Christmas Day perhaps.

DAY 6

BIG BEND NATIONAL PARK, TEXAS

86 MILES

I climb up some rocks for the sunrise. The view may be better, but I still prefer my old place. I have no phone signal here either, so I can't send the message I've carefully composed, using my full allowance of characters: a trait of the frugal text messager abroad.

I go and visit my neighbours for the daylight tour of their campervan. One of their leisure batteries is flat. I tell them about their night light, they were unaware; however, they did see me up on the hill this morning, but couldn't be bothered to get out of bed. That's home comfort for you; that can be hard to escape from. The van is compact to the point of cramped and has more dials and switches than a cockpit. It's an impressive piece of engineering and ingenuity, and I make appreciative noises. I feel fidgety and move my tent to the other vacant site. It's an impulsive move and a bit short-sighted, as the wind is getting up, and now I've gone and put myself in quite an exposed position.

There's a reason why people like me stay in a desert at this time of the year. I bloody hate Christmas. Say you detest summer heat, and no one minds; getting disturbed about autumn leaves is acceptable; moan about November rain and people empathise; but mention you can't stand Christmas and all you get is, "Bah, humbug!" Well, there ain't no humbugging out here, so I can be as miserable as I want. I don't believe in Christ or mass materialism, so what's to celebrate? There's nothing about this date that appeals to me. Yet, deny it as I do, I still have some obligations.

I have to go back to the "village store." In the laundry room, the only place to sit and plug in is in between the doors of the male and female showers. The spinning machines continue to grate their dilapidated displeasure, but still the Wi-Fi surfers make themselves heard above the noise. Overprivileged brats whinge about their underwhelming presents, and obnoxious Republicans blame everyone but themselves. I try to Skype my mother, but she can't hear me over the amplified consumers. I can't speak any louder, the bad connection thwacks in my earphones like a lawnmower on a cattle grid, and her webcam isn't pointing in a favourable position. The experience is altogether unpleasant. My tranquil existence has been infiltrated and eradicated, replaced with resentment and repulsion. I leave loathing everything: the people, the location, and the date.

I fill my bottle with water on the way out and go to my old camping ground, as I left my siphon hose there yesterday. On the dirt road, the top comes off my water bottle. I only know this because my arse is getting wet. I turn back and walk the trail, but I can't find the top anywhere, nor can I remember at which point I turned back. I do find my hose though. I wish I'd never left this spot. I have phone reception again, and it bleeps with Happy Christmas texts from happy friends playing happy families and vibrates missed call alerts that I'm too mean to retrieve. I make the one call I'm duty-bound to, and thankfully, it goes to voicemail. I can fake jollities for the thirty seconds it takes to leave a message. Responsibility fulfilled, I head back "home" but take a wrong turn and end up at the bloody hot springs again. I'm so annoyed; I'm in a really bad mood. It's a horrendous road, and I rode it needlessly; now I've got to do it all over again to get back. I hate this day, doesn't matter where I am.

I go and have a doze in my tent, hoping, but not expecting, to wake up in a better mood. Where did my satisfaction go? Calm, I need calm. I give the day another chance. Some inherent instinct is telling me to do something significant. I put on warm clothes against the cold wind, but it's not enough. I ride, unaware that my destination is the lodge for the all-you-can-eat Christmas dinner. It's just awful, based solely on indulging, massive motorhome Americans in their shallow need for quantity over quality, and the intrusive conversations that penetrate my foul mood match the bland and unnecessarily excessive offerings. I hear a lot, but no one is saying anything.

"What time you got on that computer of yours?" says an instantly dislikeable man with an annoying moustache and hesitant wife.

"21:30; it's on UK time."

"You use military time in the UK?"

No, we just have the ability to count beyond twelve. "What are you doing out here?"

"I'm heading to Mexico." Shit, why did I say that?

"On a motorcycle?" comes the predicable response.

"Yes."

"On your own?" he continues with trembling facial hair.

"Yes, I've done it before, and I've heard it all before," now take your Fox News negativity and frightened little existence back to your isolated and fortified box, where your digital clocks tell the same time twice a day. I'm rude, but I'm so tired of ignorant people pissing all over my travel plans. The only redeeming features of the meal are the stolen creamers for my morning chai and a dump in the porcelain toilet. So this is Christmas. I go back to camp. It's cold, cloudy, and windy. It's time to move on, but it's not time yet. The borders probably won't be open during the holidays. I walk to the river and take photos of cracked mud on the river banks. I lose my lens cap and have to retrace my steps.

The sunset can't come soon enough, and when it does, it's dull. I've endured enough. Wearing just my thermals, I get into my sleeping bag, but soon I'm too hot. I can't read the print in my guidebook, even with my headlight and glasses. Then in the night, it gets so cold I have to zip up my tent, so I can't see out. God, I hate this day.

Day 7

Big Bend National Park, Texas

133 miles

Oh yeah, that was a cold night; my water bottle has an icy crust. I still get up for dawn. Why wouldn't I when there's only eleven hours of daylight? My climb rewards me with a beautiful sunrise, but it won't warm away the chill in my hands. My marmite is so solid it rips the bread as I try spreading it. More southness is needed. It's almost time to go to Mexico. Today is my second least favourite day of the year. It would have been my dad's birthday. I've had a really successful year, achieving a dream of getting my book published and the unexpected bonus of it being well received. I'd love to be able to tell him that. If I was still a loser, I'd miss him less, that's sobriety for ya!

I have a trial pack, a new system, but I'm not leaving until tomorrow. I do some laundry and have a half-hearted wash with some half-boiled water. All I seem to be doing is waiting for tomorrow to arrive. When I realise this, I slap my wet face, go for a ride, and find a new road. I come across an authentic and restored stone and thatch dwelling, which would once have housed a family who would no doubt say that all I've experienced here is nothing compared to the lives they lived. Before the all-you-can-eat salad bars, entry charges, and convenient paving to vista points. I'd have loved to have got here earlier. But I can't help that I'm a twenty-first century man. Still, the silence remains the same (most of the time).

This is America's least visited national park. Its distant neighbour, the Grand Canyon, has fifteen times more visitors in a year. I wonder if this is to do with location or vicinity. Is it because it's not on the way to anywhere or is too close to somewhere else? I ride on to a canyon, the sides of which divide countries. I walk a trail that ends when the chasm narrows and both walls become river banks. It would be all the more impressive in the right light, in warmer times, and with a better ambiance. The domestic row of a family on the vista trail echoes off the walls; all this yelling just for a photo, and what memories will that photo bring? I take a different path, I always have.

Back at camp, I run over hills to photograph another stunning sunset. The best so far. I'm getting more in touch with the beauty of the desert; the plants and the occasional wildlife. I think my photos are getting better too. I'm more used to the scale. I focus in, instead of trying to capture it all in every shot. I could spend more time here, but it's too cold for comfort again tonight. The moon has steadily been getting brighter. I think I need to make a sacrifice. It's time for the ravioli . . . and no desert. I feel a growing need for a taco and cerveza. It's been a very dry week.

DAY 8

CHIHUAHUA, MEXICO

269 MILES

My water bottle doesn't rattle with frozen fragments this morning. As it starts to get light, I can see that's because it's solid ice. I decide I'm not going to climb the hill for my dawn patrol. But then the whole sky turns purple. Yes I am. It's too enticing to miss. I run out of the tent like I'm late for work. It's the best sky yet.

I pack my bike with numb fingers, and when the sun shines on me it's with a warmth I wasn't expecting, making it hard to decide what to wear. Stupid bloody soft panniers. Even without the ravioli, there's still no room. At 9:30, I'm ready to leave. I ride to my neighbours' campervan, but they're still in bed. I circle their vehicle leaving my tracks in the dirt. My imprint says, "Adiós . . . you weren't up."

I stop at the visitors' centre to throw out my rubbish and have a brief KLR conversation, only to have rubbish thrown back at me. "You're going to Mexico? They kill babies and fill them full of drugs to get them across the border. Take a gun. No, take two." Have you ever been there? Of course you haven't. But I have. Whose account do you think is more accurate? Be afraid, live in fear, listen to your TV, trust us, spend your vacation dollars at home, sing your anthem about

239

being brave and free, but don't, whatever you do, go and visit your southern neighbour. In fact, don't even get close. Go to the Grand Canyon instead. It's pissing me off, because I'm listening. I know the score. I know, I know, but I'm on my own. I have no one to help me defuse this negative bomb that's just been dropped on me.

In the last thirty years, I've spent a lot of my life in the US. I love so many aspects of the country: the hospitality of people who are as varied and diverse as the climate and scenery. I've ridden the spectacular Colorado Rocky Mountain roads and witnessed the colourful, unfeasible beauty of Utah from the saddle of many an inappropriate motorcycle. The more I've travelled the more my world view has inevitably expanded, and with this I've become more defensive and less tolerant of international ignorance. Beyond America's exceptional scenery are some very misinformed views. It's not the ignorance that angers me, it's the proud, adamant, unquestioned, misled belief of certain patriotic types that there is only one way; only America, and the information they have is right. No country is perfect; no government is innocent. And patriotism is a fine quality; it rarely offends me. But here national devotion manifests itself in arrogant and deluded views, rarely perceived from firsthand experience. Only one third of the population has a passport, which means the majority get their sporadic and selective world news from an agenda-driven media, and it's just wrong.

Deep breath: out with anger, in with calm, tranquillity now. After six days of positive solitude and tolerated company, I ride out of the park. I've ridden 400 miles around it, and all I've seen is how much more there is to see. I think it's safe to say after my two-day sprint down here that I've slowed my pace appropriately. I decide to try and find Bob. I've seen him a few times coming the other way as we've been returning from our evening rides. I see a trailer with a few bikes outside. That'll be him. If he's home, the sound of my engine will be enough to bring him out. But despite my deliberately slow turnaround, he doesn't appear. This morning I seem to be circling company like a coyote stalking prey. I'm about to pull back on the main road when in my mirrors, wearing only a towel and with a face full of shaving foam, a breathless figure bobs into view. Here is a man who has not only met riders going to Mexico, but amazingly, when they return too. He wheezes some recommended routes to me, saying the seventy miles from here to the border town are spectacular. To put both our minds at rest, I say I'll see him in a few months. Apart from anything else, it's just good to speak to someone who knows my name.

One man's spectacular ride is another's commute. It does, though, despite my scepticism, live up to the hype. The road follows the Rio Grande. There are canyons, hoodoos, and extreme undulations, down into tight bends. It's not unlike the Laguna Seca Raceway circuit at times. Over a blind hump and speeding down into a corkscrew bend, I can feel the limitations of my cheap Kenda tyres. If only I had a fork brace. If only I didn't have the bike loaded with luggage. If only it was a Ducati. Still, it's an enjoyable journey to a shitty destination. Presidio is perhaps designed to encourage you to keep going and cross into Mexico; not that I need any encouragement. Bob's burrito suggestion only increases my urge to leave. Kids scream in the restaurant, and I wait over half an hour to receive what I didn't ask for. I wonder why I ever bothered to order overpriced Texas Mexican food, when two miles away is the real deal. The only satisfaction is gleefully leaving without tipping. I'm going to Mexico now.

It's an easy transition. For a country that's world renowned for being so difficult to enter, it's remarkably easy to leave. No goodbye. No "submit your visa." No exit stamp. No "have a nice holiday." I disappear out of the country like truth in a news report. I ride into Mexico and stop in an inspection bay for a brief check of my documents.

"¿De dónde eres?"

OK, ¿De dónde eres? ¿De dónde eres? I know these words. Come on Flid, think! On the spot Spanish has never really been a talent I've possessed. Oh, now I remember. Where are you from? I know the answer too. Go on Flid, say it. My comprehension is slow; however my response, although delayed, is enthusiastic . . . and wrong. My reply isn't understood. I have an arsenal of Spanish words, and that alone makes it my second language. I revert to my first.

"England." I just know the name in Spanish will come to me later.

"Ah, hooligan!" comes the reply. That says a lot. That's your one-word response that sums up my nationality? It's true the names of certain countries can conjure up instant preconceptions: Kazakhstan—Borat, Iraq—Gulf War, Guatemala—earthquake, and so on. But we know, as a nation, there's more to us than hooligans. Likewise, the inhabitants of other countries are equally varied, but one-word generalisations are easy inaccuracies. It doesn't offend me though. It's not said in a way that is meant to. Listen, amigo. You should hear what they're saying about you over the border.

"You will need a vehicle permit."

"I know. Where do I get one?"

"Just there, Señor. Your bike will be safe here."

I go to the motor vehicle booth. The lady is helpful and friendly, although annoyingly, having such a new bike puts my deposit in the highest bracket. I pay the same as the driver of a $100,000 motorhome, but I'll get it all back. It's only my credit card company who takes their whack by finding the lowest then the highest exchange rates in their favour, depending on whether they're taking or giving.

I am processed with easy efficiency and professionalism. I'm free to go. It's a rare border crossing that is a comfortable temperature: no traffic, no queues, no touts, no confusion, no shouting, no corruption, and no delays. And contrary to the forums of fear, I'm not gunned down by an infighting drug cartel. I'm waved out of the customs compound and onto the street of food stalls. The air is filled with the smell of tacos, meat, and fish cooking over coals and wooden embers. There are stalls selling all things Mexican—sombreros and ponchos, but no dead babies full of drugs. I can't find a bank. I have no local currency, but that's the only concern I have. Less than a mile from the border and less than five minutes into Mexico, there's a screech of tyres and a crunch of metal at the lights as a car drives into the back of the truck waiting beside me. I've seen a dropped ice cream get a more hysterical reaction. I love Mexico!

Once I'm out of the little town and can see for miles, I think it's safe to stop for a wee. I'm back in the country where I began the year. It's all coming back to me now. Somewhere beyond my active memory is a force that recalls how much I like it here—how good it is for my soul—and it is this force that pushed me into renting my house and breaking free from the British winter. It drove me to buy a bike and ride back to a land that takes away the tension. Or at least it should.

The road to Chihuahua is barren and brown, sparsely populated by both the permanent and transitory. It's a little daunting, more from what I've read and been told than from what I see or experience. On the plus side, it adds to the exhilaration and butterflies. My tank is full, my bike is running well, and it's less than three hours to the big city. There's a checkpoint, and unlike the border patrols in Texas, this one has smiles, no alarm or suspicion, and no paranoia or fear-inducing authority, just a little inquisitiveness, a genuine welcome, and a blasé ¡Buen viaje! And that's all the contact I have until I'm waved through the next checkpoint, where the only negative experience is my annoyance that, once again, I have my judgement swayed by the go-nowhere-do-nothing, ignorant, nay-saying keyboard warriors. Their loss.

I remember *libre* means free and avoid the toll road all the way into Centro de Chihuahua, where I find a bank that spews pesos into my fingerless-gloved hand, before my unattended bike can become a victim of the opportunist. In fact, it appears to go unnoticed by the early evening city shoppers. I can't find the recommended hotel I'm looking for, and the low sun is in my eyes. The hotel I do come across has a homeless bum, who's clearly mentally unstable, sitting on the step. Although he's minding his own business, I can't imagine he's generating much business. There's budget accommodation and there's plain undesirable. After three laps of the one-way system, I give up on my guidebook map, made all the more complicated this year by the donning of glasses to read the bloody thing. I put the book back in the tank bag, hit the side streets, and look through my open visor for a sign. Within a few blocks, I find a hotel; in a few more blocks, I find a better one. The bike isn't off the road, but the twenty-four-hour reception will keep an eye on it for me. And the day is done. That's how you change countries: with a little common sense, a basic awareness, lots of smiles, and a relaxed and gracious attitude. I knew that. I don't know why I doubted myself.

Now, for the little things on the list. I've been camping for a week and definitely need a shower and shave before hitting the town. As I pass the receptionist on my way out, I get a nod of approval at the transformation that's just occurred in the bathroom. I'm no longer the sweaty, stressed, pannier-laden scruff who entered an hour ago.

I need some thin socks for the imminent, upcoming heat. The sock shop epitomises Mexican hospitality and helpfulness. They split a pack for me and even give me a calendar. I wander the city and stop at a convenience store for a hot chocolate on the way home. The young checkout girl asks me a question I don't understand. Her boyfriend is leaning on the counter, keeping her company through her shift. He could be seen as an intimidating youth, but he points a plastic bag out to me. Oh, right. I get it. Thanks, but I think I'll just take the chocolate in the cup.

DAY 9

CREEL, MEXICO

175 MILES

Travelling towards the equator from the north at this time of the year means the days get longer, but daylight is still limited, so I keep my desert habits and get up at first light. I have a little plan. A long ride round the one-way system, but a short push across a vacant plot is a carwash with a power washer. So without warming the engine, I push the KLR along the pavement and across a derelict lot to a place of high pressure removal, to rid the bike of its layer of road salt and all the other filth that coats it. The cold engine doesn't crackle and steam as I soak it. Unfortunately, I don't know Spanish for soapy bubbles, so can't tell which option on the dial I'm choosing.

Wow, what a transformation! It looks gorgeous when it's all clean. Whilst it drip dries, for the first time in a week, I head out to find and order breakfast. It's not so tricky, I know to look for a desayuno sign, and I know I want huevos rancheros. The restaurant owner, a tall thin man with a permanent smile, has lived in the US and travelled all over Mexico too. He speaks English to me. He's an electrician by trade, though I'm not quite sure how that led him to own a one-table breakfast diner in a northern city backstreet. He didn't say. He wants to talk about women he's known and which beaches he found them on. I'm

244

not about to interrupt. Mexico, like every other country on the planet, has its problems. The people seem aware of them, but accepting. It's an aspect of life here, but it doesn't seem to overwhelm them. I tell him I'm going to Oaxaca, pronounced war-huck-ar because of the way the "x" sounds in Spanish (although not always, as Oxxo, the national chain of convenience stores, jumped on the gravy train of logical pronunciation).

In any case, Oaxaca is a long way away. I took an indirect route the last time, and I'm doing it again this time. Copper Canyon is too good to miss. I get a smile from the owner that says, I know you know the dangers and have heard the warnings about that place, so all you're getting from me is this knowing smile. "Radio Gaga" is playing from the corner of the room, the door is open, and the sun is shining down on the dirty street. My eggs are perfect, my coffee instant, and I've got that exciting foreign feeling, but it comes with the comfort of vague familiarity. It almost feels like respect; I came, I saw, and I came again. Welcome back, Flid. We missed you. This could all be in my head, but I'm relieved and content to be here, and for less than £2 I'm fed with the breakfast I craved, and it comes with a side of wellbeing. The next song to play is *D.I.S.C.O.* I say goodbye before it sticks.

The other side of an impossible junction, my gleaming bike catches my eye. It just adds to the feel-good feeling. It is D—Delightful. It is I—irresistible. It is S—Shit, the song has stuck.

So has my marmite. With the warmer weather, it's liquefied and leaked, and the handle has broken off my saucepan. I blame all this on my soft panniers. The bike may look better, but the luggage is a disability. It doesn't just disable the aesthetics, anyway; sleek and desirable is not necessarily a favourable look—not that I have to worry about portraying that image; the bike's just cumbersome. The tank saddlebags keep shifting forward and pressing against my knees. It's an invasion of my personal space. It's like sharing a bus seat with some alpha male athlete who can't close his legs due to his giant steroid-filled testicles. I resent the intrusion. I'm thinking perhaps the savings made on tyres and panniers were a false economy, and again, I consider the bike that got away.

Until my rent money comes in, I'm on a very tight budget. That's why I haven't had a drink so far this trip. No point pleading poverty whilst standing at the bar pouring beer down my neck. This isn't *EastEnders*; this is barrel-scraping reality.

An associated symbol of Mexico is often the sombrero and poncho wearing, guitar playing, tequila drinking hombre sitting with his back to a cactus; the very effigy of lethargy. The reality, however, is that a lot of the country is high-altitude snow and ice, especially in December. Mexico is like a chilli that has been taken out of the freezer and put in the oven for a minute. It's hot on the outside, but cold in the middle; and as for the seedy bits, if they exist, I don't see them. For some stupid reason, I ride up to Creel at 7,000 feet. Why? Because I sort of promised to revisit the place I stayed in last time. They don't even know

I'm here, so it's an unnecessary ride. I take the high road through pine forests and frozen puddles, and past pickups with huddled hoodies in the bed.

I've come into town from the other end and can't grasp it at all, until I cross a bridge over a railway and rotate my mental map. At the complex, I'm greeted by someone I don't recall. He informs me the guy I made the promise to, and who helped with the production of my website last year, isn't even around. The restaurant is closed, the supermarket empty, there's no hot water, and the heater doesn't do the basic fundamental action that gives it its name. I shouldn't have revisited the past. I know better than to go back. I only go forward.

Day 10

Rodeo, Mexico

383 miles

I can see my breath in the room and frost on my bike seat when I wipe the moisture from the window. Time to turn this trip around. On an empty stomach, I go forward into the cold but deserted roads that skirt Copper Canyon. I make sure to stay on the paved bit. I could drop 6,000 feet into the warm and humid canyon, but it would only be a brief respite, as what goes down must come up, and I know the road out is horrendous.

I'm wearing the four layers, both top and bottom, that I left Denver in. It's a high-altitude, low-temperature ride: a hundred miles of twisting, deserted road. I only pass one car. That's the out-of-season bonus. In Guachochi, I have the same breakfast as yesterday. I've stayed here before. I remember the fuel station opposite the hotel. I make a stop in hope of a nostalgic view—the beautiful, voluptuous receptionist. As my tank is filled for me, I look out across the road but don't see her. She wouldn't remember me anyway. Or maybe she would; the one who drained his oil in her backyard. You should never go back.

I have no confidence in my tyres. I let out some air, but their handling is still not reassuring. They grip like condensation on a window and can run off unpredictably. Two hundred miles of scenic roads is worth the self-imposed invitation. I've ridden this road before; I'm sure I have, but not a single thing I see is familiar. Wait a minute. Yes it is. The military checkpoint at the T-junction, I remember that. The soldier has his face covered with a mask and sunglasses. He's impossible to read; it's intimidating. That's why I always flip up my helmet and smile. It stops the guessing. I'm waved through. They're preoccupied with a bus they've just pulled over. It's going to be one of those ride-until-dusk days—a mileage eater, a destination achiever. I squeeze past an Arctic that has tried to reverse up an embankment. The trailer has dropped onto the rear driving wheels of the unit and he is well and truly stuck, I can feel his fatigue, humiliation, and frustration. The best thing about being a truck driver is when you're not one anymore.

The road straightens, the cloud gets higher, and there is even a blue patch, but the sun won't shine through it. It's just a dull Saturday. My mind wanders. I think the girl I lost my virginity to has her fiftieth birthday today. Her daughters are now older than she was then. My lifestyle remains the same; only the dates have changed.

Cars wave when I stop, and pedestrians wave when I ride. And if I return a wave, all hands go up. It breaks the train of thought. I think I've stayed in that town back there, but I'm not sure. I consider the story line of *Zen and the Art of Motorcycle Maintenance*. Isn't it about a return? I couldn't bloody write that, could I? I wouldn't know if I'd got there.

The sun decides to reveal itself just as it's going down, which happens to be when the road turns to face it. It's the best scenery of the day; it coincides its descent with mist rising from the valleys. And that's the last view through my visor before my helmet is placed on the concrete floor of a perfectly reasonably priced cell for the night.

I walk the street and stop at a stall with the enticing smells of the freshly cooked. Yes, I think I'll point to that and nod enthusiastically. An elderly couple already has their order, and they help me with mine. It feels like it's a special treat. Well, it is Saturday night. I scurry back to my concrete box. The smell of grilled meat and melted cheese distracts me from the four walls of chosen accommodation. Through my amber tinted window is the shadow of my bike mirror so I know it's still there. Well, the mirror is at least, possibly taped to a plastic chair. But it provides enough comfort to induce good sleep.

Day 11

Concordia, Mexico

267 miles

It's hard to tell if the light coming through the amber window is natural or not, but the echoes in the hallway and the banging doors are definitely real. I'll assume it's morning. Due to there being no restaurant, nothing delays me leaving. And due to a change in time zone, it's still later than I thought.

Last night's burrito doesn't look so appealing this morning: limp, leftover, uneaten, unloved, lying there unrefrigerated and congealed. I decide I'm not having it for breakfast; it's best just left alone. I feel a bit alone too. I'd like some sunshine and some wow in my day.

So back on go the layers, minus one, as I'm sure I'll be dropping in altitude today. I pay a quid to miss Durango—missing the capital of the state that is, not giving a local beauty queen a pound—and use the toll road. A pound well spent all the same, as the toll road crosses ravines and cuts through mountains. Best of all, it's smooth and new, and there isn't a single red light. Nor, unfortunately, is there a fuel station. I ride 120 miles before breakfast. Perhaps that's why I'm feeling a little down. I try and think where else I'd rather be. I can't come up with anything. This is due to lack of imagination rather than contentment, and it doesn't make me feel any better. I pull over for a protein bar. It's over a year old and has more crumbs than crunch, but I need to put something into my gnawing stomach. I'm stopped for five minutes, no longer, and surprisingly, I find I have reception on my phone. I discover this because it rings; a very short call from a lovely ex. It's all I need though. I feel OK again now. Although I'm unsure if it's food for thought or mental distraction that changes my state of mind.

Going onto reserve takes me off the toll road, and I indulge in El Espinazo del Diablo Highway (The Devil's Backbone), one of those prestigious, twisting mountain roads that will provide adrenalin all the way to the coast. I really need to eat something, though, if I'm going to enjoy this. I stop at Fanny Restaurant, a place of infinite joke possibilities and limited menu. Annoyingly, it's one of those places that questions your presence in their establishment, and all I can get is coffee. Strangely, they all come out to wave me off. My stomach keeps on churning, and my tyres continue to handle with as little confidence as a hungry gringo with inadequate Spanish. Maybe a fork brace would sort it out. A periodic procession of GSs comes the other way. I'm not sure if they're a club or a tour, and not many wave, so I make defensive presumptions about them from inside my helmet. They'll fit right in at Fanny Restaurant. Nothing about their bikes, company, or quest generates envy. Even though today my spirits are low, I wouldn't travel any other way.

The dark days of the unmanageable mortgage are gone, along with youth, and now with some rental income I have the frugal freedom to continue through hemispheres. I'll settle for half a hemisphere though. The descent is steady, and soon I drop through the Tropic of Capricorn. Hairpin debris changes from pine needles to petals, butterflies fill the air, and bug splats obscure my vision. It's time for a change of clothing. I've made the transition from the dry, brown death of winter to the green, humid jungle, alive with chirping and swarming, flying and crawling. I get bitten just taking off my thermals. Do I care? It's better than frostbite. Warmth at last. My clothes are strapped on all over the bike, with a little gap between the tank bag and dri-bags to fit my skinny arse in. Smells once more fill the moist air: flowers and food. Kids run beside me in shorts, not inhibited by clothing or the cold. Why would you live at altitude when this climate is so close?

A new highway is being constructed. Concrete stilts cross valleys, and tunnels have been bored through cliff faces. It's an extravagant project. The road I'm on will be all the better, if the new one takes the lumbering, lane-hogging vehicles away. I make a few dangerous overtakes, as do the oncoming trucks I come wheel to grill with, as I round a blind corner. I have some impure Ducati thoughts. I've got to sort this KLR out. I've never been dissatisfied with one before.

I wallow round the last of the Devil's Backbone Highway and into the last of the light. Then in Spanish, I manage to find and book a place that I can call home tonight.

Day 12

Concordia, Mexico

0 miles

There's a strange noise outside this morning. I've not heard that sound since I left England. What is it? Rain, bloody rain. I conquer snow and extreme cold. I brave bland, brown lifeless plains. I endure high-altitude, blind hairpins on reluctant tyres. And what do I get for the first bona fide feel of southness? Bloody rain and a forecast that says it will last for the rest of the week. I make one of those easy decisions that isn't obvious until it's voiced. The bike is under cover, I have Wi-Fi and satellite TV. There's a supermarket across the road. And how hard will it be to get a room on New Year's Eve? I'll stay una noche más. There was a stupid '80s band called Yellow Dog who sang a stupid song called *Just One More Night*. It gets sung in my head far too frequently when I'm on the road.

Just like the end of the world and Christmas, this other significant date on the calendar will pass me by without any real celebration. Although there is a ritual that I perform at this time every year—the ceremonious changing of the diary. In the last pages of the current one, I write a summary of the year by recalling the significant moments that are stuck in my head and my heart. Then I go to the front page and look at the list of what I wanted to achieve. I don't do resolutions, just desires. This year has been the best ever, and the only thing not accomplished was reliant on someone else's input—loser! I open my new diary and make a list of goals for the coming year, the first entries being last year's failures. Some are as recurrent as road tax, only this year, for the first time in a decade, "get book published" is not transferred. However, "sell house" is.

"How's ya diary looking for next week?" a slimy Amway salesman once said to me, hoping I might be his next step up the pyramid. "Well, it's empty. Ask me at the end of the week." At the end of the year mine doesn't go in a recycle bin, it goes in a fireproof box.

I wander to the supermarket. Finding crisps is a bit of a challenge, and the assistant and manager volunteer to help me with my search as I mime eating crisps as a vague clue. We all enjoy the game, and they seem happier than I am when the crisps are found. Patatas fritas, oh right, that makes sense. Spanish usually does. They do, however, seem disappointed when I've found all my needs and the game is over. Monkey nuts were the hardest.

What the hell did I do with a day off the road before the Internet? 2013 is occurring around the world, and I read updates as it does. I leave some groups and unfriend some people on Facebook. It's all very liberating.

Outside, they seem to be preparing for a party. It was always going to be loud, wherever I stayed. I miss my desert tonight. I want an early night and an early start. My evening passes engaged in conversation with a like-minded, but vegan, biker girl on an Internet chat thingy. Then I push a pillow against my head, so the fireworks, barking dogs, and revel yells don't break through my sleep.

Day 13

Punta de Mita, Mexico

264 miles

Feeling smug is far better than feeling hung over. The noise of the festivities faded with the darkness, and I leave my room into a peaceful, but messy dawn.

The morning is damp, tropical birds screech, and the sticky, thick moist air is reminiscent of something I can't quite recall. I settle for the memory of riding on the back of a moped after an all-nighter in a Goan jungle once, wide-eyed, but coming down from some tribal trance experience. It's a good memory, even if it's not the right one.

The first ride of the year, especially after a day off, is all the more enjoyable. I've got warmth at last. It may be induced by cloud and humidity, but it's still warmth. My clothes don't restrict me, my bike is willing, and no one is about. I ride into a new year. Whoohoo! This is what I love to do. The smells are so lush and thick, I can chew on them: fruit trees and flowers, cactus and creepers, life and growth; not like that dormant winter that lurks above the cloud-covered hills.

I take the toll road to Tepic. Nothing very inspiring is occurring inside or outside my helmet. I blame the deadening of my brain from a day on the Internet. The bike has a noticeable increase in power now that I'm down at sea level. I use the throttle more and the gears less. Overtaking is effortless, and the momentum gets me to the rain all the faster, so I decide to stay on the toll road. I hand over peso notes at every toll booth and fill my already bulging pockets with more and more change.

After one such pay booth, I see a Spanish-registered Triumph, so I pull up for a chat. He's quite arrogant and is clearly fully sponsored. I should know better, but I ask him how come. He's a writer—yeah mate, we all are— got a book out in Spain, round-the-world motorcyclist, blah, blah, blah! It starts to rain again, but it doesn't stop his bragging. I put my helmet back on, and still he continues. Now he's moaning about it being an uneventful trip; nothing significant to write about. Well, you just met me, didn't you? His dreary monologue could never be anything but the blandest paragraph in this chapter.

I ride through flooded streets towards the coast, stop under a tree where rain, gathered on leaves, drips concentrated, enlarged drops on me that make the bread go soggy as I try to make a sandwich. It's such a pathetic sight it makes me smile. No one has ever enthused about soggy bread. There is a procession of traffic coming the other way—the New Year exodus, hung over and homeward bound. I'm glad I stayed where I was last night; also I expect room prices will come down now that the festivities are over. I'm really very wet. My boots and gloves have leaked, and I'm not noticing anything except headlights and brake lights. I'm cold too, but it's not much further to the recommended "well-kept secret" of a resort.

First impressions are not good, but then no beachside paradise was ever enhanced by rain. The first room I find has UK prices and is four times my budget. The next is affordable, and I'm too uncomfortable and wet to shop around further. It will do, despite the stink. As I climb the steps to my room, I see the place overlooks a sewage plant. I hang up my wet clothes and discover the ones in my panniers are wet too; stupid soft panniers.

I walk the streets in search of food. The first place ignores me. Americans, too rich or lazy to walk, ride the streets in golf carts. I end up at a pizza place run by Westerners with prices to match the language. Fed, but not fulfilled, I leave the damp, dull restaurant. Outside it's dark and raining, and I dodge open drains and pond-sized puddles back to my room, stopping on the way for a hot chocolate. Here they don't even offer to put it in a bag.

It's capitalist holiday hell. Some fucking recommendation this turned out to be. There is the sound of sloshing as the sewage is processed, and the smell hangs in the clammy night air. I mentally prepare myself for a long, wet ride tomorrow. I can't wait to put my feet into wet boots in the morning and get out of this shit hole.

Day 14

Near Lázaro Cárdenas, Mexico

361 miles

You can tell a lot about a person by their idea of idyllic. An acquaintance in Denver painted a pretty picture of this place, but for me, the only appealing thing about being here is leaving.

When the darkness turns to grey, I see palm trees lurching violently as the wind gusts off the sea. The skyline is poured concrete, and rusty steel pylons outnumber palm trees, and satellite dishes distort what little authenticity there is.

None of my damp clothing has dried through the night, but the fact that I think it must have makes putting it back on less miserable. Pushing warm feet into wet boots is not as bad as I thought it would be; it's better than staying. I'm on the road by 7:30AM. I don't glance back. No sunset, no sunrise, no second chance. I don't want to see any more of these sewage-saturated surroundings.

With an open jacket, what has festered in the night is beginning to dry in the morning breeze. I ride into Puerto Vallarta. Fat Americans walk small dogs that bark at skeletal joggers, who in turn totter along the promenade in day-glo Lycra, towelling sweatbands and with iPods strapped to their emaciated arms. This place caters to the affluent and unimaginative, with omnipresent Starbucks,

Dominoes, Staples, and Remax real estate. It's all male dance attractions and foam-filled night clubs. High-density tourism housed in Soviet-style blocks, painted white, with a palm tree stuck into the concrete and a Sheraton sign bolted to a scaffold pedestal. It's a thoroughfare of carbon monoxide and insipid life.

I chat to a guy on a KLR at the lights. His bike seems to be running fine, but he's not leaving. I don't understand why. The road is confusing, and the south of the bay seems impenetrable. I find myself on cobbled streets direction-less and frustrated. There are some crucial junctions without signposts. I start to see things I recognise, as I've managed to turn myself around. All I had to do was keep the sea on my right, but now I'm back at the bloody airport. I've done a complete circuit. Two and a half hours and I can still see where I started from. I can't for the life of me get out. Maybe the place is deliberately designed this way. It would explain a lot.

The right road takes me inland and into torrential rain. Is that a speed camera that just got me? No, it's lightning. When I stop for fuel, I hear the thunder. The road is flooded; the fields are flooded; the rivers are flooded. There are rockfalls on the corners. I let a car pass me just before I aquaplane across washed-out road. Oncoming vehicles project puddles at me with such force I feel the darts of water pierce my jacket. I can't get any wetter; I'm even breathing in water from the scarf across my face. Another rock to avoid, but this one has legs and a shell—a turtle crossing. It's too wet for photos, but a turtle says it all. It's wet, and that's all there is to it.

In these situations, I have to have optimism. I have to assume I'll ride the storm out, despite no end being in sight. It can't really rain this hard for the whole day; it's too extreme. After three hours, I see dry road ahead. However, it's still raining. I must be moving faster than the storm though. I eventually leave it behind along with the hills, as the road leads back to the coast and into a sunny evening. There's no traffic; the road is windy and warm; my flapping jacket is drying out. Unfortunately, my sheltered crotch isn't. This is better; much more enjoyable. So enjoyable I go onto reserve after I've left all opportunities behind me. "I'll fill up at the next one" is a philosophy I should have abandoned long ago. There are no excuses. Actually, I do have one. I've been waiting for this weather all day, so didn't want to stop. In fact, I'll use that excuse twice. I've also finished my water and haven't bothered to replace it. So now, even a wild camp is out of the question. How can I constantly manage to do this to myself? It's the most annoying aspect of my own company. I have a firm talk to myself, but I'm not really listening. I'm watching the sun setting, and anyway, I can justify anything.

In a one-horse town, there's no need for a fuel station. I find the man with the hose, who leads me to his stable. Inside he has some big drums; they are symbols of relief—and he also has a clever siphoning technique. He sells me five litres of mileage, and I get some water too. Now I have more options. Two miles later is a camping sign. I don't need any more options. I ride onto the beach and under a cabaña. For £2.50, I have a legitimate place to pitch my tent and somewhere to hang my clothes in a sea breeze. I watch the last of the sunset as I eat fish quesadillas in the open-air, palm-thatched restaurant.

In the space of ten minutes, a nightmare situation can become a dream scenario. It's the perfect example of a day on the road. Leave a shitty place, find a worse one, get lost, get soaked, believe, endure, persevere, make a stupid mistake, get help, and finally fall asleep on a beach with a full tummy and the sound of crashing waves. And it's all the more appreciated because I haven't trundled to this spot in a golf cart from an air-conditioned hotel. This is how a hard road rewards the persistent.

Day 15

Near Acapulco, Mexico

302 miles

Sleep by the ocean, woken by the sunrise. My panniers are drier, my maps more crispy, and the mozzie coils less droopy. Only the boots remain moist.

Today for breakfast I stop at a convenient Oxxo. I get yoghurt out the fridge and press the button on the coffee machine. It fills my cup . . . and keeps on going. I grab another cup . . . it too fills, and the flow continues on. Grabbing a third cup, I call for help. I should have filled my cup from the jug the dispensing machine is designed to fill up, not the machine itself. Luckily, I know the word for sorry, but not the words for "that I've spilt coffee all over the counter and the floor, and I've made a load of unwanted extra coffee that no one will drink, and I now have two other cups of the stuff getting cold." Still, they can see it isn't deliberate. I was looking forward to sitting on a barstool at the counter in the air-conditioned shop to drink it, but now I'm too embarrassed and sit outside on the curb by my bike.

The coffee is super strong. It has amphetamine qualities. I find myself speeding through a police check, feeling like Spud from *Trainspotting*. "You're the dude with the gun like. I'm merely a traveller passing through. Well, obviously I'm passing through, but I'm getting good vibes here, eh?" I'm not stopped.

This is the best time of the day to be riding. It's going to get hot; I can just tell. But for now the day still has a freshness about it. A lizard crosses the road in front of me: weather prediction by wildlife. Next is a tarantula. And there are also a lot of dead and bloated dogs along the roadside. I'm not sure what this says about the weather; perhaps they went out in the midday sun, madness. There are a lot of little bugs in the air too. They get into my ears and are really itchy, but I can't get at them. Some futile instinct has me hitting the outside of my helmet, unsurprisingly, this makes not the slightest difference.

The ocean-hugging road has plenty of sweeping, swooping corners, and on the best ones vultures sit on posts doing what vultures do: lying in wait—quite possibly for an Englishman with bad judgement and dodgy tyres to add a touch of variety to their accustomed mad dog diet.

I'm riding with my cuffs open. I've basically made a net out of my jacket, and I've cast it; eventually something gets caught in it. It's a bee. It gets to my elbow, and upon discovering there's nowhere else to go, it stings me. I'm lucky I don't react to such things, well, not in a profuse sweating, difficulty in breathing, violent convulsions, and finally death kind of way. My reaction is far less dramatic; just a lot of repetitive swearing, which stops me from screaming like a little girl. I find a pharmacy.

"Do you speak English?"

"More or less."

"In that case, I've been stung." But I was willing to perform the mime I'd rehearsed in my helmet to back up my simple sentence. I'm given a cream that isn't in my extensive first-aid kit. So I'll hang onto the mime until I have to silently illustrate an actor, a yoga enthusiast, and the lead singer of a major '80s pop group in the next game of charades.

My feet are very hot and damp. It's not a nice environment down there in my boots. There's little I can do about the festering foot decay, but I'm only a day away from sandals.

I'm not going to Acapulco. I have not the slightest want to go to such a touristy place. OK, I have a little want, my first childhood awareness of Mexico was cliff divers, nothing else, and there's a part of me that would like to witness the display, but not the part that has to ride into town in this heat with such a loaded bike, find a room, unload everything, get a taxi to the cliff, and pay tourist prices to get hoarded and hustled. It just seems like too much effort. I take the bypass in the hope of finding a place like last night. I don't; instead I find a rip-off little hovel run by a sweet little old lady who would be all the sweeter if she hadn't just charged me so much for my room. It doesn't even have a seat on the toilet, which makes it a squat really. I have trench foot and don't feel like walking anywhere. The beach is full of pretentious restaurants and Mexicans on quad bikes. I go back to the main road and buy five tacos for a pound from a street vendor. It's noisy and dusty, trucks thunder past as I sit at the curb side. But I don't mind. Tomorrow I'll be in my own idea of paradise.

Day 16

Puerto Escondido, Mexico

237 miles

I love this bit; another early start that will lead to a change in status. Stop riding and start researching. It's a long way to come just to sit in front of the computer. I've flown over oceans and ridden across borders just to relocate to a place where I can prepare for the proper trip in the spring. I can see how this might appear confusing, but to me it all makes perfect sense.

Sunbeams streak through the misty-morning fire smoke that hangs under the palms. I have scratched Oakleys, ripped gloves, and although my boots are nearly dry, my feet are uncomfortable. Even my smart wool socks can't solve this problem. You'd think I'd been on the road for ages; I do feel a part of it all.

I get stung again. No, not by the money-grabbing little old lady, but another bee. It flies through my visor, and when I stick my hand in to find where it's got to, it leaves its calling card on my cheek. Out with the cream again. I'm getting used to it now.

Today seems to be about the destination, not the journey. I ride erratically. Everyone is driving badly; there just seems to be a madness in the air today. Inevitably, it ends in crumpled metal and bloodshed. Not mine, but sobering to see all the same. Not that I've had a drink this trip, Sixteen days on the road and no alcohol, mainly because, well I just want to see what refraining would be like. I want that delayed gratification feeling of the first beer when I reach the beach.

A bridge takes me over a wide, clear, fast-running river. It's too attractive to ignore. I take the track down to the sandy bank for a bathe. This, for me, defines overland, independent motorcycle travel. Some people call it adventure. I'm not sure how adventurous it is, but this is definitely something you wouldn't do on your commute to work—stopping by a river and having a wash, then spinning out on the sand, standing on the pegs, up the track back to the road. That's what you do when you go away on your bike. I think this defines the freedom of the trip, self-contained, independent, and taking the opportunities that come my way, not preconceived or researched, just an in the moment impulse that needs no explanation.

It occurs to me, about a month too late, that if I'd looked at the photo from last year, I could have seen the name of the place where I'd stayed, called them, and reserved the room I wanted, the one with the ocean view. Great to consider it now I'm within twenty miles of the place. I know I'm getting close when I start to see the moped-riding, short-wearing, surfboard-carrying, semi-permanent locals who have made this paradise their home. Now I've become one of the many; no acknowledgement is needed. I'm feeling a little anxious; what if the place is fully booked? I should have thought about this earlier.

It's taken two weeks to ride 3,800 miles through snowy, barren, frozen lands, through storms, humidity; and heat. And I've finally made it to my beach of choice. I'm recognised. I'm remembered.

"There's one room left."

"I'll take it."

"The lock doesn't work, amigo."

"I'll fix it."

The price for a month's residency has me questioning my calculations. Is it really that cheap? I unload the bike, shower, and ride in sandals and shorts to Super Che to get supplies, Super as in market; Che as in Guevara, it's not revolutionary or a Safeway to ride. I park up next to the other bikes, some of them have pannier racks, their aluminium boxes stashed in the corner of a hotel room and their top boxes replaced with a milk crate for the food shop. Both tyres and riders are balding, the paintwork fading, and their hide skin tanning. These are the people who know where the cool rides are: to the secluded beaches, the jungle waterfalls, and to taco heaven. They've taken the baggage off adventure biking so they can take the narrow tracks; the lost or undiscovered highlights beyond the guided tours. The return-on-a-tankful overlander, the Canadian snowbirds who've traded rust from salt roads for rust from salt air. I know a few of them. I know the supermarket aisles too, where everything is. I get my washing powder and food supplies. I don't know of a supermarket with a better view. I stand in the checkout queue and look out of the smoked glass over a bay of white breakers. Even if Tesco Club Card points bought blow jobs, I'd still shop here. Back home whilst my laundry soaks, there's no need to delay my gratification any longer. I walk to my local off-licence for a six-pack of Modelo.

I'm here. I'm back. In the evening, I wander without knowing I'm heading there: to the place where ribs are barbecued. The toilet block has changed since my last visit. I pop my head inside a new thatched hut, and I'm handed a joint.

I sit at a table, sip my beer, and listen to the music. Led Zeppelin is followed by Boston. I push my toes into the sand, lean back on my chair so my hair falls away from my neck, look up at the canopy of palms above me, and I feel the feeling. It says this is where I'm meant to be. I remember now. Sometimes it's OK to go back.

Puerto Escondido, Mexico

171 miles

Chill for too long and you will simply freeze. Entirely the wrong metaphors for hot, southern, Mexican beach life. Every day is 35° Celsius, and the only time I reach for something with sleeves is to watch the sunrise from my little balcony, the chai in my mug cooling as the daily, inescapable heat returns.

I'm not doing what the beach has to offer. I'm not skydiving or sea diving, dolphin watching or surfing. I just want to sit quietly and do some trip preparation; devise a strategy to win the battle against red tape and obtain the visas for the next journey whilst my tenant funds this warm and frugal homeless lifestyle of mine. My mates drink in the post-Christmas gloom of a British pub, envying my escape, but the cost of their third pint exceeds my daily budget.

I live on muesli and avocado, with a treat of street tacos for dinner. If I avoid the posh and tempting seafront, I can live pretty cheaply. It's so easy to form a routine, regardless of location, and within a week I have one. Writing, research, emails, Spanish lessons, siesta, and down to the beach for sunset. I'm sitting on the beach one evening, pointing my attention-seeking lens at the orange sky, when a surfer dude approaches me, and I jump out of my little moonrise daydream.

"You're clearly a professional photographer. Could you take some photos of me surfing? I'll pay you."

I'm not professional, but if he pays me, then technically, I suppose I am, so I agree. I soon discover that they're a vain bunch, surfers. They say they want the photos so they can check their posture, their technique, their position, and so on. But actually what they really want, much like us bikers, is the perfect picture of them being confronted by and overcoming the most challenging and beautiful of environments. I take his photos, he buys me a big fat burrito, and the next morning he comes to my room to see the results on my laptop. I dump them on his memory stick; he's ecstatically happy and buys me some beer. Then he goes off and tells his surfing buddies.

Within a week, I become Mr. Surf Photographer. I'm "in" with the beautiful people: the super fit and über cool. I point my lens in exchange for beer and burritos. I have a trail of pretty surf chicks and cool dudes coming to my door with memory sticks and high-fiving me with pure delight when they see what I've captured. My Facebook friends are all becoming younger and better looking, and their profile photos are the ones I've taken.

My little routine has gone right out the fly screen. There is some productivity, I get on the forums in the hope that someone can shed light on my awful Kenda tyres. The suggestions change nothing: vary pressures, loaded, unloaded, check bearings, spokes . . . I'm even reassured it's a characteristic of the tyre. In desperation, I take off the front tyre, which has no "Direction of Rotation" arrow. The tread pattern looks symmetrical, but I turn it around anyway, and what do you know, it handles like a . . . well, like a cheap tyre as opposed to a gyroscope.

When one surfer chick asks what she owes me one day, I say, "Twenty minutes of your time." Her frown soon fades when I say to go clothes shopping with me. She's the prettiest of motorcycle accessories—too young for baggage and too naive for protection—a pillion in flip-flops and cut-offs. Beyond bike enhancements, I have no sense of style or fashion, and I need an advisor. She's good too, the right girl for the job.

"This one is too gangster. No, not that one, too dad. Or that one, too gay."

"Oh, really. I thought it looked pretty good."

"This one brings out the colour in your eyes."

"Eyes? Does it? OK, thanks. I'll take it."

So now I'm the coolest dressed surf photographer on the beach. I can't walk down the street without doing the surfer handshake with every dude and dudette I pass. Or if they're on the other side, they do that other sign, the one with the thumb and pinky finger pointing out. I think it might mean "hang loose," but the way I do it, it's kind of more like "hang up."

When I should be spending my days researching the visa situation for Iran and the 'Stans, I find I'm surfing photography websites and learning my cameras capabilities. If there is a downside to all this hanging out with petite girls and rippling guys it's that my browning tummy is growing with inactivity and cholesterol payment. They talk waves and techniques, heroes and legends, and I listen and inadvertently learn. I should be doing my Spanish. They speak of the meditation, the spiritual connection, the unity with nature. It all sounds great. I try and relate it to riding.

The day the Internet crashes, everyone comes out to play. The pool is crowded when the pasty surfers of cyberspace venture out of their rooms. And me, I choose to ride up the mountains. In two hours I'm at 6,000 feet, and for the first time since Copper Canyon, I experience the discomfort of a chilling temperature and the thrill of a twisting road.

The beach crowd doesn't believe me. Firstly, that I've ridden out that far, secondly, that elevations of this kind are actually very close, and thirdly, that it is so much cooler than the beach up there. That's when I realise that, although it's a privileged insight into their world, I'm not a surfer. Bikes are my thing. All the waves in the world will leave me stagnating. I've come here to be free of distractions, and I've ended up with a better social life than I've got at home. I've mastered some new photographic techniques and learnt more capabilities of my camera, so it's been useful in a way, but I've lost all motivation and enthusiasm for the mission I came here for. I've seen thirty sunsets; some with whales, some with waves, some in the company of a wounded surfer, and some just high on my balcony. This month turned out to be a major contributing factor to the U-turn in *Eureka*.

It's time to ride again. After all, this is a bike trip, right?

Day 47

Oaxaca, Mexico

169 miles

I experienced my first earthquake last night. In the dark silence, Satan ripped up the rug in the cavernous hell beneath the bay. The rumble came from the north at the speed of sound and shook my bed like a poltergeist before leaving like a petulant exorcism and slamming the door behind it, which created an aftershock, and I experienced my second ever quake.

My possessions are scattered across three rooms. I can't blame that on the quake though, just a month's residency at this place. It's a bigger mess when it's gathered together and there's no finesse in my loading the bike. Next time good tyres and hard panniers.

Slow speed and slow thoughts as I wind my way back up to the high-altitude spine of Mexico. I'm putting the layers back on, blowing away the malaise of the beach, and reminding myself that, although I may have developed the eye for a good surf photo, I retain the mind for a good ride. And this is what I do. Sixty-five mph; I haven't been that fast in a month. I haven't done it with confidence at all on this trip. The bike is transformed. A directional tyre without indication; what an oxymoron.

Leaving Puerto Escondido is like dumping a girl. I know I wanted to break away from the place, but every bus coming towards me has the name above the windscreen. I get a pang of regret; reminders everywhere. I long to go back to the familiar. I have to get logical to quash my heart's yearnings. This isn't new experience, watch-and-wonder riding, this is Steve McQueen, over-the-fence escapism, and I have tunnel vision to the next town.

I ride into Oaxaca, not looking for the place I stayed at the last time. I need something new. I find the place I stayed in last time and pay the price for my lack of adventure.

The city centre has colonial architecture; its beauty all the more appreciated after a month of coasting—cobbled streets and market stalls, churches of carved figurines standing between pillars with dramatic lighting that brings me to a stop. The stone courtyard invites community; skateboarders stunt on the steps and guitarists play in the acoustic corners, which resonates round the square. A building that unifies, an evening attraction; without preaching or praying, its presence alone attracts. What a novel idea. With low lighting and a stationary subject, I change my surfer settings for a slower shutter speed.

Day 48

Zapotitlán Salinas, Mexico

177 miles

The fan keeps the mozzies and the sound of barking dogs away. The morning has a freshness that is more than a brief respite from the omnipresent heat. This is a genuine coolness.

I'm heading for the Gulf Coast to meet a friend from my last trip here. I have three days to do a two-day trip. My road mind debates what I'll do with the extra day. I get out my guidebook—the brick I've been carrying and have barely looked at. I discover there's a cactus desert a day's ride away. My dithering morning turns into rushed and excited preparation.

I love being on the road. Just this. Waking up warm, looking at my guidebook, and with the freedom of the solo traveller, making a decision, loading the bike, looking at the map, and heading out.

I find my way out of town straightaway, which is always a little bonus. I take a toll road to fast-track me to the better scenery. It's 35p, but sod it, I am on holiday. The cactus desert destination is forgotten about; it's the journey that's taking my attention. It's always about the journey. The road twists up to 7,000 feet, but the temperature stays comfortable. The cliffs and rocks have multiple subtle colours and the dark blue, high-altitude sky is a complementary backdrop.

Big cathedrals in little towns, high-plain beauty in a comfortable climate. I stop to photograph a bell tower with a skirt of bunting. A teacher waves on her way to class, as does the truck driver on this lonely road. It's as though it's compulsory. Even a passing Polícia Federal shows his hand through the tinted window of an ominous-looking Dodge Charger.

It's one of those rides that can't be captured; this feeling, the next perfect bend that brings into view a whole new scene, which has me slowing down and contemplating premature camping. This, in turn, gets me thinking about supplies. If I get water and some food now, I'll have twenty-four hours of self-contained independence.

The town is tiny, and the stares say I'm rare, but I find a shop that caters to the overloaded rider with its limited supplies. Back on the main road, as if just stuck there, the ground becomes a pin cushion of cacti, towering bigger than any plant pot could contain. They cover the hillsides as far as I can see. Protruding out of the undulating landscape, they make the place a descending hot-air balloonist's worst nightmare.

Just as I'm contemplating a wild camp, I see the little triangular sign that means I won't be breaking any laws. There's a campsite a few miles up ahead. The sign actually says botanical gardens, a phrase they must have picked up from a glossy magazine. I go to the hut that says administration; a little English is spoken. No, I don't want the tour. I just want to camp. My £2 is taken. I think I've just financed the opening of the fridge, because the beer it contains is swiftly distributed among the three workers or employees or partners. I'm shown to a space next to a newly built sleeping quarters. The boiler is lit so I can shower, and the door is left open.

I have some whiskey in my panniers, and as I can already smell alcohol on my host's breath, I offer some. It's not only accepted, but exchanged for a short walking tour. He's very proud of his botanical garden, or at least that he's staked a claim in this natural cactus desert and put a few slightly inappropriate buildings on the land.

After I've set up my tent and finished the whiskey, I take my camera for a walk about. There's a wooden viewing platform. The bottom ladder has been removed, probably to deter me from climbing up; it doesn't. I look down upon the prickly spires of this dehydrated forest. It's good. It's OK. It could be better. Those big, cold bottles of beer that came out of the fridge would enhance this scenario no end. I ride over to the admin building, "Sorry, none left. Have some of ours."

The guitar is out, and the laughter is unstoppable, so I share a beer. "Are you a musician?" I've been hearing this all my life. No, I just look like I could be. I can't play the guitar, but I can pose well with one. Just stand me in front of a Marshall stack.

"But you can sing?"

"No, I really can't."

"Sing *Yesterday*!" One of them starts singing it. He loves The Beatles.

"Oh, not the Guns 'N' Roses song then?" The fact that I know the words and have an English accent, although not Scouse, is all they need, and when I get stuck on the next line they help.

"OK. Look, I'm going to get some more beer. I'll be right back." The sunset is probably not going to be as memorable as this sing-along anyway. Once again, it's shorts and shades to the shops. When I get back, I put four cans on the table, and the workers serenade me with *La Bamba*. They all have such good voices; strong and in tune. One of the guys is younger than me, has seven kids, and hair that's thicker and without a trace of grey. It's incredibly unfair.

They point at my bike. "¿Mundo?"

"No, just Mexico."

"Where else?"

This was never my intention. I only wanted a beer for the sunset, but I do happen to have a map to show and tell. Unfortunately, it's inside the cover of my book. I just show the map and then the photos. It feels a little like I'm at Motorcycle Live again.

"So that's you?"

"Yes, but I just wanted to show you the map." It's too late though. Out come the phones for photos of me and the bike. Then they insist that I eat with them tonight.

Whilst we wait for a taxi, the eldest of the three men, who speaks no English at all, tells me a story sentence by sentence. I understand the gist, and what I don't is translated. It's a gentle story of old times in these parts that his father and grandfather knew. It's passed on to me proudly and with patience, and it's so in keeping with the setting.

So with my camera and valuable documents left in the tent, I follow their taxi on my bike. A restaurant is opened for us, people are summoned, and the book is shown around. It's basically turned into a passport. More beer is brought; I'm invited, they insist; it is their treat. I meet at least five of the seven children, the wife, the sisters, and the uncles. I'm made to sing *Yesterday* once more (not *Yesterday Once More* by The Carpenters). I must say I'm sounding pretty good. I'm in harmony with my understudy prompter. And then it's on to *Hotel California*. Can I leave; can I? No, the storyteller has another story for me about the sacred cactus that occasionally produces fruit; a fruit that can be fermented into an alcoholic juice: a prestigious and potent brew. But the story has an agenda; this juice is only available at a certain bar, and I'm invited by the storyteller to come and drink two glasses of the juice with him.

"Oh, go on then."

Now my bike is left on a main street, my possessions are slowly getting scattered. We go into the centre of the dusty town and into a building in the main square. I'm ushered in. It doesn't look much like a bar to me, and I've seen a few. No, this is the president's office. He's a man with bulging biceps that a T-shirt won't cover. He shakes my hand.

"I am the president of the town," he tells me. And in case I don't understand, he adds, "Bill Clinton."

"Hi, I'm Tony Blair," I hear myself saying. It's received with a laugh. The book, which hasn't been in my possession since it came out of the pannier earlier, is now shown to Mr. Muscle and his sidekick. Who, they say, will come and visit me tomorrow. Then it's to the bar. Oh, what I'd give for my camera now. The barman has two customers and more character than an Oscars ceremony. A dusty demijohn is brought out from under the bar, there's the sound of shuffling, a shot glass is cleaned and put on the counter. It clearly doesn't come out much. It's filled with a cloudy liquid and passed to me. Would this be happening if I wasn't travelling alone, if I hadn't got the book out?

OK, here goes. I'm not going to shoot it back. The story was long, the fruit is rare, and this is a drink that deserves respect. I sip it. Thankfully, it's palatable, and as it goes down there are no surprises. The tension in the bar relaxes. Or is it me? The barman, I notice, has unfeasible hair; I would never suggest it's a wig, but it definitely needs adjusting. His contempt for me is just beneath the surface of his obligated service.

A younger man sits on a chair with his back to the wall, but his body is a straight forty-five-degree ramp. My eyes move up it, from his cowboy boots balanced on their heels and crossed on the floor, up the long thin legs covered in faded denim, and to a red shirt and waistcoat. His face is obscured by a battered cowboy hat. Smoke rises from beneath it. How lawless a smoker in a bar seems now. When he leans forward to take his glass from the bar, I see he has a long face and missing teeth, but he's still strikingly handsome, with sharp cheekbones covered in dark, weathered skin. This guy is cool. Very cool. I just know there's a ponytail down his back. I want him to be my friend. The other customer is sitting at a right angle to him, also with his back to the wall, but closer to the door. He's wearing a '70s brown leather jacket and has a round face with a grey fringe hanging over a forehead of ravines, which don't quite frown. He has the look of a man who's seen a lot of trouble, but probably avoided most of it. Music plays at a level that keeps awkward silence away and invites conversation.

"Scorpions," says the thin, dark dude.

"Where?" my body language said, but thankfully not my mouth.

"*Wind of Change.* They are German, no?"

Yes, they are. And so the ice is broken with my new, cool amigo. He's seen Pink Floyd in Texas—The Momentary Lapse of Reason tour we establish—and as we chat, my glass is refilled. My hosts are very drunk, but I don't seem to be. I say that this is one of the coolest bars I've ever been in. There's an exhalation of disbelief.

"Don't you believe me?" I ask the '70s trouble avoider.

"I believe everything," he diplomatically replies. Although I'm not sure just how good a philosophical life choice that is. My hosts are now slurring drunk, and I think perhaps a little jealous that my attention is being held by stronger and stranger characters.

I've held my drink, I've established my presence, I've met everyone, and annoyed no one. This, it would seem, is a very good time to leave. I think I'll just say goodnight. I head out of the bar and into an empty street: the kind of bar I'd imagine the clientele are either thrown out of, crawl out of, or are removed from and relocated to a room with more bars . . . across the windows. I must say I feared a more severe effect from the cactus juice, which, if the whole scenario were ever turned into a cartoon, would have been poured from a jug that would doubtlessly have several Xs on it and perhaps a skull and crossbones.

Dogs probably bark, rats may scurry, and I stride purposefully in the direction of the place I last saw my bike. The author is leaving the bar.

I frequently try, and occasionally succeed, in living in the moment. Fully aware of what is around me, appreciative and undistracted, "the moment" is a very important place to be. I spend at least half my life considering the next bit; the other half is divided between reminding myself to acknowledge the here and now and actually managing to immerse myself in it. It's a very satisfying state when it's achieved, because when it passes, as it inevitably will, that moment can be recalled with perfect clarity. This particular moment is such a moment, and the cactus juice could well have contributed to this total recall. The bike is where I left it, the keys are in my hand, and the directions in my head. I start the bike, and by the time I've selected third gear, the refreshing wind I'm passing through brings me back to the full awareness of what I'm actually doing—riding out of a small town and into a cactus desert with inadequate protection and no concern about it in the least. I never ride at night, so I'm unaware of just how bright my full beam headlight is. It shines off the towering pillars of prickle and gives me a sense of insignificance. Taking the dirt track back to my tent, I know this is one of those moments that just has to be experienced firsthand to understand the feeling it brings.

I fumble with a bread roll and avocado, making a just-got-home-from-the-pub snack. I'm stumbling around the sandy ground repeating, "Yo soy borracho," with an ever-increasing emphasis on the rolling of the *r*. "I am drunk," I tell the silent night, and it doesn't disagree. I eat my wonderful roll, drink enough water to quench, and leave enough in case of a parch in the night. And that is the end of a day that reminds me that regardless of what you call it—adventure, overlanding, touring, prolonged holiday, independent travel—it is, irrespective of the label, why I do what I do; just one of those rare and magical days you occasionally get on the road.

Córdoba, Mexico

90 miles

The night seemed to go on and on. I'm not sure why; maybe it was the cactus juice, still, every time I woke I drank water and now at first light, there's not a trace of a hangover. I get up for some silhouetted cactus sunrise shots. I don't think camera technique is the most important part of photography; awareness is. It's not about the scene I'm capturing or whether I'll ever look back at the photos. The fact that I'm making time now to notice the sky change and to see the effect the light has on the landscape is reward enough. Recall is great, but you can't beat being here.

I boil my kettle and instinctively start to pack up. The sun warms me out of my fleece, and two hours after it came up, I'm ready for the road. Yesterday was a moment in time; I don't want to stretch it or string it out. I measure friendship in depth, not length, and last night I fell into something deep and meaningful. This morning, I'll ride off and remember it—a sense of mystique for all concerned. Despite my transient lifestyle, I've never got any better at goodbyes. My leaving unannounced is genuine. Handshakes, gratitude, promises, and pleasantries always feel a little contrived.

With nobody's concern but my own, I head for the road and soon find myself looking over a wide, cloud-covered valley. A new day, a new view, no preconceptions. This too would have been a good place to watch the dawn, but you can't do it all. I stop for fuel before I need it to eliminate any possibility of stress entering the day. The pump attendant gives me directions and I avoid the historic centre of Tehuacán, which perhaps might have been worth the increase in traffic and tension. I'll never know. The road rises to a chilling 7,000 feet, and a snow-covered volcano comes into view, along with the first signpost for Veracruz, where my friend lives. I'm very early.

Sometimes it's pure luck that saves me. I stop to photograph the winding road into a valley because it seems quite a popular theme to post on Facebook. The cars are doing strange things on the hairpins. They seem to be switching lanes. For a brief moment they're driving on what I consider the correct side of the road—the left. What kind of a safety measure is this? On some, but not all, the hairpin bends you're required by the markings to switch lanes. If I hadn't stopped and seen this going on, I'd have been leaning with all the confidence my tyres can allow and gone head on into an upward-coming vehicle. Now with some knowledge and understanding, but still a dyslexic disability, I head down into the valley. But even with the arrows painted on the road, I still can't bring myself to switch lanes.

The beach was good, but this is better. I'm over the surf scene now. I'm back where I belong—on the wrong side of the road. I smell barbecued chicken. I want barbecued chicken. I see barbecued chicken. It's still early, but I stop, order, and eat barbecued chicken. It's meaty and filling and meets all the expectations of the desire that brought me to it.

The towns become more frequent. In fact, there is no gap between them. They're hot and ugly, busy and best avoided. I cross railway tracks, and things become industrial and polluted. After one too many red lights, I decide the toll road has the most appeal.

I reach Córdoba. There's no point in going any further today. It's a city of big cars, big money, and bad driving. It smells of mafia, but it doesn't feel dangerous. I find a hotel in the centre, where the manager is super friendly and my bike is parked in an underground security car park, which is good for peace of mind, but it does mean any excursions today will be on foot. I've come to the city too early. I feel too captive, bored even. I'm not used to waiting. Time has been passing at just the right pace all year, but it's suddenly become a drag. Somehow, with all the choice the city has to offer, due to a lapse in imagination I find myself boiling water in my room to make a pot noodle for dinner. Predictably, its utter shit.

Days 50–55

The State of Veracruz, Mexico

894 miles

I always tell myself I'll go back to bed after I've seen the sunrise, and I do, but not until about fourteen hours have passed.

The manager said I could go up onto the hotel roof and photograph Citlaltépetl, the snow-capped volcano that is Mexico's highest mountain. I'm east of it now and perfectly positioned to see the rising sun paint the snow pink. I always find it implausible that I can be standing in the warmth looking at a peak that seems so close, yet is so cold it has glaciers running down it, but that's our wondrous planet for you. The volcano looks a bit like Kilimanjaro, only more pointy. It's the high point of my morning. With daily practice, both my photos and my Spanish are improving, but my pictures still speak more words then I can.

The manager makes me feel special and introduces me to his wife, whilst I try and wring something solid out of the watered-down breakfast. I'd better get going. I bring my panniers down the stairs and take them over to the car park. I'm noticing the drawbacks from a month's inactivity; this feels like a workout, where it used to be routine. Everyone says good morning, even the armed security guards in the car park. As I finish loading, I'm alerted to the arrival of my friend. He's outside on his F650, or maybe it's an 800. I think it's got an extra cylinder, I don't really understand; it's definitely faster than my bike. He's with a mate who's on a fully accessorised GS, but other than that, he seems nice enough. It's a busy road and no place for greetings, so I follow them straight out of town and up a mountain. It's harder riding than I'm used to, and within fifteen minutes, we're stopped by some police. I've had no contact with them at all since I've been riding in Mexico, but as soon as I'm in a group this happens. I let the semi-natives deal with the situation. We're heading into an area of unrest: farmers rebelling against greedy extortionists. Apparently, demands have gone beyond acceptable levels. We ride up to 8,000 feet and back in time. It's tranquil and traditional; a little window into the way things once were. In my ignorant bliss, the past is all I see. I don't notice the new graffiti or understand what it symbolises. It's antagonistic and provocative, displayed to scare and warn those who are aware, and all I'm noticing are the pastel colours on terracotta churches. It all seems peaceful to me. I see the fear when we head back down to the hard, fast, busy roads. My tour guides overtake everything in the relentless pursuit of something else I fail to see. I'm underpowered and overloaded. This is not my style of riding.

Back at the house, Casa El Flid has been prepared. I have the pool house to myself. Between panniers, tools, and plastic chairs, I make a space for my mattress on the floor. There is a bathroom en suite and a swimming pool outside the door. It's the ideal temporary home.

My visit is more than a space on the floor though. I'm just beginning to realise the extent of the effort made. I met my Canadian expat friend a year ago via Horizons Unlimited. He's a family man who gets his overland fix by advising, guiding, and hosting other motorcyclists passing through. He's both knowledgeable and passionate about the State of Veracruz. My status has been upgraded from "passing through, and I don't really know you" to "first class, be my guest." On my second visit, I'd limped back with a battered bike and broken skin from a blown-out tyre and the worst off I'd ever had. For this visit, it turns out he's booked his holiday to coincide with my stay, and his wife and daughter have been sent away visiting. Am I really that bad, or does *he* want to be?

A rigorous tour schedule has been planned. We're up at 6AM to ride out of the sticky, humid city before light and up to higher altitude. When we stop, I instinctively park in the shade, then realise it's winter and push my bike into the sun. The trees are bare, and the grass is dead and brown. It's hard to comprehend how close this season is to the tropical, palm-lined Gulf Coast city we left this morning. The tourist beach fraternity see little of Mexico's high side; perhaps viewed from the plane the awareness doesn't quite generate enough intrigue. For me, it's wet paint. Knowing isn't enough; I have to touch it, to come up here and make sure. We ride up to 9,300 feet. Bikes aren't our only common ground; my mate is a keen photographer too and has an eye for a good photo. Where I see a church, he captures the shadows. When I watch goats being herded down a track, he sees the sun beam through the dust they disturb.

We ride up to a geothermal tundra, a place of pipes and tanks, high-pressure steam and pylons turning natural resources into power. The pipes arch and bend around the landscape like a Windows screensaver. This place is not in the guidebooks; this is the privilege of local knowledge, and I'm sworn to the secrecy of its location. "Mate, I couldn't find it again if I tried." I've been basking in the brain-dead luxury of having a leader and paid no attention to the route; all I know is we went up.

Coming back down is not so good. Busy, crowded roads of trucks and speed bumps, traffic and overtaking; my tour guide is riding like there's no future. I could too. I could get into courier mode, but these days I prefer living as opposed to riding like I'm trying to earn one. The evening is spent playing with pictures in photo programmes. See it, capture it, distort it, and embellish it. A bit like a Fox News journalist.

After just eleven hours' sleep, there's banging on the door. We are going to the big, posh hotel where my host does freelance translation, whilst I have a big, posh all-I-can-eat buffet breakfast. He's a busy man. Back at the house, he has to clean the pool, which involves sitting in a chair with a beer in one hand and a long rod with a net on the end in the other. It looks exhausting; best I can do is empathise and open a beer too. This is perhaps exactly what I'm supposed to do. It's no accident that a playlist has been especially composed for such activities, and so the day disappears, and my only other activity is making guacamole. We talk bikes, drugs, and rock 'n' roll and then touch on the more taboo subjects of politics and America's effect on the world. What I hear are bitter and cynical comments. The big picture depresses and angers him. Although I despair of our planet's future and the hatred that is bred and fed to the ignorant, it only encourages me to maintain my lifestyle. I want to see it for myself how things are; live life all the more. What else would I do, wait for the world to get better? Based on this philosophy, I wander downtown for the carnival.

It may have been a day of drinking by the pool, but the beer is what Australians would call "all day suppers." It's not high-alcohol oblivion, just a mild sea-level merriment. So the walk down the prom is memorable. It's obviously a big deal, this carnival. It's extravagant, loud, upbeat, and lavish. Alluring ladies on strobing floats dance to a pounding bass. I'm not sure if the thumping in my chest comes from the heart or the beat.

This is serious day trip riding. I'm up at 5:30 for today's excursion. Just before the breakfast stop, I get stung again. This time it's on the septum. I look in the mirror and see the stinger is still there. Predictably, it really bloody hurts. Annoyingly, my cream is with everything else in the pool house. So a pharmacy becomes top priority, and I get some even better cream than last time. It takes away the pain like paralysis. We ride round pleasant hills, past modest waterfalls, and rocky landslides, which reveal colourful mineral deposits on the cliffs behind. The potholes are manageable and nothing today is too extreme, except, it would seem, my dress code. Just a few blocks from the house on the return, I'm pulled by the police and left to deal with it. I can't. I have no idea what my crime is. I wasn't speeding; my bike is legit, insured, documented, and registered. My mate comes back to tell the cop he'll translate without admitting acquaintanceship. It turns out my purple combats have roused his suspicion. This is a city that takes no prisoners. Naked bodies, slaughtered by a drug cartel, were recently dumped at a busy intersection in a display of power and intimidation. I've seen houses that have literally been sprayed with bullets in gang rivalry. But the big threat today is my purple combats and to what allegiance my uniform represents.

Basically, I'm stopped by the fashion police. I'm surprised I've got away with it as long as I have.

Among his many jobs and talents, my host teaches bar work. We agree to disagree. I begrudge tipping the bartender every time he serves me a drink. It's his job. If I have twenty dollars to spend in a bar I want twenty dollars' worth of alcohol, not ten dollars', worth because I have to spend the other ten dollars on "entertainment." I don't care how elaborate the display is or the rhythm with which the cocktail maker shakes. If I want entertainment, I'll go to a show. I want a drink; that's why I'm in a bar. I'm not paying the barman to serve me; that's the landlord's job. I refuse to see any other viewpoint. I'm English, and I'm bordering on alcoholism; end of argument.

So as a last supper we go to an American-themed chicken wing place. We order a jug of beer, which doesn't come. Perhaps I should have tipped before ordering? We order again, and once the beer is poured all is calm.

We're approached and greeted by a waiter, who it turns out, is an ex-student. Now suddenly the service is acceptable. Not that we see him again; he has another table to entertain. A rowdy birthday party is happening on the other side of the restaurant. As we eat our wings, a whistle is blown and all the other waiting staff, along with a person dressed as a chicken, stand around the birthday table clapping and singing *Happy Birthday*. A good tip would be stopping myself from saying, "You must be so proud of him."

Day 56

Tampico, Mexico

344 miles

It's time to load up my bike again. As I do it, I'm not sure if I'm watched with envy or relief. My host has a good life down here. There are always sacrifices: snowboards exchanged for surfboards, Canadian whiskey for tequila. I know which ones I'd choose.

This goodbye is as genuine as the see-you-again. It's always a privilege to spend time with a local family. OK, so two thirds of this family disappeared as soon as I arrived, and my friend is Canadian, nevertheless it's an insight into a way of life that actually has a great deal of appeal.

I've heard Guatemala is even better, but once again, I haven't made it past Mexico. Entertained, thrilled, and awed, my teardrop loop of a journey has reached the bottom of its curvature. I have no new experiences coming my way, just a repeat of some of my favourite ones. Before I leave the city, I withdraw 2,000 pesos from the ATM. I think I've got about three more nights in Mexico, a few toll roads to ride, and maybe I'll treat myself to a pair of kick-arse cowboy boots when I get to the border.

Just knowing that the trip has reached its point of return has certain mental manifestations. Defences drop when ends are in sight, although

I still have over 2,000 miles to go and three weeks before my flight home.

After six months of wide-eyed travelling around India in my twenties, I'd seen a lot of poverty and pleading. All travellers have their individual ways of dealing with the unavoidable awareness of their Western wealth. I've heard of people giving their entire travel budget away at a Delhi train station before turning round and getting on a flight back home. My reaction wasn't quite so dramatic. Certain scenes, circumstances, and characters would touch me in a way that made me think giving money was helping the situation, when perhaps it was only helping me deal with the situation. I'll never know. Mostly, I bought into the don't-give-you'll-encourage-them philosophy. It's a hard generalisation that I'm not even sure I believe, but I had to have a system of defence and justification because I'm not Gandhi. I can't single-handedly change a nation. Anyway, the night before my flight home, I couldn't sleep. I stood in the sweltering pre-monsoon heat of a Delhi night, and from a rooftop I looked down on a street of closed roller shutters and flickering street lights. A trader was wheeling his barrow back home for the night, and a crippled and homeless kid with flip-flops on his hands dragged his lame body after him, begging for some food from the trader's unsold supplies. It was heartbreaking. All the boy wanted was feeding. He had nothing. I had some leftover rupees and no way of giving them to him. This image sticks in my mind so clearly; I think it's because I let my barriers down twelve hours before my flight. My soft heart no longer had its hard protection. I saw a situation that, in retrospect, I think I could have fixed, but I didn't try to.

I find myself unnecessarily driven today. I pass many inviting campgrounds under shady palms along the edge of a blue sea. Perhaps if I was with company. But it's too early in the day, too familiar to my other camping locations, so I just ride on. I know that, although this afternoon's heat is uncomfortable and tiring, I'll miss it when I reach the northern altitude I'm heading towards. The next time I'm this hot on a motorcycle will be on the next trip. The guidebook and the camera stay in the tank bag, and nothing much gets seen at all. I follow a signpost to a lagoon, which never materialises, at least not to me, so that camping possibility passes me by.

It's been a high-mileage day, and as the light goes, I pull into a town that boasts a Riviera. This will do nicely, but from the height of the toll bridge I look between oil refineries and gas flames spurting from high chimneys, wondering exactly where this idealistic location is. Then, not due to meditational discipline, the moment I'm in gets my full attention. Amongst the honking of horns and the blowing of whistles, I'm pulled by the police. It's evident immediately that this is not going to end in a smile and a warning. I went through a red light, I'm told. I'm pretty sure I didn't, and even if I did, there are none around here. The fine will be £400. It will have to be paid tomorrow, and until I pay it, my vehicle import papers will be confiscated. I won't describe the act. There's nothing original or unique about it; it's as played by corrupt cops the world over.

After the disgrace of my lawbreaking has been brought to acceptable levels of bureaucracy, I'm given the option to pay the fine now. On a busy street in, if not broad, at least adequate daylight, I'm robbed the entire contents of my wallet; the equivalent of £100, or two weeks' accommodation.

Two things I find it very hard to do are to part with money and to keep my mouth shut when somebody desperately needs yelling at. But the only way to win this game is to shut up and obey. The other way to win, and I know because I've played it before, is to only have a token amount of money in my wallet. It's been this way the entire trip, on every trip, but today, knowing I'm on the home straight, I'm not practising what I preach. This morning for the first time, and because I thought it would be the last time, I didn't distribute my wealth. It's all there in my wallet, inviting and accessible, and the fuckers take the lot. There will always be corrupt cops, and they'll never amount to anything. The money will bring them no good. If the bullying little bastard buys crocodile cowboy boots with my money, he'll know deep down when he stands in front of the mirror that they'd look way cooler on me.

Ironically, none of the junctions after this incident have traffic lights that work. Perhaps they need my money to pay for a repair or an electricity bill. These narrow-minded, thieving bastards can't see beyond their greed. What they never bother to consider is the knock-on effect of their actions. Thieves only think of themselves. I'm cleaned out. All those street tacos to save a few quid, all those musty rooms with corrugated mattresses, and the savings from my bad diet and aching back go to line a pig's pocket.

I'm not destitute, not even desperate. I'm just bloody livid, as much at myself for being blasé. I find a bank and replenish my funds, half yelling my misfortune to someone who catches my eye. "It happens," is his realistic reply. And that's how it is. Mexicans are lovely. They say good evening. Where are you going? Where are you from? My hatred needs to be focused, my anger harnessed. It was an individual, not a city or a nation that robbed me. They are as susceptible to this as I am.

I find a shitty hotel, walk out, and ride to a shitty beach, ride back, find a shittier hotel, and get a smelly room with no windows. I sit on my bed, eat a sandwich, and sulk. I don't want to do anything better tonight, I've got so much loathe to give.

DAY 57

WEST OF LA ROSA, MEXICO

416 MILES

My watch says 6AM, but it's still dark. I'm not sure if this is due to the lack of windows, or perhaps I rode through a time zone. I get up anyway and go to the underground car park to load my bike. When I go out to reception, I see it's bright daylight. Where did that come from?

My knee-jerk reaction is to leave this country as soon as I can. I'm still angry about last night. As I ride out of town, people are going to work; the beds of pickup trucks are full of coffee-drinking labourers. They all wave and smile. It gives me perspective. I'm lucky; I'm riding, and it's not to work. I feel my cheeks push up against the lining in my helmet. I'm smiling too; even a motorcycle cop waves at me. Bad apples; a few degenerate motherfuckers. Forget about it, accept it, and move on. I can't change anything about the experience except how I deal with the aftermath. They can take my money, but they only win if they take my joy too.

The pickup trucks and smiles continue all the way out of town. It occurs to me that this is a Tuesday morning in mid-February. Just how many happy faces would I see on a Colchester commute today?

It's a road of progress; no traffic and no tolls, and it's a lot cooler today too. I stop to put my bike trousers on. Standing in a lay-by in my underwear and struggling with my bungee cords, a Polícia Federal car pulls up next to me. Not again. But they're not interested in me and my fading tan. I feel the security of armoured protection again. In the heat, my heavy, black motorcycle clothing causes fatigue, which I think is more likely to cause an accident; however, when the weather cools beyond combats, it's the best of both worlds. I dress responsibly, and the bike is less bulky now too.

My next dilemma is which road to take. I have pesos to pay tolls, but the roads are free in the US, although rooms cost more, and the bottom tip of Texas is only a day away. I have to go west as well as north, so I think I'll stay in Mexico a little longer and bear left. The cloud is high, and I run parallel to a mountain range. New roads; I love new roads. Excitement is just a diversion away. With this scenery, the feeling of urgency subsides, and everything seems better.

The city of Monterrey is another surprise. It's immense and has beautiful, modern, high-rise glass and steel extravagant architecture, sandwiched in a valley of jagged mountains. I don't really have any needs that a city can offer, other than a craving for a big, fat burger. However, the thought of exiting the highway into the metropolis is not appealing. I continue through the city on the elevated toll road while passing several enticing exit ramps, but I just can't make myself turn off. Maybe the next one. This noncommittal approach has me making an avocado and tomato sandwich on my top box in a dusty truck stop lay-by outside of town. Oh, well.

Distances are longer than I expected. It's been a long day, and I'm tired. As I pass through a flat area of low bush and cacti, I divert off the road and ride the soft, white, dusty surface to a hidden spot. It's desolate, peaceful, and not the sort of landscape I've ever camped in before. I pitch my tent and run around taking photos of spiky silhouettes against the sunset. I start to feel tiny prickles in my hands. I must have brushed against a bush or something. I spend the last of the light with tweezers, pulling out tiny barbs that I can't see, only feel. That's the second evening in a row that's been ruined by a bunch of pricks.

Day 58

Camargo, Mexico

366 miles

Sometimes, especially if I'm away from any kind of civilisation, it occurs to me the only things in the world that matter or affect me are this side of the horizon. However, this morning I wonder if there has been some major natural or man-made catastrophe that I'm unaware of. Is this some kind of nuclear night or has a giant meteor cast a shadow over the planet? Surely it's going to get light at some point. I give up waiting, put on my headlight, and get fully dressed, not just for protection from the cold, but to avoid getting any more prickles in me. I even dismantle my tent with my gloves on.

Wake in the night and on the road for first light would make for good progress if it weren't for such a photogenic sunrise. I pass the occasional discarded and dilapidated building; crumbling stone and rain-washed rendered, their isolated location leaving little wonder as to why they would be abandoned. Only why would they be built here in the first place?

I'm not sure which country I'll sleep in tonight. Will I make it to the border, and does it even matter? I find a skinny little back road heading north. It's a dead-straight, flat track with a row of telegraph poles that run along the side. Together they head into a heat haze, which obscures distant mountains that I don't think I'll be going over. The road and the landscape is void of any human or development, and that alone makes it exhilarating. As I continue, the scrub clears to leave a soft, white, dried-up lake bed. It screams to be ridden over. I'm not the first, judging by the tyre tracks. It's so vast it takes all perspective of scale away. I suppose this is drug cartel country. Northern borderlands have that reputation, but it's empty, and the only threat I see is that of a breakdown; dehydration, and decomposing. I suppose this could be seen as a bit hardcore, but those who think that have more imagination than information. It's not that bad, just once again the excitement of a vast and desolate landscape.

The border town is signposted. It's 330 kilometres away and it's 3PM. I'm no closer to making a decision. I ride into the town of Camargo. It looks OK. I find a cheap hotel, which still has Christmas lights wrapped round the trunk of a palm tree. I think I'll stop here.

In the evening, I look in a few boot shops, but most are too small. They don't cater to fat European feet. There's one pair in a Jägermeister/KTM colour scheme, but with my skinny jeans the boots go over, not under them. And although the painstaking design is on full display, it's not a good look; too gangster, too dad, too *Brokeback Mountain*, or something, and they don't match my eyes. I'll stick with the second-hand Alpinestars I wore here last year. Another trip does not require another outfit. I spend my money—corruption notwithstanding—on travel, not clothing, and I think I'm all the richer for it. My eyes are tired and wild; maybe my previously owned bike and gear complement them.

DAY 59

BIG BEND NATIONAL PARK, TEXAS, USA

269 MILES

Mr. Dawn, that's me. I just can't help myself. I want to live all of the daylight hours from the very first hint to the very last trace. I'm hoping the day will warm up. My shower does eventually; just as I'm ready to get out, the hot water arrives. I'm glad I stopped here last night. This morning I feel fresher and there's no pressure in the day, much like the shower.

I have a long, straight ride to America. I calculate my fuel, and I think I have enough. After I leave the town, like yesterday, there is absolutely nothing on or off the road. I recalculate my fuel. Yeah, I'm sure I'll be OK. It's not scary this empty space, not boring, not insignificant; it's just the road to the border. There are three military checkpoints. You'd think after all this time in Mexico that my Spanish might have improved more; it's disappointing and so frustrating. Not that I need it, the checks are brief and easy. I reach the border town of Ojinaga, and fill up with cheap Mexican fuel. There's one last boot shop at the border town, but I have a desert to revisit and an international frontier to negotiate. I'm not going shopping.

I get to indulge in the luxury of understanding the language again. It comes with the irritation of incomprehension. I'm asked by immigration where I am coming from, and I try to remember the name of the town that still has my boots on the shelf, but that's not the answer they want.

"Mexico? You're coming from Mexico?"

Yes, I'm on the Mexican border on a motorcycle. Where do you think I'm coming from? Has your brainwashed education for this placement really left you unable to realise that you were not posted to an international airport? The question is irrelevant, and my destination, before you ask, appears to be the land of ignorant authority. But I'll keep my mouth shut while you charge me a processing fee that my pre-approved visa blatantly states I'm exempt from, because I know I'm dealing with someone whose respect hasn't been earned by humility, understanding, sensitivity, or wisdom, but is demanded with the donning of a uniform.

I have one more destination. I've been thinking about it repeatedly since I left. I'm going back to the desert that inspired me so much on the journey down. It slows my pace, warms my bones, and is so silent I can hear my breath and exercise my mind. I take the winding canyon, border-hugging road that was so much fun the last time, but it doesn't seem as good in this direction. I hope this isn't a precursor to the desert. Have I made it better in my memory than it was in reality?

As I approach the park, a Moto Guzzi comes past me, parks up on the other side of the entrance pay booth, and waits for me.

"Hi, Graham," says the rider. It's Bob. I'm flattered he remembers my name. It's a talent Americans seem to excel at. Bob was one of the few people who actually expected me to come back from Mexico alive, and my return reassures him that death by disembowelment does not wait across the Rio Grande. We have a little chat, but in this park of five-hundred-million-year-old rocks, I have to hurry and get to the ranger station for my back country camping pass. I top up on fuel, and whilst here, I grab a microwave burrito. There's a crazy, skinny, long-haired Asian girl hanging around. She seems to know the cashier very well. She thinks I'm from Mötley Crüe. It must be my fingerless gloves. She's got looks that kill; so wishing for once I had a kickstart. I get on my bike and head for a new place to camp. I have it all to myself, pitch my tent, and as the stars come out, a small ranger in a big truck exercises his authority, saying by law I should re-pitch it ten feet over. Then he gets all passive aggressive and says I can leave the tent where it is, but that's probably where people "use the bathroom." Now he mentions it, I can smell shit, but it leaves when he does. Unfortunately, his negative vibe is louder than words and in an empty atmosphere with nothing to overpower it; it loiters around all night.

DAY 60

BIG BEND NATIONAL PARK, TEXAS

73 MILES

That confrontation last night with the little power trip ranger really annoyed me. It's not why I came here, and his antagonistic manner was about as welcome here as a McDonald's would be, although a bacon-and-egg McMuffin would hit the spot right now. I boil the kettle and climb the rocks for the sunrise. False peaks and a genuine unfitness soon have me warmed up. I have a 360-degree panorama and can't see a single trace of humanity. I do, however, find a track. It must be the one that leads to Balance Rock. I wander down it. "Fallen and wedged rock" might be a more accurate description. But after my initial underwhelming, I see it for what it is and appreciate it as best I can.

Rather than the signposted attractions, I prefer the unlabelled and unfathomable vastness of the place. I can imagine it being an ancient sea bed as I look out across the rippling rocks, but this landscape was formed by shifting tectonic plates. I bet it was noisy here then.

I walk back along the road, contemplating another run in with Mr. Short of Arse and Temper. This is an area so large and with such a low population that his attitude has had a disproportionate effect upon me; anyway, I don't see him and I don't see a McDonald's either. As it's been a long walk with no supplies. I have a big healthy breakfast before moving my tent to the regulated position. Not because I'm conforming, it just keeps it out of the wind. With my door open, I lay inside and enjoy writing a Word document on my laptop, trying not to be pressured by a dying battery. I hear a vehicle. It's a ranger pickup truck with two female rangers in the cab. They're really friendly, to the point of even taking my rubbish away for me. Now the vibe is good again. Despite this, I decide to pack up and move on. I go to the lodge for lunch, charge my battery, and top up on water and Wi-Fi. That Asian girl from last night is my waitress. It turns out yesterday was Valentine's Day. Thankfully, my inbox isn't full of love messages, so I'm able to get on with business. The London Bike Show is on, and there's a photo of Sam Manicom promoting my book. Man, that feels good. I show the waitress the photos. She wants a copy and gives me her address, email, phone number, and everything. What would Nikki Sixx do? Somehow, it's become 3PM, and I need to find a new campsite. "See ya around, babe," I'd probably say if I was Nikki Sixx.

When I get to my site for the night, I find it's occupied by a campervan. Inside is a French-Canadian couple. "It's OK," I tell them. "I'll take your space." They invite me for dinner. So after putting up my tent, I walk to the river for a wash then head over to the neighbours. Turns out it's the girl's birthday, so we have a stir-fry and lots of wine, listen to Leonard Cohen, and despite the mood of his music, we laugh the night away. Birthday girl flirts like mad with me, and it's getting a bit embarrassing. The camper is too small for a threesome. What would Nikki Sixx do? I miss the sunset, which is the whole point of being here, but company doesn't always come on cue on the road, so I'll top up now, and tomorrow I'll go back to my solitary site.

Day 61

Big Bend National Park, Texas

69 miles

Excited by the prospect of the park's ultimate location for a sunrise, I wake again in total darkness and head for the canyon on foot. It's hard to follow the river, and my headlight batteries are failing. I don't want to walk through the tall grass, as I have no idea what may be lurking there. The canyon walls are so tall I can see their black shadows against the lightening sky. For an hour, I walk towards them without them appearing to get any closer. As dawn breaks, I start taking photos. I either need to get a wider angle lens or find some smaller canyons. I have to get creative and use the reflection in the still river to capture their height.

People who sleep lose out on so much. Not that I'd tell them that, and even the most touristy of attractions can be viewed in relative solitude before or after hours. I have the place to myself, and once the rising sun has flattened the creeping shadows, I take the path into the canyon. The echo is so prolonged I can practically see the sound waves bouncing off the walls when I make my primal howl. There are grooves in the canyon walls, presumably gouged by rocks trapped in passing glaciers. Well, that's my geological explanation; I don't really know. The lines run parallel, but are at a thirty-degree angle to the river. Obviously, the water is level, but there is an optical illusion caused by the uniformity and by the formation of the gouges. I stand on the sandy bank playing with perspective until I lose my balance. As I walk back out, I know I've seen this canyon at the best time the day can offer. A tripod-carrying photographer is coming up towards me. He has a lot of equipment, but unfortunately, clearly not an alarm clock, so I hope he has some skill in Photoshop, or he's in for a wasted trip.

I thought the walk back would be easier. I'm not convinced this is the right way. I see some footprints, but they aren't mine. I come to some still and shallow water, have a full wash, and continue the walk back commando. Back at the campsite everyone has left, and I enjoy my breakfast in solitude. I lie in the sun; already seven hours have passed since I got up. I'd better get going; my preferred camping ground will be vacated today. I pack up and leave the park to get supplies. Ten gleaming Harleys are parked outside the restaurant. I can't imagine I'd have the kind of dining experience in there that would produce positive ramblings if I were to recount it. Summed up, generalised, and avoided,

I leave them without the chance to prove themselves to be anything other than how I judge them to be. I do have a chat with some other motorcyclists at the village store, though, so I'm not completely antisocial. I decide to stop for a bottle of wine, seeing as it's a Saturday. Loaded like a tramp's trolley, I ride all the way to the other end of the park and to my long-awaited, secluded camping spot. I feel the day, my actions, my life slow down; this place is as good as I remember. I open the wine, go up to my hillock, drink from the bottle, and talk bollocks into my voice recorder.

Here in this timeless expanse the only seasons are the rise and fall in temperature. Here my little life shows its insignificance. This place demands a belief, not necessarily a religion or a faith, but you can't ignore it. You can't bury your head in your busy day and forget how everything came to be. This place may not give answers, but it makes you aware that there are questions you have to ask. The desert is as silent as the shadows that cross it. Mountains reflect the ever-changing light, borrowing the best colours from the sun when it rises and sets.

I text DRob, but I get a crap reply. He doesn't get it, he's so married these days. "He's so out there these days," he probably says to his wife after reading it.

DAY 62

BIG BEND NATIONAL PARK, TEXAS

115 MILES

It's only 3° Celsius as I sit on my little sunrise hillock. I left my stall up here last night on purpose. It's like staking my claim on the terrain; it gives it a more personal feel. As I watch the light disperse and the shadows cross the plain, I feel that this is a turning point. I think that perhaps deserts are my new thing. Grander, more remote, and utterly silent places could be my new pursuit in life, which makes going to Iran seem like a logical step in fulfilling this quest. I have a prolonged breakfast and shed my clothes as the day warms up. No one comes out here; the road is too rough to enforce rules. The two things I don't have enough of are power and water. With a bigger container and an inverter, I could prolong my independence. The laptop dies before my inspiration dries up, and the water runs out before I'm ready to leave.

The tap at the ranger station has a plaque above it, which reads "Federal regulations prohibit bathing or washing dishes at the fixture." I have one dish. I look around, make out I'm filling my water bottle, and accidently let the water overflow into my dish, which is sitting on the ground underneath the tap. So technically I'm splashing it, not washing it. It's my get-out clause. I have to get more fuel. I need some oil too; my bike chain is rattling it's so dry. Back home,

I do a little bike maintenance and realise there's a fly in my wine bottle. I get it out, but can't ignore the fact that it's been in there for some time. It seems like unfair compensation for not drinking the whole bottle last night.

I go off to explore the "ruins." The further I walk, the more evidence there is. It's not ancient life, but a nineteenth-century, rusty, cast-iron stove and some cooking utensils, which were probably freely washed at any available water source. I'm deliberately stomping around, as this looks like prime rattlesnake territory, and I don't like the idea of riding the dirt road with a tourniquet around a bitten limb.

My aimless wandering has me gravitating back to my hillock. It's a kind of lookout post, as well as a landmark and vista point. I pick up stones of interest, look closer at their weathered time lines, then find myself replacing them in the indentation they've left in the sandy floor. Because I realise they belong there and wouldn't look better anywhere else, replacing them is very satisfying, even if the operation borders on the limits of sanity. I feel a little like Bob Geldof playing Pink in *The Wall*. making patterns with the remnants of his recently wrecked hotel room just as he's about to become *Comfortably Numb.*

The silence is interrupted, not by a knock on the door, but by the sound of rushing wind, but I can't feel it. I see the spiky desert brush bend and bow in the near distance, and the sound of its dry rustle is brought to my ears on the breeze that proceeds this brief and passing gust. Slowly, this containment of wind about twenty feet long comes closer, passes over my tent, and blows my socks, which are airing on the bike mirrors, and then it passes on. It's the closest I've ever been to seeing wind. Like a package passing by, it was visually and audibly evident. I stay up here, looking down at the route I just walked. And now that I've slowed to the desert pace, I simply stay put and wait for the sunset.

I become aware of my heightened senses. I feel the change in temperature as I walk down to the flat of my camping area, which has been in the shade for thirty minutes longer than my viewing point. It has cooled noticeably. I can also smell the oil I put on my dry and dusty chain earlier. 3-in-1, the earth I've been walking on, the wind I've seen, and the fire of the fading heat from the departed sun; simple individual elements that created this harmonious landscape. If I hadn't slowed my pace, it would seem monotonous. To rush through this area is to miss the subtle fascination in every step. From an open visor it would be a blur of indistinguishable land, but viewed from a motionless stance it shows its complete perfection.

I've got what I came for. In company, impatient, this would never occur. It's an experience that, viewed from the wrong situation, could be seen as pretentious, but it's as genuine as this planet can provide. Pretentious to me is a conservatory, on show to the elements, but unfeeling; a bubble in the outside world, as natural as a resalable plastic bag.

I'm in my resealable sleeping bag by 8PM. The night is so silent that I'm woken by a gnawing sound. It's not my tummy. Outside my door, a mouse is nibbling the peanut butter off my Swiss army knife. It's not bothered by me at all. In the distance, I hear wolves howl. I try not to let it bother me.

Day 63

Big Bend National Park, Texas

138 miles

If I was with company, they'd be infuriated by how slowly I pack up. But I'm not, which is why I'm packing up in just my underwear and sandals. Regardless of how slowly and carefully I load the bike, there's never enough room for everything. My pace doesn't increase much when I leave. First and second gear seem fast enough, though I'm sure no one rides these roads this slowly. I go and get water and Wi-Fi. I can't seem to live without either.

Someone says, "Nice to be back in touch with the world, eh?"

"Depends on what the world has to say," I respond too quickly, and that's the end of that conversation. The world, and specifically my tenant, has something to say. The drains are blocked, crumbling, and subsiding, and the bathroom is full of cracks as it falls into the abyss. He thinks the structure is unstable. Bollocks! I make some calls. My insurance company tells me before I even mention the problem what my policy does not cover, and drains happens to be one of them. I arrange for someone to take a look at the problem. There's nothing else I can do, except, that is, to pay more attention to the way I load my bike. My sandals and shorts have fallen off the back. I realise soon enough, turn around, and find my frayed and scruffy shorts, but the sandals have gone. I ride

303

up and back, but they aren't there. Someone must have seen their prestigious designer name and stopped to pick them up. Bollocks again!

There is a dirt road that follows the Rio Grande. It's the only one I haven't ridden. I've heard it's sandy and tough going. It's not that enjoyable, and the only thrill comes from how far out I am, where the isolation wows me again and I don't have to bow down to the laws on water usage. I take enough with me, and I'm free to go wild in the country, at least for a little while. I'm not giving the landscape my full attention though, as I'm preoccupied with thoughts of my crumbling, clay drainpipes. Half remembering, songs play in my head, the same lyric over and over until I become aware of it and deliberately change it to another half-remembered song. "I'll do better, yeah I'll do better." It's a little more catchy and won't revert back to the last one.

I'll be home in ten days. I didn't want to think about it, but now it can't come soon enough. I decide I should be in a place where I'm contactable, so reluctantly, I head back to civilisation. The park fuel station attendant remarks on me filling my tank again.

"The problem is I can't seem to stop riding," I say.

"That's not a problem," he replies.

The lodge and restaurant are the high-altitude part of the park. At 8,000 feet, there are views that look out through a V-shaped window in the rocks across the plains. It's the park's most popular attraction and, therefore, the most populated part. I haven't seen it at its classic sunset time, as I haven't wanted to ride back in the dark. I suppose for my last night; I should camp in the high-density campground.

I pay my fee and find a gap in the concentration of campers, then wander off for the ultimate sunset view. Surprisingly, there are very few people around.

Annoyingly, that's because it's cloudy. There isn't a hint of changing colours, and that's the only reason I'm here. The sun drops behind a veil, and the only evidence of its descent is that now it's bloody dark. I seem to have ended my visit on a low. Predictably, the site is noisy all night. I make a midnight chai and a marmite sandwich and wait impatiently for an appropriate time to make my dawn escape.

DAY 64

BOTTOMLESS LAKE STATE PARK ROSWELL, NEW MEXICO

378 MILES

Rebellious defiance or desperation, I'm not really sure, but I head to the sunset point for the sunrise. It's pretty good actually, watching the light spread across the Western plains. It's certainly better than last night. That's it then, I'm off. As I ride out of the Chiso Basin and down to the desert floor, the temperature drops too. I just don't get this environment; there's more to it than meets the eye, and I thought I'd met most of it by now. One last fill up. The happy hippy cashier isn't working, so once again, I leave a place without any goodbyes—not Bob, nor the skinny waitress; she seemed a bit on the wild side anyway. I check one last time to see if my sandals have been handed in. They were bloody expensive; not to me—I got a bargain—but I can't afford to replace them.

As I ride north out of the park, I hope the next 800 miles will not be filled with thoughts of subsiding footings and disappearing shoes. It doesn't take long though, before I'm fully focused on the ride. The bike was a tool with which to see the park, but once again, it has a starring role in the journey. I know there is a border control up ahead. I also know that they have one question. "US citizen?" With my helmet on and one simple "yes," I'd barely have to stop. But if I reply honestly, I'll have to go through a rigorous inspection and interrogation. Well, that's what happened last time. The inquisition won't be in Spanish, so I can't use a misunderstanding as an excuse for giving the wrong answer. The more I practise saying "yes" in an American accent, the less convinced I am that I'll get away with it. I suppose I'd better be an honest Englishman. As I ride under the canopy, I flip up my chin guard and pull down my bandito bandana.

"US citizen?" asks a youngish and almost hip immigration officer.

"No. UK."

"Can I see your passport?"

I pass it to him, picture page open. Used foreign visas tend to generate unwanted conversation. He looks at my photo, and as he looks up, I pull my Oakleys down my nose and smile.

"Cool, dude," he says, and I'm free to go. Well, I wasn't expecting that. He didn't even ask where I've come from.

Oh, and by the way, I've got a dead baby full of drugs in my top box.

The road has been freshly sealed, sprayed with tar. I know how this can coat a bike, thrown up by the tyres and flung into every inaccessible crevice. So I ride the yellow sideline like a tight rope. The concentration required is probably quite good for both mind and balance. However, there's a far shallower experience that gets me very excited. I pass a Google Street View vehicle, its all-seeing camera strapped to the roof like an anorexic Dalek. Wow, I'm going to be on Google! It's a ridiculous reaction; the real joy should be managing to live an existence where you're *not* seen on Google. Particularly, as my next action, once the car has become a dot in my mirrors, requires stopping on the side of the road for a wee. The omniscient witness is going faster than I realise, and I have to force the flow and pretend I'm fastening my luggage as Big Brother drives past me. In the town of Pecos, it stops at some lights at the junction over the highway, and I pass it again. This may seem like excessive detail, but it's expensive to put photos in books, and out there in cyberspace is a photo of this moment, if you care to look.

In Carlsbad, I stop for fuel and break into my penultimate one hundred dollar bill. I think I'll just about manage on the money I have left, but I'll probably have to sell the bike when I get back to Denver. I'm on the oil route. I pass several busy terminals and am frequently battered by the tankers that pass me in a slamming burst of wind, leaving a turbulent slipstream behind them. Terminal velocity, no limiters, no tachographs; oil wells are the hole of the law in Texas.

When I get to Roswell, I stop at a camping ground, but it's closed. I'm told there's a state park twelve miles away where I can camp. I'd better stock up. The supermarket is an alien environment to me, and with all my bike gear on and my plastic basket I feel like Little Red Riding Hood's satanic twin. It's no surprise I get no wolf whistles. Jonathan calls me. A big snowstorm has just blown in, and they have eight inches and counting in Denver. He finds it hard to believe I'm camping tonight when I'm only a day away. It's not that cold here. The temperature is campable, but I'm perhaps the only one who thinks that, based on the fact that I'm the only camper in the park. I may be here some time. I erect my tent, cook my chunky soup, and stare directly at a dulled disc falling gently behind storm clouds. The wind has blown shut my clear-run window. The new time zone is irrelevant; only the weather matters. And like time, it will pass; these things always do.

Day 65

Bottomless Lake State Park
Roswell, New Mexico

43 miles

The dawn doesn't call me, but the time difference does. I wake from dreams deeper than the "bottomless" lakes. I'm in another overrated theme park. Balancing Rock was nothing more than a fallen boulder, and this place, Bottomless Lake, is bloody not. I take a morning stroll to circulate the blood and throw in a stone to check the watery depths. "A little deeper lake than expected camp ground" I suppose wouldn't have the same attraction.

When the visitors' centre opens, I go and break the ice with the grumpy volunteer. I get some Wi-Fi and discover it's snowing 200 miles north of here in Santa Fe. I speak to Jonathan again, who confirms it's still snowing in Denver too. Much like the exaggerated fear stories of Mexico, the snow reports are threatening that this storm is bringing "a winter's worth of snow with it." Well, one thing's for sure, I'll be spending another night here. I ride back into Roswell to top up my supplies and get a hearty meal. I've discovered it's best to ask a fatty to recommend a restaurant if I want quantity over quality. I find myself in a place of overweight cowboy types. Perhaps it's a local defence strategy to prevent them from being sucked into an alien spacecraft, or maybe it's just gluttony. The waitresses are thin and efficient, weaving around the inadequate chairs of overhanging arses. Their professionalism clashes with all the time I have to kill. I have no need for fast food. I spend the rest of the day climbing around the rocks and trying not to feel like I'm trapped here. I'm mentally preparing myself for the long, hard push back to Denver, and physically preparing myself by eating lots of crisps for sustenance. It's my excuse; it's very easy preparation. In the evening, a couple wanders over to chat KLRs with me, but having started the conversation, they can't seem to get away fast enough. Was it something I said? I'd like to leave too, but with nothing else to do, I settle down for a long sleep. Tomorrow I'll do what I've been doing for most of the trip, living the wrong side of hardcore and waking up when the people with faster lives would be going to bed.

Day 66

Denver, Colorado

579 miles

First light. That will do. There's ice in my water bottle, and my stove is out of fuel, so the day starts with the inhalation of petrol fumes as I siphon fuel from the tank. My cereal has gone. I'm sure I left it on the picnic table last night, but it's not here. The plastic milk bottle dribbles enough to lighten my chai; the rest is congealed in the plastic bottle. My marmite won't squeeze onto the bagel, and my hands are numb already. I'm feeling a temper brewing.

All the wrong things are stiff: the plastic fasteners on my boots, the zip on my jacket, and the action of my clutch lever. Dismantling the tent and rolling up my sleeping bag numbs the extremities of my body. I'm swearing and grumpy. I try to calm down.

The sun starts to shine on the plains, but in my sheltered enclave the shadows remain. With all my layers on and all packed up, I get on the bike with zombie-like dexterity. I turn on the ignition and press the starter. It won't start. My mood worsens. The battery is exhausting itself, and there isn't a hint of a spark, only the smell of petrol in a flooding cylinder. If I could just turn the bloody headlight off, but for safety reasons, factories no longer offer that option. It comes on with the ignition and drains the battery further as it struggles to turn

311

over a frozen engine. It's an altogether shitty start to a very long day. I consider my options. In two hours, the rangers will arrive, and I can get a jump start. In two hours, I won't have enough time to reach Denver by tonight.

I wander round the bike and think, then press the starter again, and the bike fires up. Relief! Back to plan A. I plug in my heated jacket and get back on the bike. As I ride away from the rocky hills, the sun shines down on me with no heat in it at all. "Are you going to be my friend today?" I ask it. The answer is obscured by clouds. It disappears behind a haze that turns into a freezing fog that numbs my feet before I've even left Roswell.

The road is straight and flat, and visibility is limited by a misted visor on the inside and a frozen moisture on the outside. After only fifty miles, I need a wee. The water in my bottle now has the consistency of a flavourless slush puppy. The crystals in the air turn to snow—not happy Christmas snowman snow, but a bleak, harsh, wind-whipped flurry. It's dry and has lip-cracking qualities. Thankfully, it blows out as quickly as it blew in and doesn't settle on the road.

After a hundred miles, I stop for breakfast, take off my boots, and massage my feet. The waitress frowns, but wisely decides to make no comment. I'm stopped for no more than half an hour, yet I need full choke to start the bike again. I fill the tank, as this high, homeward speed has dramatically increased my fuel consumption. I'm too cold to save money, too uncomfortable to care. I stomp around the forecourt in the hope of bringing life back to my feet. Then I hanker down to another hundred miles, which are exactly the same as the first. I'm driven by pure determination and distracted by calculations of time and distance. Highway 285, the same road I was photographed on by Google two days ago, finally reaches the junction with Interstate 25. And again, I stop for fuel.

"Be careful out there," the attendant warns. "There's snow down in Santa Fe."

"Yeah, but I'm going north."

"North?" Then there's no hope for you, his expression seems to say.

It's less than a 500-mile trip, so why are these distances going so slowly? This always happens when I come from a land that uses kilometres to a place of miles, but still my mental calculations aren't corresponding with the glance I took on Google Maps yesterday. Even on the Interstate, New Mexico just won't seem to end. It's doing that annoying thing it did on the way down here, weaving off in the opposite direction to where I want to go. Little milestones like the Colorado border are what keep me going in such situations. It's what I need. I can't hold on any longer. I have to stop for more sustenance and so pull into a Denny's, massage my feet again, drink coffee, order the day's second breakfast, and surprisingly, eat the lot. Out of the window, I see an enticing motel sign; today's digital display daily rate is $29. I don't have to be back tonight. I text Jonathan for a weather report.

"Are you over the pass yet?"

"What pass?"

He reports that the conditions up there are freezing snow. Sounds familiar. The pass is thirteen miles away. I'm not staying here; I want to get over the pass.

As soon as I leave the restaurant, it starts to snow again. It's settling between the lanes on the highway, but not where the tyres run. I start to climb. A slow campervan towing a car is crawling up; it's spraying filth all over my visor. I want to get past and keep my momentum, but I don't want to cross this slushy, slippy divide. Gripping my bars like a lifeline, I cross the icy partition and pass the camper. I'm pushing my limits, riding a road I can't turn round on into something I'm not sure I can handle. My tyres were never good, and now the rear one is very low on tread. As the road whitens, I hold onto the bike in the way I hope the tyres will hold onto the road. I have to reach the summit; it's my next milestone. Then I can relax a little. At 7,800 feet, I reach both the summit and the Colorado border. The descent brings a dry road and a slight feeling of achievement, and this in turn, drives me on. More miles, more fuel. This fill-up should get me there. The snow is constant now, never quite settling, but freezing up my visor, and I can see it's covering the parts of me that are reflected in the mirrors. It sits on the edges of my clocks like a shop-window Christmas display.

I need to stop again, but if I do, I'll hit rush hour in Colorado Springs. My whole body is so cold now. I think of humans who have done much worse: Arctic explorers and barefoot, indigenous Siberians. But fuck it; my feet are so numb, and the wind chill is torturous! It's agony. There aren't many options left from inside my helmet, other than to start crying from the pain.

More cheap motel signs appear as the traffic starts to build up, and as filtering is illegal here, I obediently stay in lane. The thought of getting a room is blissful, but the urge to get back is stronger. The snow gets harder and the traffic slower as the daylight disappears. However, on a positive note, the wind chill has stopped, and in this crawling, inconsistent congestion, my limbs are moving, and the circulating blood is having a vague thawing effect. For the next forty miles, the traffic is stop start. A ridge of snow separates the lanes, so I stay put as brake lights diffract on my visor and make my tired eyes squint. The light is almost gone now. This has taken so much longer than I expected.

One more elevation increase, and the snow thickens. I try to follow the tyre tracks. I would never start a journey in conditions like this, so it's with sheer determination and steady progression that I face this challenge. With the final descent comes my turn off and the very last sixteen miles towards dusky, swirling, orange clouds above the dark mountains. It's nearly over. Onto the dirt road and up the driveway. I've done it. I arrive like I left, to an empty house. The bike is encrusted in snow, but once it started up this morning, it didn't hesitate or let me down again. I pat it and thank it. "Couldn't have done it without ya!"

Against all logic, I stay outside; staring, shaking, reeling. Although uncomfortably numb, I have feeling, and it's overwhelming—a sense of achievement.

Endurance, hardships, dedication; nothing feels as good as the completion of a plan. I think that's the bonus right there; going away on a bike offers so much: exploring, discovering, interaction, independence, personal achievements, and stretched reality. This can make the return seem deflating, depressing; the tyranny of a life that's so hard to escape from and so easy to fall back into: mundane re-entry to normality. Instead of looking outside and seeing I'm back, perhaps the answer is to look inside and see what I've done.

Pushing limitations with a strong desire and an unknown ability, slowly and single-mindedly. Making sacrifices, choosing priorities, seeing progress, believing, persevering, and eventually achieving. Motivation and inspiration are everywhere. So are distractions and excuses. A dream made into a plan has a momentum; it won't drive itself, but it has the ability to entice, exhilarate, encourage; and I believe all dreams are born to become realities.

EPILOGUE

And that's it. From a holiday ride to an international adventure, somewhere in between lies the label of this jaunt. A bit of work, a bit of play, a bit of endurance, a bit of new experience. Over 7,800 miles. Yep, that'll do nicely.

There was a niggle I could no longer ignore. That last leg of the trip took ten hours. It was nearly 600 miles, and it was supposed to be about 500. I rechecked Google Maps (I'm still not on it yet!). I didn't have GPS, and I didn't even have a map of the US. But I was heading north; what could possibly go wrong? Turns out there was a point in New Mexico where I should have gone east, then northeast, then north. It would have cut off nearly a hundred miles and a high-elevation mountain range. Bollocks!

I put my bike up for sale. Checking out the competition to gauge prices, there was a KLR being parted out. It had a blown engine, but came with Jesse panniers and all sorts of touring accessories. I think it was the one I'd originally wanted but hadn't bought. There's a lesson there; all those thoughts of shoulda, woulda, coulda that tortured me as I questioned my choice of purchase. But my bike performed so well, as if trying to endear itself to me, while I kept wishing it was something else. My mistake was in the choice of panniers and tyres, and I overlooked the qualities of the bike as a result. Now I can see what I would have been dealing with; probably flying away from a blown bike somewhere in Mexico. All that glitters . . .

A week later, I went from overnight plane to overland train to looking over a drain. Two unrelated incidents had conspired to make the results of a blocked U-bend appear irreversible. With some rerouting and replacement pipes, the problem was fixed. A month later, I headed off towards Iran and came across other irreversible issues, which resulted in various other U-turns and rerouting . . . but that's another story.

Other Books from Road Dog Publications

Also from Graham Field

In Search of Greener Grass [1]
With game show winnings and his KLR 650, Graham sets out solo for Mongolia and beyond. Foreword by Ted Simon

Eureka [1]
Graham sets out on a journey to Kazahkstan only to realize his contrived goal is not making him happy. He has a "Ureka!" moment and turns around and begins to enjoy the ride as the ride itself becomes the destination.

Other Authors

Motorcycles, Life, and . . . [1 2]   *by Brent Allen*
Sit down at a table and talk motorcycles, life and . . . (fill in the blank) with award winning riding instructor and creator of the popular "Howzit Done?" video series, Brent "Capt. Crash" Allen. Here are his thoughts about riding and life and how they combine told in a lighthearted tone.

The Elemental Motorcyclist [1 2]   *by Brent Allen*
Brent's second book offers more insights into life and riding and how they go together. This volume, while still told in the author's typical easy-going tone, gets down to more specifics about being a better rider.

A Tale of Two Dusters & Other Stories [1 2]   *by Kirk Swanick*
In this collection of tales, Kirk Swanick tells of growing up a gear head behind both the wheels of muscle cars and the handlebars of motorcycles and describes the joys and trials of riding

Bonneville Go or Bust [1 2]   *by Zoë Cano*
A true story with a difference. Zoe had no experience for such a mammoth adventure of a lifetime but goes all out to make her dream come true to travel solo across the lesser known roads of the American continent on a classic motorcycle.
I loved reading this book. She has a way of putting you right into the scene. It was like riding on the back seat and experiencing this adventure along with Zoe.—(★★★★★ Amazon Review)

Southern Escapades [1 2]   *by Zoë Cano*
As an encore to her cross country trip, Zoë rides through the tropical Gulf of Mexico & Atlantic Coast in Florida, through the forgotten back roads of Alabama and Georgia. This adventure uncovers the many hidden gems of lesser known places in these beautiful Southern states.
. . . Zoe has once again interested and entertained me with her American adventures. Her insightful prose is a delight to read and makes me want to visit the same places.—(★★★★★ Amazon Review).

Thoughts on the Road [1 2]   *by Michael Fitterling*
The founder of Road Dog Publications and Editor of *Vintage Japanese Motorcycle Magazine*, ponders his experience with motorcycles & riding, and how those two things intersect and influence his life.

Northeast by Northwest [1 2]   *by Michael Fitterling*
The author finds two motorcycle journeys of immense help staving off depression and the other effects of stress. Along the way, he discovers the beauty of North America and the kindness of its people.
. . . makes you feel that you are on the journey yourself. The book shows how inexpensively a rider can tour America! Buy it, read it, and you will not be disappointed.—(★★★★★ Amazon Review

Beads in the Headlight [1]   *by Isabel Dyson*
A British couple tackle riding from Alaska to Tierra del Fuego two-up on a 31 year-old BMW "airhead." Join them on this epic journey across two continents.
A great blend of travel, motorcycling, determination, and humor. —Dee (★★★★★ Amazon Review)

A Short Ride in the Jungle [1 2]   *by Antonia Bolingbroke-Kent*
A young woman tackles the famed Ho Chi Minh Trail alone on a diminutive pink Honda Cub armed only with her love of Southeast Asia, and its people, and her wits.

Asphalt & Dirt [1 2]   *by Aaron Heinrich*
A compilation of profiles of both famous and realtively unknown people who ride dispelling the myth of the stereotypical "biker" image.

Distributed by:
NBN national book network

Road Dog PUBLICATIONS
www.roaddogpub.com

Also available for [1] Kindle from amazon.com & [2] Nook from bn.com